D0078989

Event Risk Management and Safety

Peter E. Tarlow, Ph.D.

WAGGONER LIBRARY
DISCARD

WAGGONER LIBRARY
TREVECCA NAZARENE UNIVERSITY

JOHN WILEY & SONS, INC.

This book is printed on acid-free paper. ⊚

Copyright © 2002 by John Wiley & Sons, Inc., New York. All rights reserved.

Published simultaneously in Canada.

No part of this publication may be reproduced, stored in a retrieval system or transmitted in any form or by any means, electronic, mechanical, photocopying, recording, scanning or otherwise, except as permitted under Sections 107 or 108 of the 1976 United States Copyright Act, without either the prior written permission of the Publisher, or authorization through payment of the appropriate per-copy fee to the Copyright Clearance Center, 222 Rosewood Drive, Danvers, MA 01923, (978) 750-8400, fax (978) 750-4744. Requests to the Publisher for permission should be addressed to the Permissions Department, John Wiley & Sons, Inc., 605 Third Avenue, New York, NY 10158-0012, (212) 850-6011, fax (212) 850-6008, E-Mail: PERMREQ@WILEY.COM.

This publication is designed to provide accurate and authoritative information in regard to the subject matter covered. It is sold with the understanding that the publisher is not engaged in rendering professional services. If professional advice or other expert assistance is required, the services of a competent professional person should be sought.

Wiley also publishes its books in a variety of electronic formats. Some content that appears in print may not be available in electronic books. For more information about Wiley products, visit our web site at www.wiley.com.

Library of Congress Cataloging-in-Publication Data:

Tarlow, Peter E.
    Event risk management and safety/Peter E. Tarlow.
       p. ; cm. — (Wiley event management series)
Includes bibliographical references.
    ISBN 0-471-40168-4 (alk. paper)
    1. Special events—Management. 2. Risk management.
    [DNLM: 1. Anniversaries and Special Events. 2. Risk Management. 3.
Disaster Planning. 4. Emergencies. 5. Safety.] I. Title. II.
Series
    GT3405.T37 2002
    394.2′068—dc21   2002005229
Printed in the United States of America.

10 9 8 7 6 5 4 3 2 1

To my parents who gave me life;
To my wife, Sara, who shares my life;
To my Hillel students who keep life interesting;
To my children, Nathaniel and Lysandra, to whom God has
given me the privilege of passing on life.

Contents

Foreword

Many centuries ago, Aristotle wrote, "Dignity does not consist in possessing honors, but in deserving them." The Greek philosopher and teacher knew that every man and woman must earn their reputation every day through their contribution to improving society. This monumental work by the acclaimed tourism risk management expert, Dr. Peter E. Tarlow, will help ensure that you and your organization receive the honors you will deserve. Through the pages of this volume, you will be able to rise each day knowing that you have made a positive contribution to ensure the safety and security of your event as well as others throughout the world.

Dr. Tarlow is a world-renowned consultant, author, scholar, and speaker in his field. His contributions to tourism safety and security have been praised in media around the world. He has provided excellent advice and counsel for the United States federal government Bureau of Reclamation, Department of the Interior, and for police departments and universities throughout the United States and other countries. Due to the generosity of the Bureau of Reclamation, he has worked with visitor centers at places such as the Hoover Dam, the United States Park Service Statue of Liberty on Liberty Island, the Utah Olympic Public Safety Command, and the Royal Canadian Mounted Police. His professional experience, research, and all too rare common sense make this book one of the most important contributions to the event management literature since the inception of the field.

Within these pages, you will learn not only why event risk management and safety is critically important to the future of your events but also how to efficiently, simply, and easily use specific techniques and methods to reduce risk and increase success. The numerous charts, figures, and models that the author has provided will make this book a basic training manual that you can share with your staff and volunteers to further promote safety awareness and reduce your overall risk.

This book is the single most comprehensive text ever developed in the field of event risk management. The psychological, sociological, financial, operational, and political considerations of event risk management are carefully explored and thoroughly explained. By using this book, you will be addressing event risk management in the most comprehensive manner for your current and future events.

The term "dignity" is defined as the "quality or state of being worthy of esteem or respect" *(The American Heritage Dictionary)*. Therefore, achieving dignity is a noble aspiration for your event organization. Through this valuable book, you will fulfill Aristotle's ancient wish and provide even greater dignity and esteem for the event profession now and in the future. As you achieve safer and more secure events, you will also dignify and raise the esteem for the growing event management industry. Aristotle would be particularly proud of this work by Dr. Tarlow as well as pleased with your vital risk management contributions to the ever-expanding event management profession.

Dr. Joe Goldblatt, CSEP
Series Editor, The Wiley Event Management Series
Dean, Alan Shawn Feinstein Graduate School,
   Johnson & Wales University

Preface

He who destroys a life, it is as if he had destroyed an entire world; He who saves a life, it is as if he had saved an entire world."

—BABYLONIAN TALMUD TRACTATE SANHEDRIN 37A

Psychotherapists and clergy have long shared the belief that nothing happens by chance. Certainly, this book is an example of such a possibility. The seeds for this book were planted at a meeting of event and meeting planners held in Las Vegas, Nevada, in 2000. At that time, Dr. Joe Goldblatt approached me and asked if I would be willing to write a book on risk management for the events and meetings industry. To say that I was a hesitant author is much more than a mere understatement. Having spent a good part of my academic career on issues of tourism security, I was not sure that I even wanted to enter the waters of event risk management. Yet the more that I thought about Joe's idea, the more I realized that there is no better way to make people secure and safe than by keeping dangers from self-actualizing. Once I thought about it, I realized that Joe Goldblatt's call to me was not so much about the writing of a book but about the saving of lives. It is in this vein that I have written this book. I began the book with a classical tourism orientation. Coming out of the tourism industry, I had always seen events as one aspect of the travel and tourism industry. As I delved into the subject matter, I came to appreciate the events industry for what it is—an important part of our economy. The industry is more than just an economic stimulus, it is a way to bring people together, a method to exchange information, and, most important, one of the areas in which we can, to use a postmodernist term, reenchant our lives in a time of overt ratio-nalization. This is an industry that touches all of our lives. When-ever we go to a fair or a concert, a sports event, or a business con-vention, we are part of the events industry. It is an industry that covers small events such as a family wedding and major events such as a large political convention. Indeed, life would simply cease to exist as we know it were there no coming-togethers, gath-erings of people, and chances to socialize with our colleagues, family, friends, and people who share common interests.

Whenever we bring people together, there is an element of risk. Event risk should not be seen as a single factor, but rather as an accumulation of variables. Depending on the circumstances, these variables would include such things as:

- Size of crowd
- Size and nature of the event site
- Time of day
- Nature of the event
- Consumables (food, water, alcoholic beverages)
- Age of crowd
- Weather conditions
- Location of the event venue (urban, rural, etc.)

Because each event is different, no event risk manager can ever assume a position of "one equation fits all." Not only must these multiple factors be included in any equation of event risk manage-ment, but each factor must be properly weighed in light of this (or a similar event's) past history. The actual degree of risk involved, then, depends on risk formulas that examine the probability of adverse effects occurring, the direct result of the threats, and the extent to which the venue or activity will be affected by the threats.

While event risk analysis and management were always im-portant considerations in the protection of the public, the horrific events that occurred in New York and Washington, DC, on Sep-tember 11, 2001, reminded the world of just how vulnerable we all are. More than ever before, event planners will face the pub-lic's fear of both travel and events. Suddenly, the naïveté of the charmed 1990s gave way to the reality of the new millennium. Since September 11, 2001, acts of war and terrorism are factors that every event risk manager must consider; even sport events or weddings are on the front line.

Event Risk Management and Safety

The Wiley Event Management Series

alphabetically by region. From the Lower Colorado Region of the BOR, I want to thank Jim Cherry, project manager for Yuma, and Tammy Doyle; Brent Gunderson, director of security, Lower Colorado Region; Linda Limneos, head of the Hoover Dam Visitor Center; Richard Melim, police chief for Hoover Dam; and Tim Ulhrich, project manager for Hoover Dam. From the upper Colorado region, I want to thank Don Wintch, security head for the upper Colorado region. From the BOR's Pacific Northwest region, I want to thank Dale Carriere, head of security at Grand Coulee Dam, and Bernard (Mark) Albl, head of security for the Bureau of Reclamation's Pacific Northwest region. Finally, from the BOR's national office in Denver, I want to thank Elaine Simonson, public affairs specialist.

Throughout this work, my dear friend Don Ahl of the Las Vegas Convention and Visitor Authority has given me both oral and written technical advice. Don spent many hours with me discussing the ins and outs of risk management for the events and meetings industry, and has been a teacher and guide, colleague and friend.

I also received many ideas and lessons from police departments across the United States. I want to thank Ray Wood (retired) and Craig Dorris of the Orange County sheriff's office, Greg Mullen of the Virginia Beach police department, and Gary Christian of the Detroit police department's gaming division. I also want to thank Sheriff Jerry Keller, Captain Terry Mayo, Lieutenant Larry Spinoza, and Sergeant Timothy Shalhoob of the Las Vegas metropolitan police department. Additional guidance came from Chris Peña and David Wiggins of the Anaheim (California) police department, Chief David Sexton of the Long Beach (Washington) police department, and Dale Weiss and Rick Ramussen of the Salt Lake City office of the Federal Bureau of Investigation. Additional thanks go to the many people in Hawaii who helped me, including Peter Carlisle, Tom Haverly, and the members of the Honolulu Tourism Safety Unit. My local police department went out of its way to be of help. To the people at the College Station (Texas) police department, I owe a special debt of gratitude. I especially want to thank Chief Ed Feldman, Assistant Chief Mike Patterson, Lieutenant Dan Jones, and Officers Tom Jagielski and Calder Liveley.

I would be remiss in not thanking several other people. Larry Norton, who is the president of the Hillel Foundation, which serves Texas A&M University, and his entire board have encouraged me whenever I needed extra encouragement. Joanna Kuchta of Texas A&M University's School of Nutritional Science reviewed the section dealing with food safety. Additional thanks go to Elizabeth Leiter for her insights into the world of emergency response teams. A number of colleagues around the country helped me, among them Lothel Crawford, Robert and Alison DelCore, Dr. Daniel Kennedy, Gary Rockwood, and Frank Luizzo. I want to extend a special word of thanks to my friend and colleague, Jeff Beatty, for reading chapters and offering multiple insights, and to the librarians at the Federal Emergency Management Agency in Emmitsburg, Maryland. I cannot begin to thank my secretary, Mrs. J. Sue Doyle for all of her encouragement and help, nor my students at the Hillel Foundation at Texas A&M University, who have "lived" this book with me.

A special word of thanks goes to my student intern and research assistant, Brette Peyton. Brette worked tirelessly to find missing sources and to gather information. She also took the time to read every word of the manuscript and to critique it from the perspective of a university student. Without her help, this book would not have been possible.

Last but not least, I want to thank my parents, my wife Sara, who lovingly read the entire manuscript, my children Nathaniel and Lysandra, who were there to inspire me, and my stepson Joshua, along with other members of my family. It was from them that I "stole" the time to write this book; they had to put up with hearing about the fine details of risk management issues on a chapter-by-chapter basis.

To all of these people, I offer my most heartfelt thank you.

This book deals with many of the possible risks that event risk managers must confront. I have written the book from both an academic and an applied perspective. This is not a book to be placed on the shelf, but a book that is meant to provoke thought and force the reader to apply its lessons to the saving of lives.

Chapters 1 and 2 establish a theoretical framework for the discussion of event risk management. Chapter 1 examines some of the theories of risk. What risks are unique to the events industry, and how do we define what is or is not a risk? Chapter 2 challenges us to examine the metrics of risk management. How do we measure risk? What are some methodologies, assumptions, and practical means to explore and investigate risk?

Chapter 3 directs the reader to some of the more applied aspects of this book. Books are written in chapters, but life is not a one-way flow. From Chapter 3 through Chapter 8, the reader should read each chapter as part of a flowing of knowledge. Each chapter is designed to build on the material learned in the preceding chapters. Event risk in the real world is the joining of multiple factors in ever-reconstituting social challenges. Chapter 3 brings to the foreground issues of alcoholism and drugs. These problems are not only major risk producers for those who use them but also lead to ethical and legal harassment issues. Chapter 4 is a combination of theory and practice. I have devoted this entire chapter to crowd control issues. In today's world, crowd control, whether at a political rally or at a rock concert, presents an ever-growing challenge to the risk manager. Chapter 5 examines issues of fire and emergency medical services. The chapter's underlying premise is that event risk is best handled when those who manage it are prepared for any eventuality. That same theme is carried over into Chapters 6 and 7. These two chapters present the reader such issues as food and water safety, parking lot safety, the safety of paths and walkways, stages, and pyrotechnics. Chapter 7 ends with a discussion of meetings-cum-demonstrations (MCDs) and how this new political entity may impact the events and meetings industry for many years.

Finally, Chapter 8 investigates multiple challenges, including the challenges that face event risk managers as the world begins to enter into a period of possible prolonged war against terrorism. In this war, event risk managers are not only on the front lines, but they are also very much warriors for peace. It is my fervent hope that this book may help all of us to build a better and safer world.

Although I wrote this book from an American perspective, I designed it in such a way that it will be valuable to readers across the world. To be of further utilitarian value, I have included multiple appendices. In these appendices, you will find suggestions for further readings, valuable Web sites, organizations that can be of help, and important addresses.

Being a person who works in both the world of ideas and the applied world, I have written this book as a means to bridge these two worlds. As such, interwoven throughout the book are ideas and concepts along with practical information and exercises for both students of event risk management and the event risk manager practitioner. To aid in this bridging from the world of ideas to the world of action, you will find at the end of each chapter not only an active risk management listing of key terms, but practical drills that connect to each of the book's topics. It is my hope that the material in this book will help you, the reader, to engage in the greatest of tasks, the saving of lives through successful event risk management.

Peter E. Tarlow, Ph.D.

Acknowledgments

This book would not have been possible without the love, friendship, and cooperation of many people. First and foremost, I want to thank Joe Goldblatt, who mentored me, for having the confidence in me to inspire me to write this book. Joe has been more than just an academic editor; he has also been a friend and an inspiration. I also want to thank JoAnna Turtletaub, of John Wiley & Sons. She was always there to answer questions and to give a gentle nudge.

I would be remiss if I did not thank Mr. William Chesney, head of security for the Bureau of Reclamation (BOR), Department of the Interior. Bill Chesney was always there for me, providing both oral encouragement and much needed insight and information. Along with Bill Chesney, I want to thank several other people from the Bureau of Reclamation. I have listed these people

CHAPTER 1

Risk Management:

An Applied and Theoretical Sociological Perspective

*Ask not that all troubles/risks cease, for when they
do life ends.*

—*FOLK SAYING*

IN THIS CHAPTER, WE WILL EXPLORE:

- What events are and what they are not
- Theories of how we use events to facilitate leisure time
- Basic sociological theories used in event risk management
- Postmodernism and event risk management
- The life cycle of a crisis

The Olympic Games are one of the largest "meetings" in the world.
People from all over the world gather together to compete for gold

medals. Hypothetically, this meeting fosters goodwill and mutual respect. Yet, the history of the Olympic Games shows that ever since Adolf Hitler tried to turn the games into a political statement, the Olympic Games have been a challenge for risk managers. The pinnacle of that risk was the 1972 Munich games when Palestinian terrorists murdered members of the Israeli team. The Atlanta Olympic Games of 2000 were, unfortunately, part of the rule that connected risk to security and serve as an example of how even events dedicated to peace can become acts of war. The bombing at Constitution Park placed a pall over the rest of the Olympic Games. Not only did the bombing kill someone and injure many, but both the FBI and the city of Atlanta had their reputations severely damaged. One of the great lessons of the Atlanta Olympic Games is that when risk is not taken seriously enough not only is the event marred, but there is also collateral damage to other institutions and to the host location.

Scholars of risk management, history, and tourism science will long debate the Atlanta Olympic Games. For example, should the park have been left open to the public? Did the FBI merely arrest the wrong man, or was this false arrest a means to calm the public and thus encourage the public to return to the Olympic stadium? Why were the police confused as to where the 911 call originated? Who actually did the bombing? Was this bombing an act of a madman or a planned political statement that can be connected to other Atlanta bombings that took place soon after the Olympic Games? While these questions will become the fabric for both researchers and novelists, there can be little doubt that Atlanta's image suffered greatly, a great deal of money was lost, and Atlanta has had to work hard to recapture its image as the South's most dynamic city. Looking at the Olympic Games as an event provides us with some of our first principles of risk management:

1. Events and meetings are a form of tourism and thus suffer from the same sociological phenomena as tourism.
2. Events and meetings often follow the same patterns, be they mega-events, such as an Olympic Games, or mini-events, such as a community's Fourth of July picnic.
3. Whenever an act of violence occurs within the world of events or meetings, the media are almost certain to report it,

forcing the local event industry to be embroiled in acts of crisis management.

4. Perceptions about an event crisis tend to be almost as devastating as the crisis itself.
5. The farther away one is from a crisis location, the worse the crisis will appear to be and the longer the crisis will remain in the collective travel subconscious.

These basic theoretical principles form the foundation for why risk management is so important to every aspect of the tourism industry from attractions to events, from hotels to meetings. Figure 1.1 gives you some idea of how interlocked the events and meetings part of the tourism industry is.

Meetings and events are businesses; in fact, even a family event such as a wedding, christening, or bar mitzvah is a business. Events employ hundreds of people and involve large amounts of money. Event-goers pay money to attend these events, stay in hotels, and eat in public places. People are served by staff that have

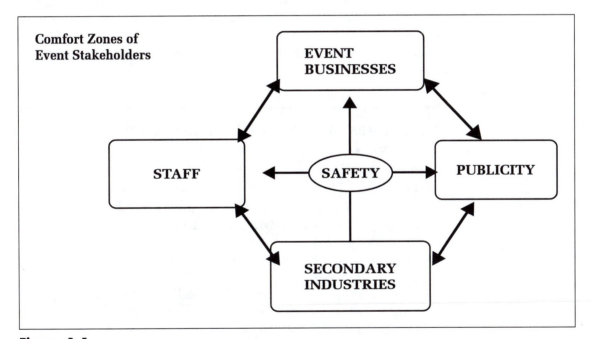

Figure 1-1
Tourism/Convention System of Comfort Zones

access to rooms, prepare food, or handle vast amounts of goods at shows. Within this system, then, there are numerous risks. The event cannot afford to have merchandise lifted, to have guests assaulted, or to have money stolen. Not only are events open to risks by staff members, but they also attract large numbers of secondary people. Among these are vendors, restaurants, gas stations and transportation providers, places of lodging, and local store owners. These people are not directly linked to the event, but earn their living due to the event. Indeed, the larger the event, the more likely that it will cause spin-off economic opportunities. All of these factors carry two risks: (1) the risk of a negative occurrence both on site and off site and (2) the negative publicity that comes from this negative occurrence.

For example, let us look at a simple event, the family wedding. Weddings ought to be both simple and almost risk free. From a theoretical perspective, everyone shares a common joy, people are either family or friends of the bride and groom, and we suppose that from the caterer to the couple all want the same outcome. Yet, anyone who has ever attended a wedding knows that it is filled with risks. From the two families fighting, to the caterer serving the wrong food, to paint on chairs, to the loss of a wedding license, there is barely a wedding that occurs without some risk and some crisis.

Examples of Event Risk Management Incidents

- Food poisoning occurs at the cake-eating contest at a state fair, and guests are taken to the hospital.
- A tent collapses at a wedding and people are severely injured.
- A local gang decides to have a "turf war" at a rock concert and someone is injured.
- Poor drainage causes sanitation facilities to overflow.
- Poor construction causes a bridge over a creek to collapse, resulting in death at a military historical reenactment.
- A bomb is planted at the Olympic Games.

As an event professional, it is important that you understand that it is significantly less expensive to manage a risk prior to the event than to deal with the crisis after it has occurred. Note also that in the world of events and meetings, safety and security issues often merge. Both safety and security are issues that must concern the event risk manager. In today's world of instant biochemical threats, it is dangerous not to view safety and security as two sides of the same coin.

According to the Travel Industry Association and the World Tourism Organization, in the coming decades event managers can expect to see greater numbers of people traveling to concerts, conventions, meetings, and sports activities. The growth of the leisure industry will increase risk, and the need to manage that risk is becoming an ever-greater challenge to the entire tourism/leisure industry. Before we can even begin to examine some of the issues in managing risk, it is essential to review how leisure time is changing in the United States. Over the last decade, scholars have noted that leisure time has taken on the following characteristics:

- Shorter vacation periods
- Competition determined not by distance but by cost of travel to destination
- Greater access to information due to the Internet and the World Wide Web
- Greater exchange of "word of mouth" information between people who have never met each other
- New opportunities for cybercriminals (Tarlow and Muehsam, 1992)

Throughout the world, both in developed and in emerging nations, risk managers in tourism and travel, and meetings and events must face and seek ways to confront crises prior to their occurrence. Risks to the events and tourism industries may come in many forms. Some of these risks are due to issues of potential violence, health and safety concerns, or unique and unexpected weather events such as floods, droughts, and hurricanes/typhoons. As Gui Santana has noted, "Crises in the tourism industry can take many shapes and forms: from terrorism to sexual harassment, white collar crime to civil disturbance, a jet crashing into a hotel to cash flow problems, guest injury to strikes, bribery to price fixing, noise to vandalism, guest misuse of facilities to technology change . . ." (Santana, 1999).

Whether they are natural or man-made crises, writers such as Gui Santana have argued that "there is no doubt that the travel and tourism industry is especially susceptible and vulnerable to crisis." Furthermore, Santana goes on to state that "Tourism is often unable to rebound as quickly as other businesses, since much of a destination's attraction is derived from its image" (Santana, 1999). The risk of these crises is the very social cancer that can eat away at the events industry. Postmodern tourism is often driven by events and therefore the industry must improve its risk management practices to destroy this potential disease.

The current period seems to be prone to great sociological mood swings. What may be seen as a risk or a crisis in one year may be ignored by the media in another year. The age of instant communication via satellite television and computers means that there is now selective knowledge and ignorance. Never have individuals around the world had greater access to information and never has there been greater levels of "information overload." What this plethora of information means is that we now have more information on how to handle risks and to prevent crises, and that the consequences of failure can be more devastating than ever before.

To begin our understanding of the role of risk management in the event and tourism industries, it is important that we review some of the historical perspectives that have shaped the role of risk management in the world of events and tourism. Historically oriented sociologists have observed the similarities that link the end of the nineteenth century to the end of the twentieth century. For example, Stjepan Mestrovic (1991) notes that just as at the end of the nineteenth century, the intelligentsia, and many around the world, live in a bifurcated world filled with a combination of hope and despair.

Event risk managers, then, must work in a world that can be very confusing as well as trying. As John Urry has noted, "Making theoretical sense of fun, pleasure, and entertainment has proved a difficult task for social scientists. There is relatively little substance to the sociology of tourism" (Urry, 1990, p. 7). To confound matters, postmodern scholars point to the blurring of sociological categories in the daily lives of people living in the developed countries:

Postmodernist vacations are usually stressful; there are few exotic places left in the world, and most vacation spots promise to deliver the same bland product—fun

. . . one could just as well spend one's time in a shopping mall. In fact, shopping frequently becomes the primary activity in postmodernist vacations. (Mestrovic, 1991, p. 25)

Examples of these forces in the world of tourism and events can be seen in the multiple conflicts that challenge the risk management specialist. How much freedom is given to a guest who may be engaged in risky behavior? How does one deal with the risks involved when a tourism or leisure event takes on a political tone?

Some of the major differences between life at the end of the nineteenth century and life at the end of the twentieth century indicate that we not only classify leisure in different ways, but that the risks involved in the pursuit of leisure have changed. Christopher Lasch has written about some of these changes, For example, he notes:

The first envisioned the democratization of leisure and consumption; the second the democratization of work. If culture was a function of affluence and leisure, then universal abundance . . . held out the best hope of cultural democracy. (Lasch, 1991, pp. 355–356)

Leisure is no longer viewed as simply idle time for the rich. Indeed, a simple list of some of the ways that we spend our leisure time would surprise our grandparents and great-grandparents. Following is a list of some of the events that occupy our time:

- Family and human life cycle events, such as weddings, family reunions, and barbecues
- Community events, such as school picnics, business outings, and holiday celebrations
- Organized shopping exhibitions
- Civil and political events
- Business meetings and conferences
- Sports events, ranging from Little League to the Olympic Games
- Concerts
- Religious gatherings and pilgrimages
- Local and national political gatherings
- Fairs and festivals

The preceding list demonstrates one of the major problems of risk management in the meetings and events industry. In the modern world, there is a great deal of spillover from a leisure activity to a business activity. Classical nineteenth-century authors of leisure such as Veblen enjoyed clear distinctions between leisure and work. In the twenty-first century, these distinctions no longer exist. One example is the major religious pilgrimage known as the hajj. On this journey, millions of Muslims travel to Mecca. How do we classify this event? Is it tourism, travel, business, or convention? Certainly all of the risks that are inherent in the other four entities mentioned are also part of the hajj. From the moment the traveler sets out for Mecca, he or she is subject to risk, be it in the form of clean water, sleeping facilities, safe travel, or crowd control. This spillover from one field to another is called "dedifferentiation." In today's modern world, it is hard to dedifferentiate between what was once a simple family gathering and what is today a small convention.

Today's mobile society has a very different view of leisure from that of past societies. "Leisure for them [us] closely resembles work, since much of it consists of strenuous and for the most part solitary exercise. Even shopping, their ruling passion, takes on the character of a grueling ordeal: 'Shop till you drop!'" (Lasch, 1991, p. 521). This dedifferentiation between work and play, as exemplified by the shop/drop syndrome, is one of the theoretical underpinnings to the understanding of risk management. As Urry observes in his work on postmodernism, "Postmodernism problematises the distinction between representations and reality . . . or what Baudrillard famously argues, what we increasingly consume are signs or representations" (Urry, 1990, p. 85). Risk management's job, then, is to keep substance from forming into the basis of a crisis, and if such a crisis should occur to contain its secondary effects.

The onset of the information age in the twentieth century has closely paralleled the growth of the travel and tourism industry. Mass tourism is a phenomenon of the twentieth century. It was only with the end of World War II that travel, like so many products, entered the modern world of mass production. This success story also contains within it the seeds of crises. With millions of people traveling daily, and with the onset of the information age, word-of-mouth/computer information spreads rapidly, diseases are carried from one nation to the next, and the potential for violent cross-fertilization, both in ideas and actions, becomes ubiquitous. For example, throughout the world, tourists have been inundated with accounts of widespread acts of violence: in schools, in the workplace, and on public highways. The spread of information, both in written and in pictorial form, has never been so ever present. For example, television and radio broadcast events as they unfold, and the Web permits word-of-mouth dialogue in computerized form to spread instantaneously. Furthermore, the use of e-mail has transformed the world into an electronic village. All this rapid interchange among people makes the life of the event risk manager even more difficult as even small events can become large crises.

Today's event guest is aware of violence not only in urban centers around the world but even in rural areas, be they in Uganda or in the United States. This vast sea of information means that event guests have greater access to information and that the events industry has less ability to hide information. What is still unknown is at what point an excess of information may cause guests simply to shut down and undergo a rejection process. Leisure-oriented risk management specialists face the irony that, as information spreads, it increases the potential for violent behavior. This violence is then reported with the potential of making today's world more dangerous than in any era since the Dark Ages. Umberto Eco illustrates this position clearly when he writes:

> *Insecurity is a key word. . . . In the Middle Ages a wanderer in the woods at night saw them peopled with maleficent presences; one did not lightly venture beyond town. . . . This condition is close to that of the white middle-class inhabitant of New York, who doesn't set foot in Central Park after five in the afternoon, or who makes sure not to get off the subway in Harlem. . . . (Eco, 1983, p. 79)*

Risk managers, then, must deal with an industry that not only is an integral part of many nations' economies, but also plays a major role in the disbursement of information. It is an industry that produces and is produced by information, an industry that sells reality and education, while creating its own postmodern realities based on simulata and plausible facts.

In such a diverse industry as the events industry, it is not surprising that there is no one single unifying theory of event risk management. This is a multifaceted industry that has yet to be defined: Are event attendees the product or the consumers of the product? Is the industry composed of tangibles or is it an intangible many-headed hydra that no one can quite tame? The events industry encompasses such diverse individuals as business travelers, people passing through a locale, people visiting family and friends, delegates to conferences and conventions, audience members, and pleasure seekers. As Chris Rojek notes, in writing about the modern traveler whom he calls the "post-tourist,"

> *[t]he post-tourist is stimulated by the interpenetration or the collision between different facets and representations of the tourism sight. The accessories of the sight—the gift shops, the eating places, the tourist coaches and other tourists—are celebrated for being as much a key part of the tourist experience as the sight itself. (Rojek, 1993, p. 177)*

Many event professionals, however, tend to divide the industry into two broad groupings: movement for pleasure and movement for work (Steene, 1999). Although in this chapter we will concentrate on the person who attends an event for pleasure, much of the material is also applicable to the person who travels or attends an event for reasons of work.

Vacations or leisure events traditionally have been a means by which people attempted to escape from the stress and rigors of everyday life. What once served, however, as a way to repair body and soul has now become a new area for victimization, and that victimization often forms the basis of the job of the risk manager in the prevention of crises.

The perception that pleasure travel to a particular location may result in the visitor's bodily harm, loss of property, or even death can destroy that locale's tourism industry or the reputation of an event. Riots at rock concerts and European football (soccer) matches, highly publicized acts of crime in Mexico, terrorist acts against tourists in Egypt, Yemen, and East Africa have all caused a major loss in revenue. These risks turned into reality serve to remind travel/visitor officials of just how sensitive their industry is to security issues. These "crises" often force two components of a nation's society, the travel/events industry and the security industry, to interact with each other and to learn just how interdependent they are on one another.

Questions of violence directly impact these industries' ability to promote a safe and worry-free experience. Vacationers, viewing their trips as an escape from their personal problems and those of the world, tend to assume that they are safe from crime, disease, and even natural calamities. Business travelers, being more cognizant of safety issues, may also shy away from high-risk locales. Although no locale can provide a perfect security/safety environment, an understanding of some of the sociological theoretical models under which visitors operate can help the student of event risk management to prepare for, deal with, and recover from moments of crises.

An unlimited wealth of data demonstrates that the travel and events industries cannot tolerate an environment that is perceived to be unstable. As noted by Sonmez, Apostolopoulos, and Tarlow, and demonstrated by the example at the beginning of this chapter, the aftermath caused by media coverage may become the second real tourism crisis: "The ensuing negative publicity often characterizes the period after a disaster occurrence that lasts until full recovery is achieved and predisaster conditions resume" (Sonmez et al., 1999, p. 13).

City, county, state/provincial, and national law enforcement agencies play a vital role in making tourists and event attendees feel safe. Convention and visitor bureaus (CVBs), resort hotels, convention organizers, and event planners are aware that a pleasure visitor need not come to their particular community, conference, or event, and therefore see any attack against the safety or security of their guests to be an attack against the essence of their industry. For example, high crime rates, especially at night, do more than just keep visitors and locals alike from frequenting downtown establishments. These crime rates produce a sociological cancerous blight that in the end gnaws away not only at the tourism industry, but at the chance for holding a particular event, eventually destroying it from the inside.

To make matters even more difficult for the event risk management professional, many security forces have only a superficial knowledge of event tourism and travel practices and theory. Few police departments are cognizant that, taken together, the travel and events industry is the world's largest industry or of the relationship between travel and their own community's economic well-being. There are several exceptions to this rule. To illustrate this point, let us examine one city, Anaheim, California. Anaheim has created a special police unit, called Tourism Oriented Policing Services (TOPS), to deal with almost every travel, meeting, and/or convention problem imaginable. A special Anaheim police unit now works with Disneyland and its convention center, focusing on the unique risks involved with conventions and travel. Some of the risks that this unit has learned to handle are risks to non-English-speaking guests, robberies at local hotels, specific crimes targeted at the convention market (such as the stealing of laptop computers), and the special risks that take place in valet companies serving the events industry. In other words, tourism-oriented policing is not just crime fighting but also understanding the risks that event-goers face and developing ways to manage those risks.

Police and other security personnel are often geared to the ideal of "to protect" rather than the marketing ideal of "to serve." The TOPS philosophy changes this equation and declares success not as "How many crimes did we solve?" but rather as "How many risks did we identify and how many crimes did we therefore prevent?" TOPS hopes to change the role of law enforcement agencies by helping them to understand how the events industry impacts a community: what its role is in gaining often needed foreign currency, creating employment opportunities, or improving a community's public image and perception of itself. Additionally, many of the attributes that attract visitors to a community also add to that community's uniqueness and quality of life. Figure 1.2 provides an overview of some of the costs and benefits of tourism to a community.

Because tourism and events are nontangible products—a "feeling" rather than a "thing"—risk management is dependent not only on concrete plans but also on attitudes held by both the risk management professional and the public. Xenophobic attitudes or simply a "take the guest for granted attitude" are felt by the industry's clients who react negatively to such attitudes, be that person an employee or simply a citizen of the locale being visited.

The risk management professional's attitude is therefore a critical element to his or her success. If these professionals resent their guests and view them as intruders, then no amount of fancy marketing will undo the economic damage done to that community's tourism or events industry. If, on the other hand, these pro-

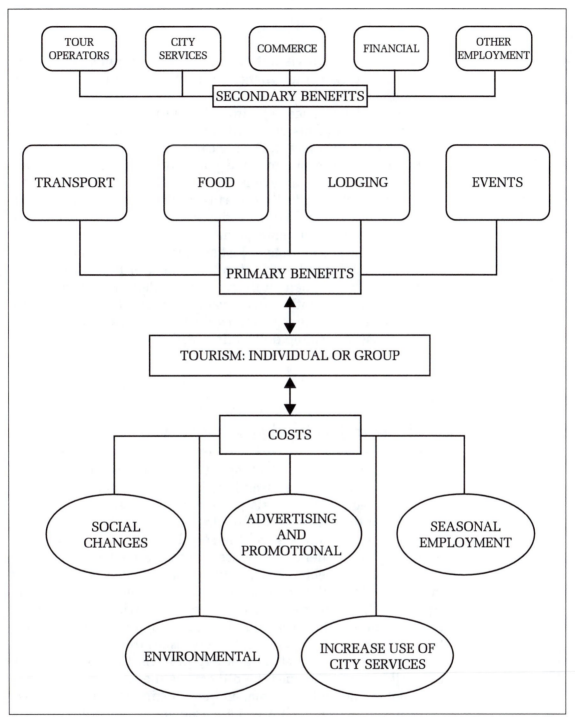

Figure 1-2
Costs and Benefits of Private Tourism

13

fessionals work with visitors with a "cheerful countenance," then the industry creates the synergy necessary to ease it through periods of crisis.

Because risk management, from the guest's perspective, touches so many aspects of his or her life away from home, the potential for a crisis is ever present. Danger can occur not only at the event itself, but also in restaurants and places of entertainment that are in close proximity to an event site, hotels, and transportation arteries. This lack of definition means that event risk management, in its broadest scope, like the industry itself, is undefined. Like a one-cell animal, risk management grows, splits, and travels throughout the social system. Just as there is no one standard and universally accepted definition for the words "tourist" and "tourism," in a like manner there is no one definition of risk management. Working with a composite industry made up of many subindustries, risk managers must deal with crises that are often like the Russian nesting dolls: crises within crises within crises.

Sociological Theories Used in Event Risk Management

Due, then, to this interlocking of industries within tourism/meetings and events, one useful method of understanding the role of risk management in crisis prevention is to return to classical sociological theories such as functionalism.

Functionalists understand the social system as a series of interlocking components. They assume that a change in any one component of a social system will produce changes throughout the system. From the perspective of event risk management, then, a problem/crisis in any one part of the industry is bound to create problems for that locale's entire industry. Due to this interlocking, functionalists do not distinguish safety issues from security issues. Functionalists argue instead that any problem that touches upon the well-being of the guest (and therefore the locale's industry as a whole) is one and the same, and any distinction between these two sides of the same coin is mere academic sophistry.

For example, let us return to our wedding. How are things interconnected? What happens if the wrong meal is served? What risks are there if a person is seated next to someone with whom he or she is having a quarrel? What crises can take place if a relative, parent, or friend has a bit too much to drink? What happens if the band is too loud, the flowers wilt, or an airplane arrives late? In each of these cases, we can easily see how a change in one aspect of the wedding can cause major problems for other parts of the wedding's social system.

G. Smith illustrates this notion when she writes: "Increasingly vicious acts of terrorism against tourists and tourist destinations, rising international alarm over traveler health [and] safety, and the growing economic competitiveness of safe, hygienic, and environmentally sensitive or "green" tourism will be relentless drivers" (Smith, 2000). Functionalists argue that, from the perspective of the tourist, a safety issue and a security issue are interchangeable.

The functionalist perspective is an important tool in our understanding of the interlinkage of tourism components. What functionalists fail to measure, however, is the intensity of the crisis. Are all crises the same? If not, how does a risk manager decide how to prioritize his or her efforts? Do risks generate "time lags" so that there is a measurable amount of time from one risk to another? Must the risk manager react to all of the system's components in every crisis? Thus, while functionalist theory sends up a red flag and warns the risk manager that the potential for a crisis is developing, it fails to provide an accurate forecast about the crisis's severity. Functionalism cannot tell the risk manager what parts of the system will be most affected and what the crisis's time frame is or who in a particular crisis may come out to be the winner or the loser. Thus, a murder in a hotel may also affect restaurant business, but the tourism scholar does not know how deep the effect will be or how long it will take to become a crisis.

A second classical way of looking at a tourism risk management system is through conflict theory. Conflict theorists assume that any social system or component-driven industry has a high potential for conflict/competition, not only between locales but also within locales. For example, a city wants to bring in more conventions. A number of businesses, hotels, restaurants, and nightspots, would be highly supportive of such a decision. Nevertheless, opposition arises from locals who fear greater competition for parking space, higher road usage, and an increasing number of social problems. In such a scenario, the events industry might find itself

in direct competition with any number of coalitions that band together to limit the number of conventions brought into the city.

In conflict theory, there are always winners and losers and
tourism/events are seen as a "zero-sum game." From this perspective, locations and events compete for space, publicity, and clientele.
This competition, in turn, is one of the reasons for the business life
cycle. Thus, a tourism or event crisis in one part of the world may
be seen as an opportunity in another part of the world. Michael Fagence, for example, writes that "the greater experience and resources
of the principal destinations seem to be capable of impeding the
growth in market share of the lesser known destinations" (Fagence,
1998). In such a Darwinian worldview, crises are merely shake-
downs in which the best and fittest survive to the benefit of the
consumer. Risk from this perspective is almost a sport in which
managers compete to determine who can best manage the most risks.

If we view our wedding from the perspective of conflict theory, we can note a number of risks. It can be argued that the people planning the wedding are as much risk managers, trying to
head off potential conflicts, as they are wedding planners. How
many of us have been to a family wedding where the bride and
groom's side may already be in conflict, or where one or more of
the couple's parents are divorced and not speaking to each other?
How popular is the photographer with the guests? How often do
waiters and waitresses lose their tempers?

From this perspective, weddings are like golf, the lower the
score, the better the game is played. Such competition, however,
does not necessarily signify the best tourism product. The history
of consumer products has shown that survival may not be based
on quality of product but rather on quality of marketing, timing, or
symbiotic name recognition. Tourism crises may cause a shake-
down in the tourism market and produce strong marketing agencies, but these crises do not necessarily translate into a better
tourism product or a better managed event.

The prism of symbolic interaction is another way by which to
analyze a tourism crisis. Over the years, this perspective, as first
understood by the sociologist Max Weber, has evolved into postmodernism and then into iconic theory. Scholars who accept this
form of theoretical paradigm argue that tourism, meetings, or special events are highly sensitive to image creation.

The basis for their academic argument is that these industries
sell memories and are "image" producers. The meetings and events

industry, for those who work in symbolic interaction, is about the packaging of a collective memory and associating it with (a) specific place(s) in time or space. From the symbolic interaction perspective, crises are interpreted in a symbolic and symbiotic manner.

An example of this symbolism is in the presence or nonpresence of a police/security force at an event site. In many event venues, a police/security presence may serve the industry as a "psychological" security blanket and a way to avoid crises. Visitors report that they feel more comfortable when they know that an area is well patrolled. In contrast, however, too many police officers in a particular location may send the message that there is a good reason to be afraid, that the officers are there as a result of a crisis, or that the area is dangerous.

Because most people connect a uniformed officer to a range of meanings, the tourism center that chooses to have a security force present must create a setting in which these security personnel symbolize hospitality rather than restraint, service over protection, and security over threat. When security departments produce negative images, they can become part of the risk crisis. For example, negative media reports about Los Angeles and Mexico City have added additional challenges to the tourism industries in those cities. The recent example of New York City police officers doing nothing while more than fifty women were molested in Central Park during the Puerto Rico Day parade has been reported throughout the world. In that case, due to poor risk management and assessment, a major crisis developed for both the city's tourism community and its police force.

The opposite can also be true. In some communities, local security forces have succeeded in becoming symbolic icons, representing not just the use of force but also a cultural attraction. In those cases, the police force is not only a deterrent to crime but also an important icon of that society. Consider, for example, the positive images evoked by the Royal Canadian Mounted Police and the British bobbies.

The aforementioned classical sociological theories form the framework for this book. You, as an event risk manager, must be aware of the following:

1. Events are a volunteeristic activity. As such, the industry must resell itself on a consistent basis. The theoretical consequences of this proposition are many. For example:

    a. Guests need not come to a particular place or return to that place. An event, then, always involves a sense of marketing. To survive, the professional must assume that brand loyalty or even desire to buy can never be taken for granted.

    b. Most guests expect a safe and secure environment. The one exception to this rule is the allocentric adventure market where people seek danger. For example, consider the rise of storm chasers or those who specifically choose to visit a war zone. Even among highly allocentric travelers, danger can be divided into expected dangers (i.e., dangers factored into the trip) and random violence (i.e., dangers that are produced in a violent manner and not considered part of the experience). The large majority of guests, however, assume that a place is safe and secure.

2. Most guests do not distinguish between the concepts of safety and security. The poisoning of food and an act of terrorism often have the same consequences. This dedifferentiation between the terms again holds a number of consequences for the industry. For example:

    a. The farther the person is from a crisis, the worse that crisis seems and the longer the crisis lasts in the outsider's memory.

    b. Guests tend to be more ignorant of local conditions than those who live in a locale. Thus, fear and rumor have greater consequences than does reality. Facts are those that seem plausible rather than those that are empirically provable.

    c. Potential visitors are often highly unsophisticated when it comes to geography. Due to geographic ignorance, fear, and media hype, a crisis in one part of a nation may affect that entire nation's tourism and even tourism throughout that region. For example, consider the drop in event attendance and general tourism throughout the eastern Mediterranean during NATO's Kosovo action.

    d. Event guests do not distinguish between one part of an industry and another. Thus, if a crisis occurs in a locale's food-handling sector, the negative publicity may produce fallout in that locale's lodging industry, attractions, and so forth. Other than a few worldwide attractions, such as the Eiffel Tower and the Taj Mahal, most tourists, especially on first visits, come to a locale and not to a site.

3. There is no one formula to describe all guests. What may be a crisis for one person may not be a crisis for another person. Classical psychographic tourism theory tends to divide visitors along various continuums. For example, we can adapt the Plog model to event risk management and divide guests along the allocentric-psychographic continuum. This typology shows the amount of risk that a person is willing to take. Another typology is that of the inner- and outer-directed event guest. In this continuum, guests are situated according to their motivations to attend an event: Did they attend this event to impress others or merely to please themselves? In all cases, the term special events covers a number of people who view different events as indications of a crisis or lack of crisis. Figure 1.3 distinguishes allocentric from psychocentric event participants.

During the last century, all forms of event participation have grown from an activity of the well-to-do to a part of everyday life. Leisure, parasitic in nature, was once the idle time of the rich. In the mid-twentieth century, leisure became a product for the working person, and once it became producible en masse, it became an integral part of local economies.

Allocentric Event Guest	Psychocentric Event Guest
Rock concert guest	Theater attendee
Ropes course participant	Conference participant
White-water rafter	Visitor to a museum

Figure 1-3
Allocentric and Psychocentric Event Participants

There are several other theoretical models that can be of use to the event risk manager. George Ritzer discusses the McDonaldization of much of the world. This thesis holds that service-oriented businesses have undergone a paradigm shift. Ritzer (1998, pp. 138–140) offers the following postulates:

- Service industries, such as restaurants and hotels, have become rationalized to the point that efficiency over service has become the goal. Risk, then, is an issue of efficiency. Where efficiency ceases, crises begin. Even the wasting of time is a risk that can become a crisis. To understand Ritzer's position, one only need observe the rage that takes place whenever a flight is delayed or canceled or there is a traffic jam on a busy interstate highway.

- Service industries must be measured in quantifiable terms. Ritzer argues that customers want to know exactly how much a vacation or event will cost. Crises may occur, then, in cases where there are cost overruns or missed places on stated itineraries.

- Service industries are seeking scripted experiences. Disney may be the best example of the scripted, or predictable, experience, though cruises also follow this pattern. Vacations, according to Ritzer's theory, enter into a period of crisis when, on a meta level, they cease to be similar to our daily lives. In other words, even what is different becomes the same in that we "script" the differences into our play.

- Service personnel are being replaced by nonhuman apparatus. Ritzer argues that the machine is slowly replacing the human. In risk management, for example, there is the use of security cameras instead of human service agents. This dehumanization of tourism means that crises develop when machines break. The breakage leads to irrationalization due to the fact that it becomes almost impossible to speak to a human being. An example of such irrationalization is the attempt to find a human being in the maze of voice mail after a crisis has occurred at an event.

- As the tourism/event industry becomes more rationalized, Ritzer argues, in the best Hegelian sense, an irrational element occurs. Within this model, a crisis is any irrational moment/occurrence/event within the rationalized tourist experience.

On the other side of the spectrum, Ernest Sternberg argues that all business, including the events industry, manufactures meaning through the use of icons, which he defines as "thematized commodity: an object, person, or experience that has acquired added value through the commercial heightening of meaning" (Sternberg, 1999, p. 4). In Sternberg's terms, tourism or events are placed within a series of contexts that give the tourist or event guest's experience "added meaning" (Sternberg, 1999, pp. 99–100). As the added meaning develops, the first, or realist, meaning becomes depleted. Thus, as Sternberg notes: ". . . one of the turn-of-the century's early realizations is that culture is a depletable resource. This is not because it cannot be used again and again—it certainly can; rather because through repeated use its marginal evocativeness declines" (Sternberg, 1999, p. 108). Sternberg's analysis helps to explain why so many locals see themselves in a state of crisis due to tourism's interaction with the local culture.

Sternberg argues then that to manage the risk at an event, the event risk manager must prevent the risk by:

- **Staging the product.** By this, Sternberg means that the "tourism product's safety" must be organized in such a way that it achieves its aims for both the consumer (visitor) and the supplier.
- **Arranging the product.** Risk management must stand out within its geographical or psychological environment.
- **Contextualizing the product.** Risk management needs to be placed within, or purposely removed from, the context of itself, be that context physical, historical, or psychological.
- **Thematizing the product.** Sternberg challenges his readers to conceptualize how event risk management fits in with the overall theme. What expectations does it meet or not meet?
- **Authenticizing the product.** By authenticization, Sternberg does not mean real or not real, but rather he asks if risk managers provide a genuine experience while still protecting the public (Sternberg, 1999, pp. 115–119, 127–128).

In Sternberg's view, an event crisis is any event in which the visitor does not receive his or her "paid-for reality" for whatever reason. If the product does not deliver a heightened experience (even if the heightened experience is rest and relaxation) into which the client can be fully immersed, then the potential for a crisis develops (Sternberg, 1999, p. 109).

Therefore, it may be concluded that there is no one single definition of a tourism/event crisis. As such, the range of solutions to these crises is as complex as the crises themselves. Following is a potpourri of examples of how different crises have been confronted. The list is not meant to be exhaustive, but rather a snapshot of different event scenarios.

Perhaps the greatest crisis that event management can encounter is the loss of life. Be this loss from kidnapping at a diving resort in Southeast Asia or a serial killer stalking the streets of a large urban center, no destination or venue can long survive capricious and random acts of violence. To combat this threat, event security specialists have developed techniques such as:

- Interacting with guests as an implicit anticrime tool. Even in cities with high crime rates, crime tends to be highly concentrated in small geographic regions. Security specialists can instruct tourists on the safest routes between attractions. These interactions, however, require highly trained security professionals in tourism and tourism safety/security.
- Developing, in conjunction with local tourism offices/bureaus and event organizers, plans to deal with event guests who are victimized by crime. Tourism theory predicts that kind words and caring after a crime has occurred can (but do not always) mitigate some of the crime's negative effects. A security officer's professionalism can create a situation where the victimized tourist leaves with a positive, or at least less negative, attitude about the locale's hospitality rather than as a vocal critic.
- Becoming ambassadors of goodwill for their product. Police and security departments may wish to consider the adoption of special uniforms that match their city's image. Such uniquely tailored uniforms remind local townspeople that their police department/security force not only serves and protects them, but has also adopted a proactive stance in helping to bring economic benefit to the community.

Not all crises are of a violent nature. As the range of tourism crises to manage is exhaustive, following are some other techniques that have been used:

- **Developing interesting jobs and creating high morale.** By creating interesting and well-paying jobs, the community's stake in its local tourism industry increases. As such, when crises do happen, the entire community pulls together to help mitigate and rebuild from the crises.

- **Improving the quality of life.** Typically, tourists and event guests visit communities with sound ecologies, good restaurants, and a multitude of attractions. These same considerations are important factors in determining a community's quality of life. By creating an atmosphere that visitors enjoy, tourism/travel officials encourage leaders in both the public and the private sectors to further improve the community's quality-of-life aspects.
- **Being open and honest.** When a crisis occurs, the last thing the tourism industry can afford is to lie. Facts about the crisis should be given to the media in a nondefensive and forthright manner. Specific people should be designated as representatives who can provide the media with clear and precise facts.

From a tourism/travel perspective, crises have certain common patterns and "life cycles." Accordingly, the risk manager should take into account the following:

- Determining what preparations are already in place and what resources are available.
- Involving the local population in the disaster. Is there special attention that can be given by the locals to the survivors?
- Considering the postdisaster healing process.
- Knowing that no place is immune. The worst possible mindframe is for you to believe that no form of disaster can occur at your locale. For example, the random shootings of tourists that have taken place in the United States are exactly that, random. So far, there has been no pattern determined as to type of place, type of perpetrator, or type of victim.
- Being prepared for a worst case scenario. In any disaster, there will be a threat of personal injury and death. Disasters mean that there will be disruption of operations, financial strain on the tourism locale or company, and damage to the tourism/travel company's image. Prior to an event, take the time to plan two or three scenarios. Tourism/travel professionals should be able to answer such questions as: What actions would you take during a disruption? Do the people in

your community, or at your tourism locale, have adequate insurance to survive a disaster? Will employees and their families have adequate finances to avoid financial ruin? Does the locale have two or three generic recovery marketing plans set to go should a disaster strike?

In all disasters be prepared for disaster fallout. This fallout can occur both during and after a disaster and can include such things as adverse media coverage, constant involvement and monitoring by outside sources, negative name brand association, damage to destination/resort's image, lowering of staff morale, and anger on the part of the victims toward their hosts.

Conclusion

There is no one magic formula to manage all forms of risk in the tourism and event industries. The professional event risk manager must always remember that crises are products of poor planning, lack of media coordination, and lack of foresight. It is the task of the risk manager to minimize the damage, maximize the aid to victims, and work to make sure that the business survives the media onslaught. Although different in nature, all crises demand that a community must be above all else: a community. Event risk managers put their efforts into minimizing the suffering of the victims and their families. Event risk management is making sure that the industry's number one concern is for its guests and their families. Risk management in the hospitality and events world manages a crisis best by caring for people and remembering that hospitality is derived from the Latin meaning "to be open and caring about our guests."

Event Risk Management Key Terms

Allocentric: The tendency to accept risk while traveling or attending an event.

Conflict theory: A theory that assumes that conflict is ever present and that we must learn to manage it as we cannot eliminate it.

Functionalism: A theory that assumes that all parts of an event are interconnected with all other parts. A change in any one part will produce a change in all parts.

Icon: Object that takes on a symbolic meaning apart from what it is. For example, a uniform may become a symbol of security.

Irrationalization: This is the result of too much structuring on the part of an organization. When rules lead to chaos and meeting breakdown rather than to efficiency.

Meeting: A peaceful gathering for a specific purpose. To qualify as a meeting, one must have more than two people, a scheduled time, and a reason for being.

Postmodernism: The theory that seeks a merging of social phenomena. For example, a business convention attendee who takes in a show while out of town.

Psychocentric: The tendency to avoid risk at all cost while traveling or attending an event.

Publicity: Information given about a business or place to people who do not know it or have not used its services in the past.

Secondary industries: Businesses that earn their money from both tourism and local residents.

Symbolic interaction: Actions are determined not by the event, but by the interpretation of the event.

TOPS: Tourism Oriented Policing Services. These are special police units developed to aid the out-of-town public and are specialists in crimes that are prevalent in the tourism industry.

Tourism: The industry that often encompasses meetings and conventions. Tourism is often defined as traveling at least 100 miles away from home and spending one night in a taxable place of lodging for either business or pleasure.

Tourism businesses: Those businesses that are directly engaged in providing tourism services. For example, an airline, a convention center, or a meeting/event planner.

Event Risk Management Drills

1. Assume that you are planning an outdoor sports event, for example, a softball tournament. List the secondary industries and tourism industries that would be impor- tant to you. Then list some of the risks involved, such as health, weather, food, crime, etc. How would each of these risks impact your event? How could a

knowledge of functionalism help you to see problems before they happen?

Where would conflict arise? Who might work at undermining your event?

What icons would make the event memorable?

2. Following are some of the major risks involved in a wedding. Under each item, you will find a list of typical things that can go wrong. How many of these can be managed? How does one prepare oneself to handle these risks? It is important to realize that you can never identify all of the risks. Each event is special and we must always be prepared to deal with unforeseen risk.

   a. Where will the wedding take place?
      - What can go wrong at this particular spot?
      - Who is responsible for the location and its working order?
      - In what type of building will the wedding take place?
      - What problems does the building have: leaks, electrical breakdowns, poor cleaning, sewage problems?
      - If this is an outdoor wedding, what can go wrong: weather conditions, attacks by animals, someone falling, trees or branches falling, surprise noise?

   b. What type of wedding is it?
      - Is this a formal or informal wedding?
      - Will a full meal be served?
      - Are there any special dietary considerations?
      - What time does the invitation state that the wedding will begin? What will you do if there is need for a delay?

   c. Who is participating in the wedding?
      - Does the clergyman or justice of the peace know the time, date, and place of the wedding?

      - Are essential people in the wedding party traveling to the wedding? What happens if they arrive late or lose luggage?
      - Is there a caterer and/or band?
      - Is the florist reliable?

   d. What types of people will attend?
      - What types of risks are inherent in these people? What do you know about them? What is fact and what is colored by your own emotions?
      - Who are the guests?
      - How many guests are coming?
      - Who does and does not get along with whom?
      - What personal grudges do people bring to the wedding?

   e. What are its special security and safety considerations?
      - Is there a safe place to hang up coats?
      - Is there a safe place for presents?
      - Is there a possibility that someone may get sick, break a leg from dancing, or need a doctor?
      - Is there the possibility of a robbery?
      - Is there the possibility of food poisoning?

   f. What resources do you have to manage the risks?
      - Has a budget been set aside?
      - Are there people ready to help?
      - Will you be paying for a police guard or security agent?

   g. What are security and safety considerations?
      - Does the site have a custodian? Will he or she be there during the event? Will you have a chance to meet with him or her?
      - Will you need to hire a police officer to handle traffic?
      - Does the caterer use bonded personnel?

- Will you need a doctor on the premises?

h. What interactions can take place? (See the section on functionalism.)

- Will Aunt Mary throw a fit because someone forgot that she is a diabetic and therefore cause a scene?
- Does Uncle Joe traditionally faint just as the groom is about to kiss the bride?

How does each component interact with the other components?

We can reduce items a to h to the following equation: The actual degree of risk involved depends on "the probability of adverse effects occurring as a direct result of the threats along with the indirect results of a threat plus the extent to which the event or meeting will be affected by the threats" (Tarlow, 1995).

3. Complete the same exercise for another more complicated event. For example, assume that you are the risk manager for an outdoor concert.

  a. Where will the concert take place?

  b. What type of concert is it?

  c. Who is participating in the concert?

  d. What types of people will attend?

  e. What are its special safety and security considerations?

  f. What resources do you have to manage the risks?

  g. What personnel are available?

  h. What interactions can take place?

How would an outdoor concert be different from and similar to a wedding? How about a sports event or a convention held in a downtown hotel?

CHAPTER 2

Risk Assessment

Try to love the questions themselves. . .
—Rainer Maria Rilke, from a letter to Franz Xaver Kappus in 1903

IN THIS CHAPTER, WE WILL EXPLORE:

- How to determine the event risk management data we choose to use
- Utilizing Gemba Kaizen in risk management
- How to conduct a preliminary risk assessment for an event
- Different types of crimes
- Event risk management packages
- Improving our listening skills

Risk assessment is as much about asking the right questions as it is about getting the right answers. Indeed, the old adage, "garbage in/garbage out" applies as much to risk management as it does to computer science. This chapter examines many of the questions that need to be asked by professional event risk managers.

Critical Steps in Conducting Professional Event Risk Management

The critical steps in conducting professional event risk management require that you assess, plan, manage, and control the risks for each event. The simple acronym APMC will help you remember these important steps. The professional event risk manager is responsible for ensuring that each of these steps is carefully completed. Professional event risk management further requires that you carefully and systematically evaluate the outcome of each event so that you can use this history (data) to make informed decisions regarding future events. The primary difference between the amateur event manager and the professional event manager is that the professional systematically completes each of these steps and concludes with a thorough evaluation of the processes and outcomes for each event.

For example, when the fire and police departments of New York City were called to the scene of the World Trade Center disaster, the leaders immediately began conducting a thorough assessment that included:

- Triage of the injured individuals
- Planning for the next steps (search and rescue)
- Management of the scene (credentialing for security)
- Control (by limiting access, providing safety equipment for the workers, and taking other steps to avert additional injuries or loss of life)

Whether you are managing a small or large event, these four steps, APMC, are essential to ensure that you have addressed each and every possible risk factor associated with your event. Once you have completed APMC, you will, as did the New York City risk experts, carefully evaluate your processes and outcomes in order to improve your performance for the next time or perhaps to prevent a next time from occurring.

To accomplish the above, we must decide what data we need and what the risks are. This leads to the eternal epistemological question: How do we know what it is that we know? In other words, a risk manager may have a lot of diverse facts, but without some format the facts are just facts. To understand this concept better, let us examine the place where an "event" is to occur. It is the risk manager who must decide if the quantity of doors is important. The risk manager will examine the site for issues of security and safety. How many entrances/exits should the site have? How many entrances are too many? What is the relationship between the number of exits needed in case of fire and the number of entrances needed as regards crowd control? If the quantity is important, then this piece of information becomes part of the overall database; if the quantity is not important, then we are dealing with a nonuseful fact. Think how important this simple judgment call is at a major jewelry show, computer show, or clothing show. At these trade fairs, there is a great deal of merchandise available to the public. For the show to be a success, the buyers must be able to handle the goods shown at the fair, yet pilferage is a major problem at such events and can cost well into the millions of dollars.

In order, then, to determine which facts are important, we must develop risk theories and scenarios. We will need to ask questions such as the following:

- **How many people will be in attendance?** In event risk management, size matters. Knowing how many people are attending an event establishes perimeters and forecasts staffing levels.
- **What types of events take place in the venue?** Take the time to study the history of the venue. If this is normally a venue for sports events, what special problems will a political event pose for you? What sports facilities can be converted and used for another purpose?
- **What type of person will attend the event?** Demographics tell us a lot about the type of risk that may be prevalent at this event. Will this event attract jewelry thieves? Are the attendees liable to become rambunctious or is this a group that has a low tolerance level for frustration? The more you know about the type(s) of person(s) you will have at the event, the easier it is to develop a risk plan.
- **How frequently do events take place in a particular facility?** Is the site used only occasionally for a special event or large gathering or is this a site that has employees who are event oriented? What event facilities, such as communications centers, does the site have?

Part of the risk manager's job, then, is to know the right questions to ask. Determining the correct questions to ask may be one of the hardest parts of risk management, yet the cost of asking the wrong questions can be enormous. If the risk manager emphasizes the wrong data, he or she is liable to miss issues and to cause a great deal of harm. This need to know which questions are to be asked is the basis of his or her decision making. A mistake here can lead the risk manager to overcollect data and thus "drown" in a pool of data, or it can lead to undercollection of data, resulting in a myriad of dangerous happenings or costly mistakes.

Unfortunately, there is no one magic formula for knowing which facts are important for the event risk manager to transform into data. Following are some suggestions that will help you to decide. At the end of this chapter, you will find a listing of common methodological mistakes.

- **Know who you are.** It is essential that you are comfortable in your position of risk manager. What are your strengths and weaknesses? Are you a person who operates more according to rational thought or more through intuition?
- **Know with whom you are dealing.** What does (do) your supervisor(s) expect from you? What type of public are you serving? What are the public's needs? What type of relationship do you have with local law enforcement agencies and fire departments?
- **List your event risk management assumptions.** We all make many more assumptions than we are willing to admit. From personal relationships to pure science, assumptions are made. For example, scientists assume that God does not directly intervene in the universe or that there is order in the universe. Social scientists assume that in decision making "the alternatives are limited and patterned and that the choices made are orderly [nonrandom] and caused by other [at least potentially knowable] phenomena concerning the person and/or situation" (Chafetz, 1978, p. 35). What assumptions do you make about the people (staff, volunteers, guests, participants) with whom you must serve and work? Do you assume that they are basically smart or not so smart? Do you assume that these are people who tend to have adult bodies and children's maturation skills? Do you expect trouble from alcoholism and drug usage or are you expecting people to need assistance with physical challenges?

- **Develop a methodology for data/information collection.** How do you plan on getting the facts you need and how will you put these facts together in a logical system?
- **Keep your paradigm options open.** Are you doing things based on "we've always done them that way" or are you ignoring contradictory data simply because these data do not fit into your particular paradigm? If so, take the time to challenge your own assumptions and determine if you are engaging in circular reasoning.
- **Don't get stuck in a political quagmire.** All too often, event risk managers get off base, simply because the politics of the situation make it impossible for them to work. Politics is the art of the possible; know what is possible and go there. Time your proposals and reports carefully.

To illustrate these principles better, assume that you are planning a major celebration in your community. It is the community's 100th anniversary and the mayor and city council really want a major celebration and do not want anything to go wrong. Now, assume that a famous movie star from this community is returning to appear at the celebration. Even before accepting the position, it is critical that you decide how comfortable you are working in this situation. Do famous people intimidate you? Can you stand up to the media scrutiny? How well do you deal with people who may be reluctant or even adverse to giving you the data that you request? Then ask yourself who are the major stakeholders. Review the description of conflict theory found in Chapter 1 and ask yourself what does each group want before, during, and after the event.

For example, our movie star may be seeking publicity, showing her in a wholesome light for a new movie she is making. The town's mayor may have a very different agenda and one may assume that other local celebrities have their own agendas. How do these different agendas shape your understanding of event risk? Is your role to be a security guard or an event manager? Does everyone in town know why you are there or did someone else hire you without seeking local approval? Once you have determined if you are comfortable with the job and with your bosses, you can begin to list assumptions about the event. Ask yourself such questions as:

- Are all aspects of this event public?
- Will the media be involved?
- Will you need security guards?

The reason for asking each of these questions is that, first, most event managers may not have considered these questions and thus you are operating from a lack of information, and, second, they allow you to conduct a reality check on yourself. How close to reality are you or are you creating problems that barely exist while overlooking problems that may be ubiquitous? Now, you need to review the material found in Chapter 1. Be careful to constantly check yourself. As you prepare for the town celebration, are you reverting to old patterns? Have you practiced good listening skills and are you willing to redo the plan if new data become available? At the end of this chapter are guidelines for improving your listening skills. Listening may be the single most important skill that a risk manager needs to develop.

Principles of Gemba Kaizen

Much of this chapter examines decision-making theory. Despite what many people believe, few event risk managers have all or even most of the data needed to make informed decisions. Indeed, in a classical hierarchical system, those on top of the pyramid, that is to say, those who have the most power, often have the least knowledge. Executives often are not on site and they often must use highly filtered information. Even if event managers could spend large amounts of their time at the point of contact, there is no way that they could be at all points of contact. Where one goes to look for information may be as important as what information one gathers. In the case of a wedding, should the risk manager only confer with the bride and groom or would he or she want to interview people such as the caterer, florist, and parking lot attendant?

The Japanese have tried to circumvent this system by use of what they call Gemba Kaizen. Gemba Kaizen is defined by Masaaki Imai as "being in the workplace; knowing what goes on at the point of production." In event risk management, we do not produce a tangible product, but risk managers should also practice Gemba Kaizen. For example, it would be hard to assess and control the risks of a celebrity wedding if the event risk manager did not attend the event.

Gemba Kaizen is a classical methodology that allows us to not get stuck in a routine that can lead to costly errors. Gemba Kaizen's eight steps include the following (Imai, 1997, p. xxvi):

1. Select a project.
2. Understand the current situation and objectives.
3. Analyze data to identify root causes.
4. Establish countermeasures.
5. Implement the countermeasures.
6. Confirm the effect.
7. Standardize.
8. Review.

Even in this system, which the Japanese developed for manufacturing purposes, choices must be made as to observation points. In event risk management, the situation is further complicated as event managers must be concerned about selling the product (the event), producing the product (the trade show, convention, festival), and being certain that the product (staging the event) is delivered to the consumer in a safe and timely manner.

The first set of questions that a risk manager must ask is: How does he or she receive information? Is the information conveyed from direct observation, from empirical or factual sources, or from intuitive sources? Following is a brief summary of the types of event risk information that can be gathered and examples of how it is used in event risk management.

DIRECT OBSERVATION

In normative research, this method is the most empirical of all. Routine inspections of an event site location, for example, may reveal potential risk. The operative word, however, is "potential." All event risk is "potential." We may state that "risk" is a future event that we treat as if it had already happened. Thus, the event risk manager cannot actually observe risk. The best that he or she can do is to assume that a particular situation can result in the potential for harm. Thus, even in the most empirical of event cases, the event risk manager must rely on his or her own professional intuition from past events. For example, let us suppose that floors have been waxed just prior to an event. While many people would argue that these waxed floors are a potential risk, until someone actualizes that risk (slips or falls) there is no way of knowing if the risk will become a danger. As long as the risk is in the future, it is only a mere hypothesis. Direct observation never answers the question "why," but rather it seeks to answer questions such as those listed in Figure 2.1.

We might argue that waxing makes floors slippery. However, the fact that the floors are slippery might make people extra cautious. Thus, the waxed floors might also cut down on slippage. The risk might take place on the floor; however, the person may be so busy watching his or her step that he or she does not see the low ceiling and bumps into it. One might imagine that older people have a higher potential for slipping, but it may be children who slip due to the shiny floors inviting them to try and see if they can slide. In a like manner, the risk may at first be seen as a risk to a visitor's health; nevertheless, the risk may also be to the building or the economic well-being of the event.

DATA COLLECTION

Data collection is the most popular tool in decision making. Event risk managers should keep careful records. For example, who slipped and where, what was the age breakdown, and did men and women exhibit different patterns? No matter how good one's data are, it is essential to remember that data reflect the past and never the future. There can be no future data, but rather we use data from past events to assume that, under similar circumstances, future events of a similar nature may occur. Of course, as the popular television advertisement reminds people: Past performance is no guarantee of future action.

---

1. Where might the event risk occur?

2. Under what circumstances would this event risk occur?

3. Who might be at the event?

4. What is the risk of conducting this event? High? Medium? Low?

Figure 2-1
How "X" Is a Risk

When we make decisions based on data collected from past events, we assume that, given a similar set of circumstances, there is a higher probability that a similar incident will occur than not occur. In the example of the waxed floor, there is no guarantee that people will slip on a newly waxed floor, but past history tells us that slippery floors are more dangerous than nonslippery floors. The assumption that the past can be a helpful predictor of the future is the basis of science. Thus, we assume that a person who is inebriated and whose faculties are impaired has a greater chance of being in an accident while driving than one who has not been drinking alcohol. Of course, there is no guarantee that the inebriated driver will be in an accident or that the sober driver will not be in an accident. The most we can do is create a working hypothesis: Under similar circumstances, there is a higher probability that a drunk driver will crash his or her car than a sober driver.

Data are only as good as the way that they are formulated. For example, if no records are kept on where people come from, then even the most careful data analysis will not reveal a distinction between local and foreign visitors. Without the correct variables, the risk manager is at a loss. Event risk managers, then, must not only analyze the variables correctly, but also know which variables to analyze.

INTUITIVE KNOWLEDGE/PAST EXPERIENCE

No matter how well the event risk manager observes the location, how well he or she analyzes it, and how much data he or she collects, some facets of the event risk will be missing. No one can observe everything, no one can collect all of the data needed, and even if such data collection were possible, there is always the potential to subdivide (analyze the data) by the wrong variables. It is at this point that risk management moves from pure science to art. Event risk managers must make decisions, often based on past experience and personal intuition. This need to create an internal professional database is one principal reason risk managers should try to gather first-hand knowledge of the entire events management industry. It is this first-hand, hands-on experience that produces the base from which professional intuition grows. Performing routine tasks, then, helps event risk managers to develop the internal databases that are needed to make informed and intuitively correct decisions.

Assessing Event Risk

One of the key ways by which event risk managers determine event risk is by conducting a preliminary assessment of the event's location and venue. This assessment means that the event risk manager needs to determine who is at risk and where the risk will take place. What are the political and economic consequences of the risk actualizing itself? Are there different consequences if a participant is hurt, an employee is hurt, and property is damaged? How much support is the administration willing to provide the risk management team? Does management understand all of the consequences of assuming a risk? Risk can often be divided into four distinct groups, as shown in Figure 2.2.

The convention industry is part of the visitor industry (also known as the travel and tourism industry), and, to a lesser extent, we may even say that weddings are part of that industry if the wedding brings in people from out of town. As such, the event risk manager's number one issue must be the safety of his or her guests and employees. Material goods can be replaced, but lives cannot be replaced. To be effective in developing an event security risk management program, we first need to understand the challenge of security and safety.

---

1. The probability of the risk occurring is highly probable and its consequences are minimal.

2. The probability of the risk occurring is minimally probable and its consequences are minimal.

3. The probability of the risk occurring is highly probable and its consequences are great.

4. The probability of the risk occurring is minimally probable and its consequences are great.

Figure 2-2
Risk Probabilities

- Workplace violence

- Violence against visitors (event attendees, conventioneers)

- Social disorders such as rowdiness from alcohol, drugs, or gangs

- Family violence

- Violence committed against property

Figure 2-3
Acts of Violence That Concern Event Risk Management

The events industry has more security and safety issues (ranging from food safety to acts of violence) than the average person realizes. Some of the acts of violence that may concern the risk manager are shown in Figure 2.3. Traditionally, event risk management crimes of violence have been classified into one or more of three categories as shown in Figures 2.4 to 2.6.

- Carjacking

- Drive-by shooting

- Kidnapping

- Mugging

- Murder

- Sexual assault

Note that acts of terrorism are included in this category.

Figure 2-4
Event Crimes of Violence

- Auto theft

- "Con" games

- Property theft

- Pickpocketing/distraction

- Vandalism

Figure 2-5
Event Crimes of Opportunity and
Nonviolent Crimes

Planning for Event Stakeholder Security

Physical security begins with planning. It is not economically feasible, or theoretically necessary, for installations and activities of every kind and character to achieve the same degree of protection. Due to monetary and personnel constraints, many sites will not be able to achieve maximum protection for the entire facility or activity at all times. It is essential that where cuts may need to be made that everything possible is considered to first protect lives and only then to protect physical property.

- Drug purchases

- Illegal gambling

- Prostitution and public nudity

- Public disorderly conduct (e.g., intoxication)

Figure 2-6
Self-Victimizing Event Crimes

Mission Exercise

The beginning of event risk management is "knowing your mission." What do you, as an event risk manager, believe your mission to be? For example, a mission statement might read: "The mission of the Festival Risk Management Division is to create a safe environment in which the guests are able to enjoy our festival in a peaceful, safe, and secure environment."

Stages

Risk management programs often have three stages. First, a program that desires to create a safe and visitor-friendly ambiance must offer good planning. This means that the program is organized for those unfortunate events with which we hope we never have to deal. Second, employees should consider public awareness and participation. Are employees allies in avoiding risk or do they simply not notice? Finally, you must implement employee and volunteer education and training. Does your program train others to work with you or is your department isolated and alone?

An event risk management department should consider a "park, walk, and talk" philosophy regarding security and crime prevention. Alternatives to standard patrols that might be considered are saturation or directed patrols and special-event units that utilize equipment such as bikes or horses. To begin to develop such a plan, think about the questions shown in Figure 2.7 and for each event seek answers that work for that scenario.

---

1. How would you define visitor activities at your event?

2. Where are the major risks to visitors at that specific event?

3. What are the major risks to the event site from outsiders?

Figure 2-7
Questions to Consider

Publicity and Crime Reduction

Publicity for your event comes in many forms: visual, written, or oral; formal or informal. Publicity is the way that the events industry informs the public about an event: what it has to offer, when it is open, and how much it costs. Events are often public spectacles and, as such, they do not exist without some form of publicity. Because many people who work in the events industry want their event risk management team to take a "quiet" approach to security issues, there is a great need for early and continuous risk analysis. It is essential that security officials and event stakeholders agree on what is or is not an acceptable risk. It is essential to remember that no risk is fixed in time: What may be an acceptable risk at one point in time may be unacceptable in another time frame. Risk is changeable and needs to be reviewed constantly. All event risk analyses should be based on the principle that there is no object, person, or reputation that cannot be stolen, damaged, or destroyed.

Event Stakeholder Risk Analyses

Because there are always costs involved, risk analyses are conducted to develop probability samples and determine how resources should best be utilized. Event stakeholder analyses consist of a number of steps, including those shown in Figure 2.8. Then:

- Conduct a hazards and vulnerability study (site survey) of personnel, facilities, items, and functions.
- Conduct a probability of occurrence assessment. What are the chances that the risk will actually occur?
- Establish a range of losses based on experience (3–5 year period). How much damage will the risk's occurrence cause?
- Compare the probability of occurrence with the risk of damage. Can you absorb the loss? What would happen if such a loss were to occur?

The following formula provides an insight into the probability of risk. Determine the probability of adverse effects occurring as a direct result of the threats and add the extent to which the site or activity will be affected by the threats.

Identification of Individuals, Items, Locales, and Functions in Terms of:

- Loss of life or bodily injury

- Total replacement

- Temporary replacement

- Unrecoverable costs

- Allied or related loss

Figure 2-8
Identifying Individuals, Items, Locales, and Functions

SUPPORT STRUCTURES

These are the facilities that supplement or make possible an event or convention delegate's stay in an out-of-town location. They include such items as places of lodging, eating establishments, transportation arteries, medical facilities, and basic city services such as firefighters and security professionals. At an event site, risk managers may want to examine such areas as the power/cooling/heating system, the visitor information center/booth, storage areas, the walls and fences around the site, and the roadways leading up to the site or through the site.

The law enforcement/security professional community and our legal system traditionally have served as our social control process. However, at special events, some people exhibit low inhibition levels and social control is harder to maintain. Event risk managers often have large geographic areas to patrol and this mixture of high visitor density plus wide-open spaces leads to the questions shown in Figure 2.9.

NATURAL THREATS

These are the consequence of natural phenomena such as a hurricane or earthquake. In the United States, these occurrences are seen as not preventable or, as they are called in the world of

- What type of equipment is best for a particular site and event? For example, heavy weapons might add extra security but could do more harm than good at a political rally.

- Does the threat of punishment act as a good deterrent in visitor situations?

- What impact might acts of terrorism have on the event's management?

- What is the potential for site disruption, damage, loss or destruction of property, personal injury or loss of life?

- How secure is the information at your event both for the attendees and for the event management?

Figure 2-9
Patrol Questions

insurance, acts of God. They may, nevertheless, greatly affect security measures and are a major risk to the event. Europeans, on the other hand, argue that the results of such natural threats are foreseeable and therefore not acts of God. To make matters even more complicated, it is often very difficult to reschedule an event. Thousands of dollars may already be invested in the venue, airline tickets, and/or speaker's fees. The event's organizers may take a very different approach to foreseeable natural phenomena, such as the prediction of a hurricane, than the risk management department, thus causing a major political problem for the risk management team.

The questions shown in Figure 2.10 should be posed as a key part of your event risk management assessment process.

HUMAN THREATS

These are traditionally those threats that are the result of a state of mind, attitude, weakness, or character trait. Some common human threats that event risk managers must assess, manage, or control

- What are some of the natural threats to your event or meeting?

- Do you have a plan of action ready?

- How well are you coordinated with other agencies such as civil defense?

- What type of communications system would you use were your site to lose standard methods of communications?

- How would you handle the political problems involved? For example, the risk management team desires to cancel the event and the event's organizers are willing to accept the risk.

Figure 2-10
Key Considerations Should a Natural Disaster Occur at Your Event

are listed in Figure 2.11. Human threats have certain common characteristics, including those depicted in Figure 2.12.

While most event risk managers wish to achieve a perfect and absolute risk-free environment, the reality is that this goal is unattainable. For this reason, event risk management departments concentrate on both prevention and protection. Most people who

- Theft

- Bombings and acts of terrorism

- Pilferage

- Assaults, economic or sexual

- Carelessness and accidents in performance of duties

- Disaffection and disloyalty of staff

- Safety hazards from equipment

Figure 2-11
Typical Human Threats at Events

- They often involve acts of carelessness.

- They often can be prevented by thoughtful planning.

- A determined person will get through almost any risk management system.

- They often involve a sense of denial on the part of the event's organizers.

Figure 2-12
Common Characteristics of Human Threats

commit crimes against event guests believe that the opportunity exists for that crime's success. Event risk managers must always operate under the assumption that there is no object so well protected that it cannot be stolen, damaged, or destroyed. There is nothing in this world that is 100 percent secure.

Event risk management should never be conducted in a vacuum. It is a good idea for event risk managers to develop contacts with allied organizations such as local police and fire departments, hospitals, and federal agencies. Figure 2.13 provides a guide to conducting the event risk management process.

Types of Crimes That Are Common Event Occurrences

The following crimes may occur before, during, or after an event. You must assess your event's vulnerability for each of these potential threats.

CRIMES OF DISTRACTION*

While crimes of distraction (CODs) are rarely noticed by the media, the victims of CODs rarely forget their experiences. How you handle a COD can determine how a visitor will remember his or

*The author wants to recognize the lectures given by Ray Wood and Lothel Crawford for their ideas and inspiration found in this section.

1. Conduct a good security analysis of the event site both before and after the event. What are your weaknesses, where are you most vulnerable? Before the event, the risk manager attempts to locate risks and develop a plan to deal with these risks. The postinspection is the critique. After the event, the event risk manager should ask questions such as: What other risks were there? What was missed? What actions might have been taken?

2. Develop a good working relationship between local security professionals and the various components of the local tourism, hospitality, and events industry. Do they know you: the risk manager? Will local public safety agencies be of help? To whom can you, as the event risk manager, turn, should you need help. These are the political questions that can make a major difference in the success or failure of an event's total risk management plan.

3. Make certain that all event stakeholders know who you are and for what each risk manager is responsible. The more other staff and volunteers understand your role and what you do, the better the chances that they will become willing team members in helping you to manage the risks at your event.

4. Develop security pamphlets/signs and other communications that explain to guests, staff, and volunteers key information as listed below and make sure that the signs are readable to all of those who are attending and working at the event. English language signs are not helpful if the attendee does not read English and you may prefer to use international graphical symbols.
   - Best evacuation routes to take
   - Exit signs
   - People and things to avoid
   - First-aid signs
   - Warning signs
   - Parking signs
   - Emergency access phones and numbers
   - Information kiosks

5. Develop a media plan to:
   - Increase safety and security awareness
   - Be prepared in case damage control is needed

6. Coordinate event risk management efforts with the local community as to:
   - Controlled hours and traffic flow
   - Advance notice of events
   - Consultation prior to event
   - Limitations and division of labor and resources
   - Policy vis à vis out-of-towners
   - Visitor information sources

Figure 2-13
Guide to Conducting the Event Risk Management Process

her visit to your event site. CODs are always remembered by the event's participant, who often blames the experience on the risk management team rather than on his or her own mistakes. The category of COD includes such criminal activities as credit card fraud, pickpocketing, and "quick change-of-bags."

Although we will never be able to enter into the mind of another human being, research shows these common elements among the perpetrators of CODs. COD perpetrators often view their victims as suckers whose money should be separated from them with a minimum of difficulty. COD practitioners do not wish to deal directly with victims, but instead prefer to be invisible. They tend to seek an immediate escape and feel no remorse at hurting another person. COD practitioners assume that getting caught is part of the "price" of doing business.

Following are several examples of common COD techniques. It should be noted that COD practitioners study their art, just as any other professional, and are continuously updating their skills and techniques.

- **Coat over arm.** In this case, the perpetrator uses the coat as a means to take a purse and then hide it.
- **Ketchup bandits.** Something such as ketchup is spilled on the victim and then while one person is cleaning the victim up, his "colleague" steals the victim's wallet or purse.
- **Luggage/bag removal.** This is common where bags are held while an event is in progress. It can take place either by the perpetrator insisting that he or she has lost a receipt or when one person creates confusion while his or her partner walks off with the luggage.
- **Rest room thefts.** These are common in places where a man hangs up his jacket or a woman her purse on the back side of a lavatory door. Men's wallets have even been stolen while the victim was using the toilet.

Pickpocketing

Pickpocketing is the number one form of COD. Event risk management departments are often unaware of the extent of this problem because many guests fail to report such crimes. Figure 2.14 lists several techniques to help guests reduce the incidence of pickpocketing.

Always Remind Visitors To:

- Use handbags with zippers and locking flaps

- Carry handbags securely with the flap close to the body

- Never carry wallets in back pockets

- Watch out for unnecessary "bumps," especially in markets and other places where there are crowds, such as at long lines or major banquets

- Never leave valuables unguarded or trust a stranger to watch valuables

- Be on guard if a stranger tells you have a spill on your clothing or spills something on you

- Watch out for strangers at ATMs or credit card machines who state that money has been dropped—on the whole, indoor ATMs may be safer

- Watch for people loitering

- Never loan money to someone who claims to work for the event

Figure 2-14
Theft and Pickpocket Reduction Techniques

Credit Card Theft

Credit card theft is another serious problem at events. The goal is to take credit cards and utilize them as quickly as possible. Credit card theft can become a problem, especially where there are booths selling souvenirs or at local stores that earn their money from major event participants. The event risk manager can use the recommendations in Figure 2.15 to reduce credit card theft.

Reviewing Packages

Events may be places where "terrorists" may choose to make a statement, and for this reason a large number of places around the world review packages prior to allowing ingress into event venues.

- Encourage visitors to keep credit cards protected.

- Encourage event sellers and concessionaires to check signatures on credit cards. The signature on the card should look like the signature on the sales slip. Both signatures should look the same!

- Look for unusual behavior. If the person seems overly nervous and/or is making a strange set of purchases (e.g., many of the same item), this may be a sign of fraud. Another sign may be purchases made without regard to size, quantity, or color.

- Encourage event personnel to seek a second form of picture identification prior to selling merchandise by means of a credit card.

- Check the expiration date. Is the card still valid?

- Ask to see a passport and check the passport's seal and the individual's photo when dealing with foreign credit cards. Handwritten passports ought to be regarded with a tremendous amount of suspicion.

- Be wary of customers who are unnecessarily talkative or who delay a selection until the salesclerk becomes upset.

- Be wary of a person who hurries the salesperson just as it is time to quit for the day.

- Be wary of a person who takes a credit card from a pocket rather than from a wallet or purse.

- Be wary of a person who does not carry a driver's license or does not have a photo identification card.

Figure 2-15
Event Credit Card Theft Prevention Recommendations

While bombs and other incendiary devices can be disguised in numerous types of packaging, the following discussion may act as a guide to help the risk manager deal with extraneous packages, bags, and so on. Such package reviews often cause a great deal of consternation, possible embarrassment, and additional time management problems for guests and participants. Figure 2.16 provides event risk managers with a number of ways to handle this problem.

- Post signs clearly announcing package reviews. Make sure that guests and participants understand that packages are to be reviewed at the time of ticket purchase or prior to entering an event venue.

- Encourage attendees to store packages away from the event venue or to leave these items with trusted people not attending the event.

- Act sensibly and sensitively. Event participants are not criminals. If a person chooses not to be searched, that person should be allowed to leave. Do not immediately assume that a refusal to have a bag examined means that the person is dangerous.

- Offer alternatives, be polite, but do not give in to pressure. If the person refuses to allow the search, explain that the examinations are the policy of the event management and that people who do not wish to have their bags searched can either lock their bags at another place or not enter the venue.

Figure 2-16
Guidelines for Event Package Reviews

Event risk managers must always consider both local laws and customs and so should modify these guidelines accordingly.

There can also be a significant amount of risk to the people conducting the package reviews. Make sure that these people are trained in package review and in anger management. Prepare written instructions and guidelines to remind package reviewers of the following:

- Do not put your hands into a package blindly; you do not know what needles or other dangerous objects may be there.
- Place the contents of a package onto a tray, then in plain sight look at the contents.
- Allow the person whose package is being inspected to return the contents to the package.
- Test cameras and beepers. Take a photo or turn the beeper on.
- Use common sense. If in doubt, do not admit the article in question into the venue.
- Smile! If a person becomes angry, smiles and agreements that these inspections are a hassle is the best policy. Let the visitor know that you are on his or her side and that you are doing this procedure for his or her protection.

Decision Making

We began this chapter with a discussion about decision making. How you reach these decisions can have major consequences for your event. Event risk managers are human and, as such, also make mistakes. Following are some of the most common methodological mistakes that event risk managers commit:

- **Inaccurate observations.** Event risk managers must always remember that seeing is not always believing. Often, what appears to be safe may not be safe at all. In a like manner, there are many people who are experts in deception. Seeing should be understood as one way to gather data, but never the only way.
- **Overgeneralizations.** It is easy to assume that all children are at risk, that all females are helpless, and so forth. These are dangerous overgeneralizations. For example, the female may be a karate expert or a homicide bomber, while the sexual assailant may be desirous of assaulting a man rather than a woman.
- **Selective observation.** Event risk managers may be so convinced that they must deal with an alcohol problem that they may fail to note other potential problems along the way. The problem may be not just alcohol but also drugs and/or sexual assault.
- **Inventing information.** All people have a habit of creating information. In fact, as any good lawyer knows, honest people may hear and see events from totally different perspectives. The mind often plays tricks on observers and providers of information. Risk managers can never accept a story at face value. Instead, they must investigate it and use good common sense. The difficulty arises when time is of the essence for your event.
- **Illogical reasoning/lack of alternative assumptions.** Mistakes are often made simply because we get stuck in one set of assumptions. The cash box may have been stolen by the local carnival troupe down the street, but perhaps it was not stolen at all but merely misplaced and the location forgotten. Often, we assume too much. In the area of event risk management, too many faulty assumptions can lead to major errors in judgment.
- **Ego involvement.** Risk managers need to be able to say, "I don't know." When we assume that we have a monopoly on

good judgment, truth, and information, we place ourselves and those for whom we are working at risk.

- **Premature closing of inquiry.** We can easily overlook an issue because we are too tired or too sure of ourselves. We are often stuck in a specific paradigm, so we simply do not see the obvious or we forget to ask the next set of questions. Because something was successful, dangerous, or not dangerous in the past does not mean that it cannot be so in the future. Immediately following the Atlanta Olympic Games bombing, a suspect was arrested and later found innocent. The resulting publicity, however, injured his reputation.

- **Mystification.** This is the way that all of us deal with issues such as luck. There is a certain amount of luck that can make the difference between success and failure, but it is a mistake to confuse good luck with good planning. Many airline crashes are avoided by good luck, but chaos theory would argue that our luck can only last for so long.

- **Not recognizing that we make errors.** All people make mistakes: Reports get mislaid, light switches get turned off by accident, and doors are not locked that should have been locked. The issue is not necessarily that mistakes happen, but rather how we plan for their happening. Do we have a backup plan for when they do occur and what is our recovery plan?

Listening and Communication Skills

One of the most important methodologies in developing data for risk management is precise listening skills. We often hear what we want to hear, or, due to distractions, busy lives, and so on, simply do not hear what we need to hear. Learning to listen may be one of the hardest things we do and most of us rarely do it very well. Figure 2.17 provides several tools to help improve your listening and communication skills.

GENERAL SKILLS

Most feelings are combinations of five basic feelings (similar to the primary colors). Almost all other feelings can be regarded as a combination of these primary feelings. When listening, see if you

In Event Face-to-Face Communication:

- *Look at the other person directly.* It is essential that you face the person who is speaking to you. Not only does this let the other party know that you care, but it also provides you with insights into the person's body language.

- *Adopt an open posture.* Many of the people with whom you may come in contact are of a psychographic nature. When dealing with these people, it is essential that they think you care about them and that you are willing to help.

- *Lean slightly toward the other person.* When we lean toward someone, our body language says "I am taking what you say seriously." The better the rapport, the better the information.

- *Maintain good eye contact.* There is a wealth of information to be gained from someone's eyes. The better the eye contact, the more people are willing to share information.

- *Try to be in a relaxed position.* You are the professional. The last thing that you can afford is for the other person to think you are nervous.

In Asking Good Questions:

- *Use concrete speech.* Avoid words like "things" and "feel." Ask questions such as: When did the event happen? What was the man's name? The pronoun "they" refers to a plural, not a singular. Using "he" and "she" can reveal important information.

- *Do not be vague.* What does an "old man" mean? Is old 20, 30, 40, 70, or 80 years of age? Get the facts.

- *Listen for themes and subtexts.* If the person is telling you about a food problem but there is always a stranger in the story, are you getting a message that is different from what the initial story may have been?

- *Listen for feelings.* Is the person telling you that he or she is afraid? Is there a control issue that is not being stated? Is anger being expressed in the guise of love? For example, "I would not tell you this but I care about Joe. . . ."

Figure 2-17
Improving Your Listening and Communication Skills

can find one or more of the following basic feelings and then determine how the speaker is expressing it (them).

- **Anger.** Many people in the United States are often afraid to express anger. Instead it manifests itself in passive aggressive behavior, for example, agreeing to do something and then not doing it. Anger can make your work a lot harder and mislead you when you are trying to collect information.
- **Fear.** Fear is a major element in event risk management. Risk is a form of fear of the future. In small doses, it can lead to a well-thought-out plan; too much fear, however, can paralyze the event and lead to overreactions.
- **Sadness.** Sadness is a normal part of life. When organizing most events, sadness is an emotion that most event risk managers try to avoid. Sadness is one of those emotions that leads people to let their guard down and to be open to a high degree of risk.
- **Joy/happiness.** This is the emotion that most event risk managers' supervisors and clients want to create. Your job is to do the risk management work so that others can experience joy with the least possible risk. However, as every event guest knows, joy often is accompanied by tragedy, for example, as many people seek joy through high levels of alcohol consumption.
- **Love.** This is one of the hardest emotions for an event risk manager. Love can create all sorts of strange problems. For example, family disputes are dangerous because they often mix passion, love, and anger. The love emotion may also mean that important information may be withheld from the event risk manager.

Listen for sensory modes and respond in kind. Try to show that you are on the same wavelength. If you respond with a different mode, hostility can often result. If you respond in the same mode, the other person may respond better. Figure 2.18 shows the relationship between the five senses and the verbs that express these senses.

How can you adapt your event risk management language to better communicate with your stakeholders? The critical component of risk assessment is open, continuous communication with all event

Sense	Verbs/Expressions
Sight	See, look, be lucid, be foggy, clear things up
Hearing	Pay attention, sounds . . . , gossip
Touch	Dig, handle, get a hold of, be easy to deal with, push people around
Smell	Sniff, be rotten, smell like
Taste	Be nasty, sweet, sour, on tip of tongue

Figure 2-18
Sensory Relationship Words for Event Risk Management

stakeholders. The better your communication skills, the more comprehensively you will be able to assess the risks at your events.

To improve your listening and communication skills, practice this exercise. Take the sentence, "I don't think you should produce this event because. . . ." As you complete this sentence, carefully distinguish between the feelings and the content of the message. Then, to further progress in your abilities, make certain that you:

- Avoid responses that imply condescension or manipulation.
- Avoid giving premature advice.
- Do not give a negative response.
- Do not patronize or placate.
- Avoid clichés.
- Ask closed and specific questions.

HEARING BODY LANGUAGE

When people are given a choice between visual body language and oral communication for meaning, most people will choose body language. To improve your communication skills, you should:

- Keep your voice low and steady and know that your voice really does sound like the one you hear on the tape recorder.
- Listen to a tape or compact disc (CD) of a person whose voice you admire.
- Listen to your voice for signs of stress: higher or lower than normal pitch or faster or slower than normal speed.
- Review your mannerisms to determine what is and is not pleasing.

INTERPRETING BODY LANGUAGE

An effective event risk manager must be able to interpret body language. You can accomplish this task by paying attention to:

- Person's use of space
- Person's posture
- Person's seeking of privacy, through silence or lack of expression

The latter is often symbolized by closed eyes, withdrawal of chin toward chest, or hunching of shoulders.

A smile is not always the same smile. There are various forms of smiles. Which other smiles can you recognize?

- Knowing smiles
- Forgiving smiles
- Presenting smiles

As you watch for body language, you must be able to analyze carefully the hidden messages that are transmitted through looks, posture, smiles, and gestures.

When listening for body language make certain you:

- Do not appear to be defensive.
- Connect with the other person; try to see things from his or her side.
- Apologize and do not argue if you have made a mistake.
- Do not take things personally; when necessary, quote an event policy or rule in a neutral manner.

The preceding discussion on interpreting body language was adapted from the book *Body Language* by Julius Fast (1971).

There are three ways we communicate with event stakeholders: through words, through body language, and through the tones and loudness of our voices. If the total message we transmit or receive is 100 percent, then about 7 percent is through words, about 38 percent is through tones, and about 55 percent is through body language. Therefore, over 90 percent of our ability to communicate is through our ability to use and interpret body language, speech tones, and vocal cues.

JUDGING BEHAVIOR: MALES VERSUS FEMALES*

It is essential that when we listen we try to be as gender neutral as possible. Figure 2.19 shows some of the prejudices under which many females have been, and often still are, forced to labor. This figure demonstrates how a person with sexual bias often unfairly reframes a statement made by a male when the same statement is made by a female. Read carefully the statements in the figure and then think of other unfair situations in which you may have judged someone not for what that person said or did, but merely because of the person's gender, religion, ethnic background, sexual identity, or race.

Effective event risk management must avoid bias when communicating with stakeholders. The more open you are to communication with others, the more effective you will be in collecting the information you need to make informed decisions regarding event risk management.

Event Risk Management Key Terms

Decision-making theory: A set of principles that explains how we make or do not make decisions.

Foreseeable natural phenomena: Another term for acts of God. It implies that humans are responsible for natural calamities due to lack of good risk management.

Gemba Kaizen: Being in the workplace; knowing what goes on at the point of production.

Hazards and vulnerability study: An assessment of the physical site for an event, what can go wrong, where the risks are found.

*Much of the information in this section was taken from or inspired by the works of Deborah Tannen, Ph.D.

Males	Females
In business we call men enterprising.	In business we call the same action when done by women pushy.
When men are contemplative, we view them as thoughtful.	When women are contemplative, they are often called overly choosy.
A man who finishes a task is praised for his follow-through.	When a woman finishes a task, some men say she does not know when to quit.
If a man holds on to a position, he is seen as steadfast in his beliefs.	When a woman refuses to budge, she is often call stubborn.
When a man has many intimate relations, he is often called "worldly."	In the same situation, women suffer from a double standard and often people say that they have "been around."
Men who say what they think are considered to be honest and forthright.	Women who say what they think are often unfairly called opinionated.
Men in positions of power are expected to exercise authority.	Women in positions of power are often called tyrannical when they exercise their authority.
We call men who know how to be quiet discreet.	When women choose not to speak, they are called secretive and when they do speak are called gossips.
Society honors tough-minded men and calls them stern taskmasters.	When a woman is tough-minded, she is often called difficult.

Figure 2-19
Are You Guilty of Male and Female Stereotypes?
(*Source:* Deborah Tannen.)

Human threats: Traditionally, those threats that are the result of a state of mind, attitude, weakness, or character trait.

Probability of occurrence assessment: An attempt to decide if there is (1) low chance of occurrence and low consequences, (2) low chance of occurrence and high consequences, (3) high chance of occurrence and low consequences, or (4) high chance of occurrence and high consequences.

Event Risk Management Drills

1. How would you incorporate listening skills into your collection of data for a festival? How might different people state problems each in their own way? What information might not be said? How might body language help in determining the types of questions that you might want to ask? How would your process differ if the event were a trade show?

2. You have been asked to turn a sports arena with seating for 5,000 spectators into an exhibit hall. What are some of the types of information that you would need to know? What questions would you ask? What would be some of the event risk management challenges that you would face?

3. You have been asked for the first time to manage a large business meeting. The corporate executives will attend, and if they like the way you organize the event, there will be some great recommendations. Review the principles of Gemba Kaizen and explain how these principles might help you. How would this methodology help you to conduct a hazards and vulnerability study (site survey) of personnel, facilities, items, and functions, as well as a probability of occurrence assessment?

CHAPTER 3

Alcohol and Events

Drunkenness is temporary suicide. . . .

—BERTRAND RUSSELL

IN THIS CHAPTER, WE WILL EXPLORE:

- Issues of alcohol at events
- Misconceptions about alcoholism
- Alcohol and the lifestyle of young adults
- Alcohol and ethics
- Alcohol and sexual harassment issues

In 1991, the international media reported on a major U.S. military scandal, called the Tailhook scandal. The part of Tailhook that was most reported on by the media was the sexual harassment aspect. There was little doubt that the lowering of inhibitions due to the use of alcohol played a major "supporting role" in the drama. In many ways, the Tailhook scandal, involving some of America's brightest and most promising young people, reinforces the principles studied in Chapter 1. In Chapter 1, we learned how individuals often develop a new persona when they are in a group or away from home.

One of these group behavior tendencies is the lowering of inhibitions. For example, during the 1991 Tailhook convention, there were both group drinking and "group-think," and both led to a major scandal involving the U.S. Navy in the embarrassing problems of sexual harassment and sexual exploitation.

The Tailhook scandal destroyed the careers of some of America's best military officers who may have had a "few too many drinks," resulting in a lowering of sexual inhibitions and common sense. In fact, the scandal was so traumatic that a naval instructor, James Berry, quoted the following from one of his students:

> *We live the lie of denial here, which is perhaps the strongest lie of all; we are like an alcoholic family that denies to itself and outsiders that there is a problem. The Naval Academy family must come out of this denial and engage in open, honest and productive communication. (http://www.inlink.com/~civitas/metro/metro59.htm)*

Alcohol and Risk

Alcohol has an established place in U.S. society. Most Americans accept the use of alcohol at special events. Nevertheless, alcohol consumption can be a major risk to the success of an event and to the lives of both those attending the event and those with whom the event's participants may come in contact. Many of us may have a story regarding a relative who had a few too many drinks at a family celebration. Communities such as Mendocino, California, have tried to create covenants for responsible hospitality as a way of controlling the negative side effects of alcohol. Some colleges and universities are known for large gatherings where alcohol is the main beverage, and the literature in event risk management contains numerous examples of alcohol consumption at conventions and meetings. Figure 3.1 demonstrates why alcohol has become the drug of choice at events.

Perhaps no place is alcohol feared more than at a function with young adults such as a university function or a concert/festival that caters to young adults. This is especially important in light of the fact that when event risk managers are polled regarding major risks at events, the top risk factor noted by both individuals and

Illegal Drugs	Alcohol
Always illegal	Not illegal for people over age 21
High probability of a jail sentence	Probability of a jail sentence greatly reduced and only for specific reasons such as "drinking and driving"
Socially unacceptable in most circles	Socially acceptable in most circles
Many people believe that its usage produces unexpected outcomes	Many people believe that they can use alcohol in moderation without major consequences
Unacceptable to all major religions	Many religions do not reject use of alcohol if kept in moderation
Does not prove "maturity"	Often seen as a sign of adulthood or sophistication
Is a danger to people on the road	Is a danger to people on the road

Figure 3-1
Reasons Alcohol Is Often Preferred at Events as the "Drug of Choice"

groups is the sale and consumption of alcohol (Berlonghi, 1994). It is of interest to note that the second highest risk for a group is the inexperience of the event organizer. From the Berlonghi study, it becomes clear that when alcohol is served, it is imperative to have well-trained professional event managers who understand the importance of comprehensive risk management.

When we understand the implications of the Berlonghi study, it is clear why organizations that cater to young adults or teenagers fear alcohol. We have the combination of young people, many of whom are under the legal drinking age, creating events often with little or no professional guidance and who may serve large amounts of alcohol. Event risk managers who work with young people state that alcohol appears to be the drug of choice. What is true in the youth/young adult community is also true in the community at large. While most conventions and large events have few illegal drug problems, alcohol can be a major problem.

Universities and colleges must face several difficult situations at the same time:

- Young people away from home often follow the sociological characteristics of a traveler. Not only are they in a state of anomie, but they tend to lower their inhibitions.
- Young people tend to experiment and desire to try new experiences.
- Fraternity/sorority parties are often seen as failures if alcohol is not consumed.
- Many of those attending the event may not be of a legal age to drink.

Universities and colleges are not the only places where alcohol consumption can get out of control. In almost any social situation where risk management is needed, alcohol can become an issue. For example, Mardi Gras celebrations in New Orleans, Louisiana, have often been described as a giant alcohol feast. The New Orleans police department reports that people who are the elite in their own communities have been known to pass out or engage in unflattering biological acts during visits to Mardi Gras. New Orleans is not the only example of such "drunken" street festivals. How often has "drunk leading to lewd/illegal behavior" become part of the sports scene? From national conventions to festivals, from family affairs to college spring break events, alcohol consumption has challenged the event risk manager to face the issue of inebriation and alcoholism.

This chapter assumes that we are dealing with non-alcohol-addicted people. We recognize that there is a whole group of people who suffer from the disease of alcoholism. As tragic as that may be, this particular chapter focuses on the person who does not suffer from alcoholism as a disease, but rather the person who attends an event or convention and simply loses his or her sobriety for the moment.

Although fraternities do not have an event professional on staff, most universities do have such people and serve as a model for other types of meeting and convention planners. That is to say, the problems that universities encounter with alcohol and events can serve the entire event industry as the model of what to do and what not to do regarding alcohol.

Meg Manning of the Texas A&M University risk management team summed up this position best when she stated: "Special events are always a challenge. Alcohol introduces an element of risk. The best way is to eliminate alcohol." Manning describes the following psychosocial tendencies after people have become inebriated:

- A person who is five feet tall often feels as if he or she is ten feet tall and wants to fight the world after drinking.
- Drinking and driving do not mix. Compounding this is the belief by many young people that they are indestructible.
- Alcohol lowers inhibitions and good sense. With hormones raging, there is a definite positive correlation between sexual assaults and amounts of alcohol consumed.

Although Manning would prefer that fraternities and sororities eliminate alcohol altogether, she, like other university officials, realizes that this goal may be unachievable. The solution, then, is not to eliminate the problem but rather to control the problem. Following are some of the methods used to contain the problem of alcohol consumption:

- Conduct the event at a location where there are people trained to serve alcohol.
- Understand and implement effective crowd control.
- Make certain that carding is coordinated by the organization's personnel.
- Make sure that monitoring is in place so that underage people are not involved.
- Do not have an open bar. Open bars encourage drinking; cash bars allow for greater control and often limit a person's ability to consume more than he or she should.
- Price the alcoholic drinks expensively so that guests drink less.
- Make certain there are designated drivers at the event.
- Maintain a list of who is and who is not 21 years of age.

Event risk managers who must host young people have a number of alcohol-related concerns. Among these concerns are:

- Driving while intoxicated (DWI)
- Date rape and "rape drugs" dropped into drinks
- Mixing of alcohol and drugs

- Tendency to brawl or fight after drinking
- Illegal hazing

To counterbalance the special problems that organizations that host young adults experience, risk managers note that they can use the organization's values to help them convince students that the element of risk is greater than they think. Risk managers can often encourage student organizations to cooperate by asking them such questions as:

- Are you practicing what you are preaching?
- What research have you conducted regarding alcohol-related issues?

Event risk managers are keenly aware of the problem of alcohol at events. The event risk manager's first line of defense against alcohol-related problems is often to meet with the event's hosts, hostesses, or sponsors prior to the event. During this meeting, the event risk manager should provide checklists to prospective clients.

It is essential that event risk managers develop a risk plan called a "lightning plan" (what you would do if lightning were to strike). Prior to an event in which alcohol is served:

- **Determine who is in charge at the event.** Is there an alcohol service manager? Make certain that you are able to identify the chain of command for the event.
- **Find out what plans are in place.** It is as important to know what plans do not exist and what plans do exist. What has been overlooked? Who forgot what? These are essential questions.
- **Determine how similar this alcohol-related event is to other events of a similar size and demographic composition.** Having a benchmark can be an excellent predictor of future problems. Do not be afraid to consult with other event risk managers and always keep a written list of essential facts and incidents after each of your major events.
- **Evaluate current alcohol management rules.** Review the McDonaldization material in Chapter 1. Can too many rules lead to overrationalization?
- **Review signage.** Be careful of what you write on signs or other sources of information regarding the serving of alcohol. We live in a very litigious society, and what you write may be held against you in court.

- **Take into account all risks.** Event risk managers are often as concerned about risks associated with alcohol that have a low probability of occurring but whose consequences are grave as they are about high-probability risks. First, never see each risk as unique unto itself. Instead, assume that there is an interaction between all risks. Thus, each risk that is added into the equation increases the total risk factor.
- **Use past experience with issues of intoxication**. If the situation "feels" wrong, take the time to listen to your feelings. It is never a mistake to err on the side of prudence.
- **Learn from other events**. Alcohol problems at events tend to be similar at many different events. A college spring break, however, is very different from a banker's meeting. Keep a careful sociological profile of these events and use these profiles to help in your planning. Be careful never to use racial profiling and never assume that a person is guilty simply because he or she falls into a particular demographic grouping.
- **Gain knowledge from other sources.** For example, visit different Web sites to see what your colleagues are doing with regards to the serving of alcohol at events.
- **Examine current insurance policies.** Insurance policies dictate what you can and cannot do at an event. Make certain that you speak to the event's insurance agent. What insurance restrictions and exclusions are enforced? What coverage do you have?
- **Use common sense.** Often the best risk management is common sense. Part of the job of event risk managers is to apply their common sense to the risk situation.
- **Don't get angry or feel superior.** It is all too easy to see a group of people having a "good time" and start to feel superior to them. Remember that your task is to help these people have a good time with the least possible amount of risk to life or property.

Event risk managers must also be aware of the dram shop laws, based on the Supreme Court decision in Samson *v.* Smith (1989). Event risk managers should understand how these laws may impact them and should consult a professional for legal advice. The basic premise of these laws is that if person X gives too much alcohol to person Y who then, in an intoxicated state, hurts himself or another person, then X can be held liable. There are a number of legal points that person Y, the plaintiff, will have to prove, including that the injury was a result of Y's drinking and that the alcohol provider knew that the plaintiff was intoxicated.

Following is a sampling of the dram shop statute in Florida. The statute is available on line at **http://www.alcoholismkills. com/alcohola.htm.**

> *768.125 (Liability for injury or damage resulting from intoxication) states in relevant part:*
> *. . . a person who willfully and unlawfully sells or furnishes alcoholic beverages to a person who is not of lawful drinking age or who knowingly serves a person habitually addicted to the use of any or all alcoholic beverages may become liable for injury or damage caused by or resulting from the intoxication of such minor or person.*
>
> *562.50 (Furnishing intoxicants to habitual drunkards after notice) states in relevant part:*
> *Any person who shall sell, give away . . . alcoholic beverage . . . to any person habitually addicted to the use of any or all such intoxicating liquors, after having been given written notice by wife, husband, father, mother, sister, brother, child, or nearest relative that said person so addicted is an habitual drunkard and that the use of intoxicating drink or drinks is working an injury to the person using said liquors, or to the person giving said written notice, shall be guilty of a misdemeanor of the second degree, punishable as provided in s. 775.082 or s. 775.083.*

Not only do states have different interpretations of the dram shop laws, but each state also has its own alcohol and beverage commission (ABC). The ABC's job is to set policy regarding who may receive a liquor license and under what conditions, what taxes are to be paid, and what the state's policy is concerning the use of alcoholic substances. Readers are strongly advised to check with their state ABC in order to comply with all regulations. Appendix 2 contains a listing of ABCs for each state and the District of Columbia. The listing gives the name of the ABC by state, its mailing address, and telephone and fax numbers. As each state has its own bureaucratic division, policies that fall within the purview of one department in a given state may be located in a different department in another state.

One of the most frustrating issues for event risk managers regarding festivals and outdoor events is that these events often become "open parties." These are events for which the risk manager has no prior list of attendees and which are open to anyone. For a number of reasons, these open parties are the most difficult to handle when alcohol is involved.

- There is a sociological tendency to act out fantasies when in a crowd. For example, on June 15, 2001, the *Jerusalem Post* reported on the Boombamela beach festival at Nitzanim Beach.

  > *The festival, attended by thousands of people, was part of a much-discussed trend among Israelis to seek escape from the cycle of violence that has gripped the land for more than six months. "Maybe people need it here because of all the tension," said Na'ama Na'aman, a Tel Aviv massage therapist who organized Boombamela's holistic therapy tents. "They want to relax their bodies, relax the soul." The music and otherworldly atmosphere couldn't quite muffle the chop of IAF helicopters headed for the Gaza Strip, some 30 kilometers south, where Israelis and Palestinians regularly exchange fire. Still, they went barely noticed by the thousands thronging the Mediterranean beach, pierced and tattooed, hair dyed red or blue or dreadlocked. A naked man and woman painted people's bodies, surfers swiveled back and forth in the sea, yoga enthusiasts reached for the sky.*

- The participants do not have a "buy-in" to the event's success. In the event mentioned previously, as in most out-of-door festivals, the participant has little or even no relationship to the event. Participants come to have a good time, not to make a political statement. Another illustration of this is Woodstock II. In this festival, the object was not to protest a war, but rather of a hedonistic nature. In such cases, risks rise as people's responsibility toward the event decreases.
- Participants may assume that they will never return to the event. Beach festivals, rock concerts, and so forth often

attract people whose philosophy is "been there, done that."
Under those circumstances, few people will worry if the
event cannot be repeated. When the crowd lives for the moment, the risk manager will have a very full plate.

- There is no way of knowing who is at the event for a good
time and who sees the event as an opportunity for mischief.
One only has to look at city-organized victory celebrations
for major sports teams. Many of the people who attend these
types of events do come to honor the members of the team,
but others may be there as an excuse to cause mischief or
worse. It is essential whenever a city puts on such an event,
or is aware that it may "spontaneously" start, that event organizers and risk managers have a plan and the means to
head off alcoholic problems prior to their start.

- These open parties can often become "joint events." A joint
event is when the gathering is co-sponsored with another or
multiple parties. For example, liquor companies will try to
become co-sponsors of outdoor events, presenting even
greater challenges to the risk manager.

The general sociological principle to remember is: *There is a
direct inverse correlation between caring about an event's success
and the abusive use of alcohol.* The best way to avoid a crisis with
alcohol is to remove alcohol from the special event. When alcohol
cannot be removed, it is the responsibility of the risk manager to
make sure that his or her policies are strictly enforced.

Alcohol and Ethics

Alcohol is an accepted part of U.S. society and special events.
However, the decisions that an event risk manager, staff, and volunteers make are as much about ethics as they are about alcohol
control. The Talmud notes that "He who saves a life, it is as if he
had saved an entire world; he who destroys a life, it is as if he had
destroyed an entire world."* Risk management and alcohol are,

*Babylonian Talmud, Tractate Sanhedrin 37a. This same concept is also ex-
pressed in the Muslim tradition. See the Koran, Sura 5 (Maa'idah) 32.

then, about the ethics of saving an entire world. When deciding how to ethically handle alcohol, first make sure that you clarify your options. Must you serve alcohol? If so, what options do you have? Then determine the risks that you are willing to assume. At what point is the risk of one life worth the enjoyment of many? Never be afraid to stand up for principle. All too many event risk managers have stories to tell about how much they regret allowing themselves to be pressured. To decide if you are making the right decision, ask yourself if you will be able to live with this decision next year. Could your plan do more harm than good? Would you want to tell your children about this decision? How would you justify this decision to the media?

Time, Place, and Alcohol

It was Albert Einstein who first discovered in the modern world the relationship between time and space. This principle of modern quantum mechanics is also true when it comes to event risk management of alcoholic beverages. Time influences people's consumption patterns, and risk managers must take into account both the time and the place of an event. Although people can become intoxicated at any hour of the day or night, the general pattern in the Western nations of the world is that events that take place after dark have a higher propensity of liquor intake. One exception to this rule may be sports events, where a person's relationship to his or her team's success (or failure) may be as much a factor as time of day. Other important things to consider regarding timing are:

- When does public transportation cease? Will the event attendees be forced to use private forms of transportation?
- Is the event in close proximity to or at a distance from the place that most people are staying?
- Is the event indoors or outdoors, during the day or at night?
- Is there a set beginning and end to the event?
- Is there a policy to close the bar or cease consumption of alcoholic beverages at least one hour prior to the event's ending?

A Guide to Serving Alcohol at Events

The following suggestions will assist you in controlling alcohol consumption at your event:

- Always serve food when liquor is present.
- Refrain from serving salty foods such as chips and salted popcorn.
- Emphasize foods that are high in protein such as meats, cheeses, and pizza. The higher the protein, the more the food functions to reduce the effects of alcohol.
- Enforce the event's rules.
- If a guest is intoxicated, help the person by
  - Offering food and coffee
  - Offering a place to rest
  - Assuming that it will take one hour to sober up for every drink ingested
  - Monitoring breathing if the guest passes out
  - Calling for emergency medical aid
  - Positioning the sleeping person on his or her side so as to avoid choking as regurgitation can be a problem; make certain that the guest is monitored throughout the night
- Carefully observe and monitor the "fighting drunk."
  - Try to calm the person.
  - Speak in low tones.
  - Attempt to get the person to leave.
  - Call the police if the need arises.
- Know your responsibilities. As the host of an event, you assume the responsibility for the safety of your guests. There are court cases where even the uninvited person is still the host's responsibility.
- Host only closed parties.
- Focus the decorations on the event's theme, not on its alcohol.
- Appoint event monitors.
- Appoint designated drivers.
- Check identification at the door.
- Always serve nonalcoholic beverage alternatives.
- Set starting and ending times.
- Do not permit drinking-oriented games.
- Monitor for intoxicated people.

- Avoid bottles and other glass objects.
- Whenever possible, stay away from "bulk distribution" of alcohol. It is much easier to maintain control over a situation if drinks are distributed by the glass/cup rather than through kegs, cases of beer, or an alcoholic punch.
- Always make alcohol an adjunct to an event. If people hear a speech, have food, see a show, or are part of a program, it is much easier to control the situation.
- Develop a "get home safe" booth. Have an easy way to call taxis or find rides to attendees' homes. It is essential to remember that adults often behave as if they were teenagers when intoxicated.
- There should be a ratio of one nonalcoholic drink to each participant at the event.

Common Questions and Misconceptions About Alcoholism as They Impact Event Risk Management

Alcoholism is a common form of chemical dependency. As such, it follows the pattern of any other chemical dependency illness. While the following questions and answers are phrased in terms of the problem of alcoholism, the information is equally valid if considering other drug-related problems. It should be noted that the information given below is only a thumbnail sketch and is not meant for diagnostic use. It is always wise for a risk manager to have a physician and other health-care professionals available for further consultations.

Q: Is alcoholism a disease?
A: In most cases, yes. It can be a symptom of another disease, but in most cases it is a treatable disease.
Q: What causes this dependency?
A: We are still not sure. It is not a result of weak character, and there is no way of predicting who will have a proclivity toward alcoholism.
Q: What are the major symptoms of alcohol dependency?
A: The need to drink is the major symptom. When a person's

drinking becomes inappropriate, unpredictable, excessive, or constant, there is a high probability of alcoholism. Other signs to watch for are:

- Difficulty in arousing person
- Slowed, stopped, or irregular breathing
- Bluish fingernails, lips, or gums

Q: Can the person be helped while gradually tapering off?

A: No. So far, no one has developed a method that allows a gradual reduction in alcohol consumption.

Q: Are there progressive phases to alcoholism and if so what are they?

A: Alcoholism is often seen as going through four phases of development. Phase 1 is the experimental stage. The person uses alcohol to feel better. In phase 2, the person begins to anticipate (look forward to) the effects of alcohol. In phase 3, the person begins to feel depressed after feeling euphoric. In phase 4, the person becomes dependent on alcohol to the extent that he or she needs it to function at all in daily life.

Q: Is alcoholism typical of any one class of people?

A: No. Alcoholism can be found in people of all ages, genders, races, social and economic classes, and ethnic groups.

Q: What sobers up a person?

A: Only time will sober the person up. Coffee, cold showers, fresh air, and exercise do not sober up a person who has had too much to drink.

Figure 3.2 demonstrates the downward spiral of alcohol dependency. Note how each downward stair takes the victim only one step closer to total defeat without his or her realizing the problem.

Planning for Alcohol at an Outdoor Event

Outdoor events are harder to control than indoor events. Event managers often fail to give themselves enough time to think through all the details that events require. One aspect of outdoor event planning that is often neglected or overlooked is the issue of alcohol. When planning an event, think through what might be your

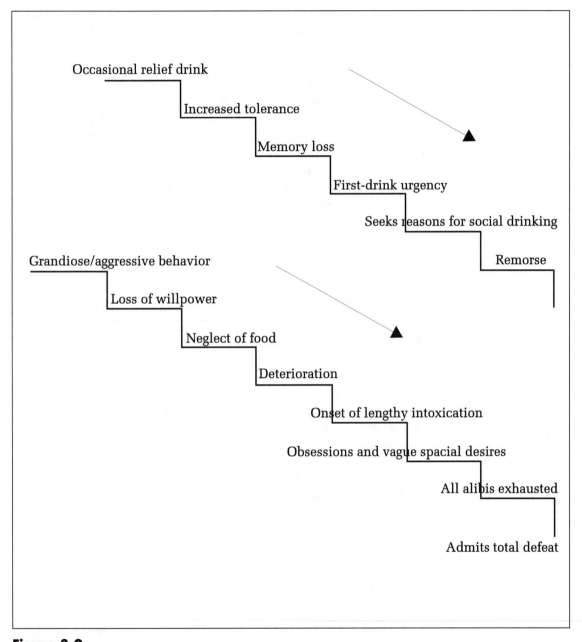

Figure 3-2
Drinking Dependency Spiral

worst case scenario. Crowds can easily turn into mobs; drinking may release all sorts of undesired urges; glass bottles or containers can easily become weapons. Many risk managers recommend that a licensed third-party vendor take charge of alcohol distribution. In that way, the event manager can be at least one step removed from the distribution of alcohol. On the other hand, independent vendors cost more and may want a share of the profits. Make sure that you meet with the local police department. It is essential that the event's risk management team have a good working relationship with local law enforcement agencies. Find out if there are restrictions to the number of people allowed, what overtime needs to be paid to the local law enforcement agencies, and which policies they enforce and which policies can be overlooked.

Reducing Liability During Alcohol Service

1. Use only trained and certified bartenders and servers of alcohol. Display their certification on the top of the bar.
2. Require, in writing, that bartenders and servers immediately stop serving intoxicated persons.
3. Require, in writing, that bartenders and servers remove the intoxicated persons' car keys and/or provide them with alternative transportation.
4. Document, in writing, and have the document countersigned (witnessed) that the incident took place and how it was handled (steps 1–3).

Alcohol Statistics

- Young people of college age consume an average of 4.3 drinks per week.
- About 86 percent of all college students consume alcohol.
- Fraternity and sorority students report a drinking rate about 3 times more than that of other students.

- Approximately 75 percent of college students state that they are aware of their university's policy regarding alcohol.
- About two in every five Americans will be involved in some form of alcohol-related car accident.
- Every alcohol-related death costs society almost $800,000.
- California state law enforcement data show that almost 50 percent of drunk drivers arrested for driving under the influence (DUI) had been drinking at a community event, a fundraiser, or an office or home party.
- The National Highway Traffic Safety Association (NHTSA) defines a fatal traffic crash as being alcohol related if either a driver or a nonoccupant (e.g., pedestrian) had a blood alcohol concentration (BAC) of 0.01 gram per deciliter or greater in a police-reported traffic accident.
- In 1999, 21 percent of the young drivers 15 to 20 years old who were killed in crashes were intoxicated.
- Seventeen states have set 0.08 gram per deciliter as the legal intoxication limit. All states plus the District of Columbia have zero-tolerance laws for drivers under the age of 21 (it is illegal for drivers under 21 to drive with BAC levels of 0.02 gram per deciliter or greater).
- In 1999, 24 percent of the young male drivers involved in fatal crashes had been drinking at the time of the crash, compared with 11 percent of the young female drivers involved in fatal crashes.
- Drivers are less likely to use restraints when they have been drinking. In 1999, 73 percent of the young drivers of passenger vehicles involved in fatal crashes who had been drinking were unrestrained.

International Events and Alcohol

In the December, 3, 1997, issue of the *Daily Egyptian* of Southern Illinois University at Carbondale, Karen Blatter reported on how foreign students "were stunned at US alcohol policy." In the case reported by Blatter, one student,

a 16-year-old, was not able to drink from the goblet of wine that was on the table in front of him. The student

*commented "I couldn't drink with the rest of my family,
. . . . It was like an insult to my family that I could not
drink in the restaurant. . . ." The student, now 24, and a
senior in physical education from Athens, Greece, said
that since he was 7 years old, it was tradition in his home
country for him to drink with his family on special occasions. Although he has been to several foreign countries,
he was first unable to drink when he was in the United
States. The student went on to say that "many cultures,
such as that of the Greek people, believe in educating
their children about the proper use of alcohol before the
children have to find out for themselves—the hard way."*

Blatter's article illuminates a growing problem. While the article quotes a university official who helps train people in U.S. law,
the official sums up a major difficulty in cross-national meetings.
As the article notes, the university official stated, "It's our law,"
she said. "Regardless of whether it is frustrating or not, they have
to abide by the laws."

A good example of how societies view alcohol can be seen in
the major debate that occurred in the state of Utah regarding alcohol consumption at the 2002 Winter Olympic Games. Utah is a relatively conservative state with very strict liquor laws. During the
Salt Lake Winter Olympic Games, it will have to deal with the
thousands of people who will visit the state. Utah's alcohol consumption laws reflect its deep religious values. As reported on
May 21, 1999, by CNN's *Moneyline:*

*Utah's legislative leaders aren't willing to make even mi-
nor changes to Utah's strict liquor laws to please foreign-
ers at the 2002 Winter Games. The state gave its blessing
to the Olympic bid on the condition it wouldn't have to
bend its alcohol rules, said Senate President Lane Beattie,
R-West Bountiful, and House Speaker Marty Stephens,
R-Farr West. ". . . I'm not a big proponent of making
changes to our liquor laws to accommodate the international community. We have a society here we are proud
of." The International Olympic Committee Wednesday
asked Salt Lake organizers to seek permission for unfet-
tered alcohol sales at the main press center, which will be
set up at the Salt Palace convention center downtown for*

some 9,000 members of the media. Thursday, Olympic officials said they had some kind of variance in mind, not a repeal of alcohol restrictions.

As international events become more common around the world, event risk managers will have to deal with a number of cultural issues pertaining to alcohol consumption. For example, many Muslim nations prohibit the consumption of liquor, at least for their local populations. On the other hand, there are a number of nations that have much more relaxed attitudes toward alcoholic beverages. People from Scandinavia, large sections of Western Europe, and Israel are used to their governments taking a laissez-faire approach and view a place such as Utah as highly puritanical. International special events not only mix people from different lands and languages, but also, in the realm of alcohol consumption, create new challenges for event risk managers. For example, in Brazil the intoxicated person goes to jail rather than the bartender or event manager.

From a U.S. perspective, event risk managers will have to deal with four possibilities, as shown in Figure 3.3. In many cases, the United States is becoming a very good destination for foreign corporations to hold events. In all cases, the person(s) involved are always held liable to the laws of the nation in which the special event has occurred.

This means that in some countries, as we have just noted, for example, Brazil, there is greater emphasis on personal responsibility regarding alcohol consumption, while in other nations, such as the United States, the risk manager or bartender may be held negligent. To make matters more difficult, courts have held that if a U.S. corporation holds an event outside of the United States for

U.S. Event/U.S. Participants	Event Held in U.S. for Both U.S. and Foreign Participants
Event Held Outside of U.S. for U.S. Participants	Event Held in U.S. for Foreign Participants

Figure 3-3
Four Possible National Scenarios

U.S. citizens, then the risk manager and corporation (sponsor) may be sued upon return to the United States.

Alcohol and Sexual Harassment

Although sexual harassment issues can take place in a nonalcohol situation, alcohol abuse can be one cause in the lowering of inhibitions and the increase in sexual harassment problems. The FIPG fraternity-sorority risk manual states that "Legal liability is a reality in sexual abuse incidents." It then goes on to state: "The [fraternity/sorority] chapter may be sued if an incident of sexual abuse occurs at a chapter function." Sexual abuse (harassment) is different from sexual assault (rape). Sexual harassment is an unwelcomed giving of sexual attention when the person has indicated that he or she does not desire such attention. Sexual abuse can be either verbal or physical. The *Texas Law Handbook* (p. 96) defines harassment as follows:

> *A person commits an offense if, with intent to harass, annoy, alarm, abuse, torment, or embarrass another, he: Initiates communication . . . and in the course of the communication makes a comment, request, suggestion, or proposal that is obscene. . . .*

While physical abuse may well be worse, it may also be easier for security personnel to spot and prevent. Verbal abuse is a more difficult problem to contain. When liquor is mixed into a situation where both sexes are present, people are away from home, and event attendees may not know each other or have the idea that they will never see the other party again, the probability of sexual verbal abuse increases greatly. Because sexual verbal abuse is often subjective, the risk manager must be especially sensitive to how different people, cultures, and ethnic groups may react to any of the following situations:

- Unwanted whistling
- Uninvited comments/jokes about a gender trait
- Sexually suggestive sounds
- Sexual statements about another person's private sex life
- Continual requests or demands for sexual favors, especially if accompanied by overt or covert threats to the person

Physical sexual abuse may be easier to spot. Event risk managers need to train their staff and volunteers to monitor the following activities:

- Obscene gestures
- Staring at another person's private parts
- Inappropriate touching, pinching, or patting
- Moves to coerce sexual relations
- Assault

Risk managers cannot train everyone who comes to a public event or conference regarding sexual harassment policy. Risk managers, however, can work hard to make staff sensitive to the issue and to factor in the fact that alcohol can lead to a decrease in inhibitions and an increase in sexual harassment problems. All event risk managers should have in place a sexual harassment policy and all staff should be trained as to this policy's implementation. One of the first things that an event risk manager must do is to make sure that his or her staff is sensitive to this problem. Staff members should never tell sexually oriented jokes on company time and they should be fully versed in all sexual harassment procedures.

Staff members must stop harassment as soon as it is noted, keep careful records of the incident, and encourage the person being harassed to file a formal complaint against the harasser. When an incident takes place (or is reported to have occurred):

- Consider reported incidents in a serious and professional manner.
- Notify the event or conference's management immediately.
- Refer all calls/comments to the event spokesperson. Do not answer media questions, but refer the media or legal representative to the proper spokesperson.
- Make certain that the event's lawyer is advised of the situation.
- Make certain that the police are notified about the incident and are told who the accused person is.
- Conduct a preevent assessment of the facilities prior to the event to determine if there are physical site issues that may lead to harassment. Always check for open closet doors, examine lighting inside and outside of the event, and follow the rules of CPTED (crime prevention through environmental design). For example, examine shrubbery and trees. Do

they contain places where someone may be abducted or taken by surprise? How easily are telephones accessed and are there emergency numbers that do not need coins?

Remind event staff and volunteers that no one should have to:

- Be subjected to rude or unwelcome speech
- Be forced to deal with someone who is inebriated
- Be forced to be in physical proximity with another person
- Be forced not to change his or her mind
- Act the same way with all people
- Respond positively when he or she desires to respond in the negative

Sexual harassment is a major problem for event employees. For example, a guest is at a restaurant or bar, has a few too many drinks, and as his or her inhibition levels become lower, begins to see the waiter/waitress as a piece of property. Indeed, this phenomenon occurs whenever there is a situation in which the public is served and the event professional's job is to make the guest or customer happy. Even where tipping is not an issue, such as on airplanes, flight attendants report numerous forms of sexual harassment by both men and women. Because people often conduct themselves in an inappropriate manner when they are away from home and under the influence of alcohol, it behooves the risk manager to teach his or her staff how to recognize and report the following traits:

- Threats to staff or attempts to intimidate staff as a means of gaining sexual favors
- Paranoid behavior (world is against me) or statements such as "You are only rejecting me because I am . . ."
- Overly moral righteousness, "I'm good; you're not"
- Blaming others for one's mistakes; for example, "The waitress was coming on to me because of her provocative uniform"
- Romantic obsessions or statements

Liquor can also make a guest become violent, especially when the liquor has helped the person to lower his or her sexual inhibition levels. When one is both sexually infatuated with another human being and also violent, the situation can become extremely dangerous. Professional event risk managers, working with the proper law enforcement professionals, should develop policies that allow them to isolate the violent individual as quickly as possible. In cases such as sexual harassment, it is easy to assume that one case is like all others. Be careful to remember that each situation is unique, think before you act, stay calm, and remember that it is your responsibility to protect the harassed employee. Customers/guests sometimes use the power of the purse to try to control the harassed person. No employee should ever fear that profit is more important than life. No one should be subjected to harassment, be it harassment of a sexual, racial, religious, or ethnic nature. When someone who is intoxicated becomes belligerent or harasses other people:

- Do not let nonsecurity personnel try to disarm the person.
- Determine what the security department can do to help in the post violent recovery phase.
- Follow your preset policy guidelines.

Following are some questions about sexual harassment and assault that are important to consider:

Q: Is sexual assault motivated by sexual desire?

A: Sexual assault is not motivated by passion, but by the desire to humiliate or dominate another human being. Most sexual assaults take place in high-risk situations, such as hitchhiking, walking alone at night, and so on. While it is not a good idea ever to put oneself in a high-risk situation, and certainly sexual assaults do occur under these circumstances, there are a large number of sexual assaults that occur between parties that have known each other. Events with high levels of alcohol consumption can be prime areas for sexual assaults.

Q: Do people invite harassment or sexual assault by the way that they dress?

A: These actions can happen to anyone, dressed in any fashion and of any age group.

Q: Will the majority of sexual assailants continue until they are caught?

A: Yes, there are many repeat offenders and often sexual harassment and assault are not reported.

Event Risk Management Key Terms

BAC: Blood alcohol concentration. Persons with a BAC of 0.01 gram per deciliter or greater involved in fatal crashes are

considered to be intoxicated. This is the legal limit of intoxication in most states.

Fighting drunk: A guest at a special event who becomes violent due to too much alcohol.

Joint event: When an event is co-sponsored with another party.
This can become dangerous when the co-sponsor is an alcohol distributor or tavern (a place that generates more than
half its income from alcohol).

Lightning plan: What you would do if the same situation were
to happen again; how to handle the unexpected.

Murphy's law: If it can go wrong, it will.

Open parties: Parties that are open to the public. These are the
most difficult to handle when alcohol is involved.

Sexual harassment: An unwelcomed giving of sexual attention
when the person has indicated that he or she does not desire such attention.

Event Risk Management Drills

1. Assume that you are the event risk manager for a young-adult rock festival. What
are some of the problems with alcohol
that you might encounter? Develop a risk
strategy that manages in a just way both
students who are over 21 and students
who under 21 years of age. Include the
following assumptions:
   a. The institution and festival do not
   want negative publicity.
   b. The university does not want its students arrested.

   c. It is a hot evening.
   d. There are no classes the next day.
2. Prior to organizing a spring break festival,
describe a meeting with the local police
department. What are some of your alcohol and sexual harassment concerns? How
would you explain your training procedures to the local police department?
3. Develop an alcohol training session for a
citywide event. What issues would you
include? List the risks that seem to be
more pressing and explain your reasons.

CHAPTER 4

Crowd Control

From the five boroughs of N.Y.C., sixty soulless
monsters came, not knowing each other, they all
found each other all in agreement: water all the
women with ICE and bring them to tears.

—POEM FROM "CENTRAL PARK: WATER FIGHT, FLIGHT AND TEARS," 2000

IN THIS CHAPTER, WE WILL EXPLORE:

- The history and types of crowd control
- The sociology of crowd control
- The lessons learned from crowd control disasters
- The different types of crowds
- Various theories of crowd control and management
- Some of the ways to control crowds

According to the Lake Chelan (Washington) Police Department, in the mid- to late 1980s city officials had to cope with a major problem. During the holiday weekends of Memorial Day, Fourth of July, and Labor Day, the "city's family oriented slow paced environment

85

was shattered by thousands of screaming and inebriated young adults who seized the entire city and its residents, including it's [sic] police department."

A headline in the May 27, 2001, edition of the *Jerusalem Post* read: "Soccer fans crushed at Maccabi Haifa game." The paper went on to report that "Maccabi Haifa's championship celebrations came to an abrupt and sad halt last night when 35 fans were injured, two of them seriously, as they were crushed against the perimeter fence at Kiryat Eliezer stadium while trying to make their way onto the playing area. Eight minutes from time, as fans from the east stand tried to charge onto the pitch, they were restrained by policemen who refused to open the gate despite the mounting pressure." The Haifa soccer event took place a short time after the soccer stampede of May 9 in Accra, Ghana. In that incident, some 126 people were killed when the crowd lost control. To make matters worse, during the Ghana soccer riots, some survivors reported that police fired tear gas at fans. The fans threw bottles and chairs onto the field, sending panicked spectators running to the exits where they found the gates to be locked.

College spring break is another event that can often turn to tragedy due to poor crowd planning and management. Cancún, Mexico, reports more trouble each year during the week of spring break than throughout the rest of the year combined. Virginia Beach, Virginia, took years to recover after a fraternity convention turned into a riot in 1989 and destroyed a good part of the city's downtown shopping district as well as its tourism industry. It took years for Virginia Beach to recover from the physical damage and negative publicity that these riots inflicted upon the city. As shown previously, sports events are another opportunity for disorderly conduct. Many American cities have experienced the tragedy of a winning sports event rapidly degenerating into a riot with millions of dollars being lost and lives and livelihoods being destroyed. When an event includes youthful indiscretions and alcohol, then the event risk manager faces a potentially extremely explosive situation.

One example of this was reported in the November 12, 1998, edition of the University of Oregon campus newspaper, *The Oregon Daily Emerald*. The newspaper declared the need for action by stating in an editorial that in light of "recent riots, the University needs to reconsider its approach to student behavior off campus." The article by Giovanni Salimena further stated that: "Although the University claims to have its hands tied when governing student behavior off campus, community members are demanding the University take a more active role in curbing students' violent behavior, such as the Halloween riots." The Halloween student riots resulted in 12 arrests, 1 stabbing, and 100 citations for drinking and driving while under the influence of alcohol.

These examples appear to confirm what the French writer Gustave Le Bon theorized when he wrote *La Psychologie des Foules* (1895) in which he stated that the world was now entering an "era of crowds." According to Erika King, "Le Bon and his fellow fin de siècle French and Italian crowd theorists perceived crowds to be increasing both in pervasiveness and power, which they viewed with alarm, for all feared the social disorganization and anarchy which both could result from and indeed had resulted from the barbaric impulses of individuals in such groups" (King, 1960).

These examples are just a few of the many incidents where crowds have lost control and turned peaceful events into moments of terror.

When people riot, they cause a great deal of destruction to both property and life. They also create negative impressions of the event destination, which become part of that area's collective memory. For example, one year after the New York Puerto Rico Day parade became a riot, the *New York Post* continued to publish negative stories about this event. In an article dated June 5, 2001, the Reuters news service reported that "a business group on Madison Avenue urged its members to close during the Puerto Rico Day parade scheduled for Sunday, sparking criticism Thursday from New York's mayor and Hispanic leaders." Because the parade goes down Fifth Avenue, a block from Madison Avenue's exclusive businesses, in 2001 the Madison Avenue Business Improvement District group distributed leaflets to merchants reading: "We would advise that your establishment remain shut this Sunday . . . [and] the removal of expensive merchandise from your windows." The flyers also referred to the parade date as a "difficult day." This reaction one year later illustrates several basic concepts:

- An event remains etched in a locale's collective memory long after the event has ended.
- When an event is not managed correctly, postevent damage control can be more expensive than proper risk planning and control.
- One negative event can influence other events that occur in the same locale.

Parades, demonstrations, and sports events are not the only crowd management challenges facing event risk managers. Event risk managers are keenly aware that almost any event can quickly change from leisurely fun to chaos and even death. In fact, in the 1990s over 150 people died at rock concerts. All events—sports events, concerts, young people's "happenings," political rallies, to name a few—may degenerate from orderly gatherings into disorder, chaos, and riots. These disorders can destroy a destination's reputation and its economy, and, at times, they can even define a city within the nation's vocabulary. The Woodstock music festivals have become part of American "cultural" history. All event risk managers must understand how an orderly crowd can be transformed into an angry mob. They should also know how mobs work and what precautions can be taken, in conjunction with security professionals and law enforcement officials, to ensure that an orderly event does not disintegrate into a destructive mob.

These disorders often begin with large groups of people who soon become a crowd and then turn into a mob and riot. The progression from peaceful crowd to a riotous mob can take place in every corner of the world and at any time of the year. In the United States, small communities such as Seaside, Oregon, and large cities such as Los Angeles, California, have both suffered from riots. While all crowd control has similar components, Figure 4.1 shows how these "human hurricanes" can be classified.

To manage crowds, the risk manager must first have an understanding of the sociology of the crowd. Therefore, we will first look at the sociology of a crowd and investigate how crowds become mobs. Then we will examine some of the techniques used in controlling crowds and some of the resources for orderly crowd control such as fire prevention.

Sociology of the Crowd

The Nobel Prize–winning author, Elias Canetti, has written the great classic on understanding crowds. Indeed, anyone who is interested in this subject should read his massive 470-page book, dedicated to the sociology and psychology of the crowd. Canetti's book, titled *Crowds and Power,* contains a vast encyclopedia of

Type of Incident	Contributing Factors
Festivals (music festivals)	Drugs, alcohol, sudden noises, fighting, gunfire
Political	Speeches, planned violence, drugs, gunfire
Street events	Alcohol, drugs, boredom, fighting, sexual acts
Sport events	Alcohol, drugs, boredom, fighting, sexual acts
Student events/parties	Alcohol, drugs, sexual promiscuity, tolerance by authorities

Figure 4-1
Event Crowd Control Factors

classical thought concerning how crowds develop, gain power, and have the potential to move from an orderly assembly of human beings into an uncontrollable mob. Canetti builds his premise on the following principles of the crowd:

- Humans have a desire and a fear of being touched by the unknown.
- To deal with the fear of being touched, humans set boundaries.
- In crowds, there is a loss of fear of being touched:
  Crowds create equality.
  There are no distinctions in a crowd.
  Crowds have tendencies to grow.
  Open crowds have no boundaries.

In other words, when we find ourselves within a crowd, we both enjoy the contact and, at the same time, fear it. Being surrounded by people can be reassuring; however, on the other hand, sociologists have long recognized the concept of the "urban blasé." To understand an example of Simmel's theory, one only has to observe people on an elevator or on crowded public transportation such as a subway car. Note how no one looks another person in the eye. We are there; yet we set an artificial boundary around us. Eyes rarely meet; we do not smile at the next person. Ironically, although humans tend not to make facial contact with their unknown cohorts, they do not seem to be afraid to be touched by strangers. In crowds, we accept the fact that we will be bumped into by others. We have no idea who the other person is, indicating that crowds have neither rank nor prestige. Finally, anyone who has ever been stuck in a highway traffic jam due to an accident on the other side of the road understands that crowds tend to attract other people. Our normal curiosity causes crowds to grow.

It is worthwhile restating that from these basic premises, Canetti's theory provides the event risk manager with five major attributes of a crowd:

- Crowds want to grow.
- Crowds create equality.
- Crowds seek to become denser.
- Crowds move and seek direction.
- Stagnant crowds seek rhythm or discharge.

These attributes are essential in understanding the basics of crowd control.

For example, let us assume that a person has just fainted and we suspect that he or she may be the victim of a heart attack. In reality, the best thing for the victim would be for the crowd to move away, call for help, and give those in charge room in which to work. Yet, anyone who has ever been in a situation similar to that described above knows that people immediately begin to gather around the victim. To make matters worse, numerous people proclaim themselves to be experts, freely giving advice that has not been sought. Others soon join the crowd as people "crowd around" the victim. Soon the crowd tends to move (usually into the circle), causing event risk managers and other professionals to beg the crowd to leave. These attributes are essential for a risk manager to understand if the risk manager is to take control of the situation and prevent a bad situation, in this case a heart attack, from turning into a tragedy.

To a great extent, the New York Puerto Rico Day parade of June 2000 stands out as a dramatic applied example of much of Canetti's theoretical work. In an article published in *Salon* (June 15, 2000), Bruce Shapiro notes that "With Amadou Diallo, the cops went too far. In Central Park, not far enough. But guess what? It's the same problem" **(http://www.salon.com/news/feature/2000/06/15/central_park/print.html).**

The Puerto Rico Day parade of 2000 spawned a tremendous amount of violence in New York's Central Park. The festive spirit disintegrated as a mob of young men and women sexually assaulted at least 24 women, including a 14-year-old. One woman, Peyton Bryant, went from one police officer to another, begging for help as the mob attacked other women. What shocked the nation was that these attacks took place in broad daylight. Furthermore, the attacks were in close proximity to police officers who were watching over the parade route. The Puerto Rico Day parade escalated from a water fight to stripping women's clothing and near rape. Yet, as one witness reported, "I went over with my camera and started shooting but the cops just stayed there. . . . I saw girls getting groped, getting pushed down. The cops knew what was going on" (witness David Grandison as reported in *Salon* magazine).

The following are lessons to be learned from the Puerto Rico Day riots:

- Train law enforcement personnel to listen.
- Remember that police officers are there to serve the public.
- Take responsibility when things go wrong; do not shift the blame to others.
- Statistics are important but so are individuals. Do not dehumanize an event by switching to a statistical mode.
- Develop as much contact with the public as possible.

New York Congresswoman Carolyn Maloney (Manhattan, Queens) viewed the Puerto Rico Day fiasco as a form of violent crime/harassment, which she defined as crimes motivated by gender bias, race, sexual orientation, religion, ethnicity, disability, or national origin. She noted that this type of event creates a climate of fear that keeps a particular segment from participating fully and freely in society. After receiving news of the riot, Maloney issued the following statement:

> *This Sunday, all of us were shocked and horrified as women began to tell their stories of being surrounded, stripped, robbed and harassed by a gang of men in*

Central Park. There is only one thing that unites these victims. They are from different countries, different ages, different races. But all of them were women. The mob went after these victims simply because they were women—and they humiliated them because they were women.

Types of Crowds

The French author Gustave Le Bon has dedicated much of his scholarship to the study of crowds. Le Bon divides crowds into two main categories: the heterogeneous crowd and the homogeneous crowd. The heterogeneous crowd is composed of the following:

- The anonymous crowd, for example, street crowds
- The planned crowd, for example, assemblies and juries.

Likewise, the homogeneous crowd is composed of the following:

- Sects, such as political or religious
- Castes, such as the military or working caste
- Classes, such as economic classes in socially fluid societies (LeBon, 1895, p. 156)

Le Bon's use of the word "crowd" might be more akin to the modern American use of the word "group." From the perspective of event risk management, we will only concern ourselves with the first of his subcategories, that is, the anonymous crowd or the aggregate that becomes a crowd. Le Bon's work is most useful in his understanding of what he describes as the "criminal crowd." Le Bon notes that: "The usual motive for the crimes of crowds is a powerful suggestion, and the individuals who take part in such crimes are afterwards convinced that they have acted in obedience to duty, which is far from being the case with the ordinary criminal" (Le Bon, 1895, p. 160). Le Bon's basic argument is that people in crowds are open to suggestive behavior that is highly different from the way they would act as mere individuals. Many risk managers might take exception to the ideas of Le Bon or argue that his understanding of a political crowd's turning into a pogrom is no longer valid in the twenty-first century, yet his basic premise leaves room for contemplation. That is, when individuals enter into a collective mind-set, they engage in behavior that is counter to their normal way of acting.

Perhaps of greater value to the modern event risk manager is the work accomplished by Elias Canetti. Canetti presents us with a much more sophisticated view of crowds, dividing the crowd into such groupings as:

The invisible crowd. The crowd that forms to represent a dead person and soon turns into a riot.

The bating crowd. The crowd that forms for a specific goal, which is clearly marked and easily obtainable. The lynching mob is an example of this type of crowd.

The fleeing crowd. The crowd that perceives a threat and flees from it, often in panic. Risk managers should seek to avoid this type of crowd at all costs.

The prohibition crowd. The crowd that refuses to do what is asked, instead obeying a self-proposed prohibition. This type of crowd has often been viewed in a political context, but it can also be borne of a crowd that is coming for entertainment purposes and suddenly adopts a cause.

The reversal crowd. The crowd that seeks to overturn the political status quo. These crowds are defenseless but, due to their numbers, gain strength and often gain control.

The feast crowd. These are people, according to Canetti, who are in a crowd only to celebrate. They have no purpose other than to have a good time.

Interestingly enough, Canetti also uses a number of symbols to understand crowds. Among his principal crowd symbols are fire, the sea, and the rivers (Canetti, 1973, pp. 75–90). Canetti sees fire as similar to a crowd: Fire spreads, it can be sudden, it can have multiple parts, and it is destructive. Thus, he states, "Fire is the same wherever it breaks out: it spreads rapidly, it is contagious, insatiable; it can break out anywhere, and with great suddenness, it is multiple and destructive; it has an enemy, it dies; it acts as though it were alive, and it is so treated" (Canetti, 1973, p. 77). On the other hand, he argues that crowds are like the sea: They are dense and cohesive, they are never entirely still, and, like the sea, while a crowd is alive it never sleeps. For Canetti, crowds are like rivers, because their origins are often taken more seriously than their goals.

Throughout this chapter, we will be referring to different types of crowds. One way to understand crowd types is to borrow from the tourism sciences some of that discipline's relevant theories. Following you will find two other theories that will serve to help identify crowd types.

In 1973, Stanley Plog first introduced what has come to be known as the Plog model of psychographic tourism (Plog, 1973, pp. 13–16). This typology divides people along a continuum, ranging from the allocentric to the psychocentric. Plog tells us that the allocentric person is one who looks for "thrills" or adventure. He or she is a risk taker and is not afraid of danger. The other extreme is the psychocentric person. This is a person who tends to worry about his or her safety/security, takes few risks, and tends to be fearful. Few people are at either extreme of the continuum, but rather hover around its middle. When we think about these two personality types in regard to crowd control and risk management, Figure 4.2 will be useful .

Another way to view event attendees when considering crowd control is through the inner-outer-directed continuum. The inner-directed person takes the position that he or she is less interested in what society says than what he or she believes to be the right thing to do. On the other hand, the outer-directed person is interested in what others think; for this type of person, fashion is important as are the impulses of the crowd.

Putting these two theories together produces a series of quadrants. It is useful to be able to determine into which quadrant a particular crowd falls as you attempt to predict the group's future behavior (Figure 4.3).

Crowds do not always listen to those in authority. Anyone who has observed a riot at a rock concert or at a sports event knows that, despite the best efforts of the authorities, people can turn from individuals into a mob. A television program on MSNBC interviewed people who have participated in what the British call "acts of hooliganism" (sports riots) (MSNBC Investigates, May 23, 2001). These people are often professionals and upstanding members of their community. Yet, once part of the mob, these individuals undergo a loss of individuality and inhibitions, shame disappears, and often the hooligans seek to perform for others in the crowd. Police departments from around the world report that

Allocentric	Psychocentric
Wants excitement, will tend to ignore security personnel's warnings	Wants fun without danger, may be overly cautious
Free with money	Is frugal with money, may worry about being overcharged
Bores easily, will not complain to security until after an incident has occurred	Tends to complain about everything from people watching him or her to atmospheric conditions
Person will climb onto stage and seek crowds	Person wants to enjoy show and avoid crowds
Troublemaker—wants to challenge	Does not want to stir the pot or make trouble
Single	Family oriented

Figure 4-2
Allocentric/Psychocentric Event Crowd Characteristics

crowds at events that turn into riot situations tend to follow the above-stated principles. For example, let us examine the case of Michigan State University.

Soon after Michigan State University (MSU) lost to Duke University in the semifinals of the NCAA basketball tournament on March 27–28, 1997, a student riot erupted. As reported in the *Detroit News*:

> *During the incident an estimated 10,000 people filled the streets of East Lansing, smashing store windows, igniting bonfires and burning cars. Damages were estimated at $240,000. The drunken crowd included students and visitors from around the state. A year earlier, students rioted when the MSU administration announced that*

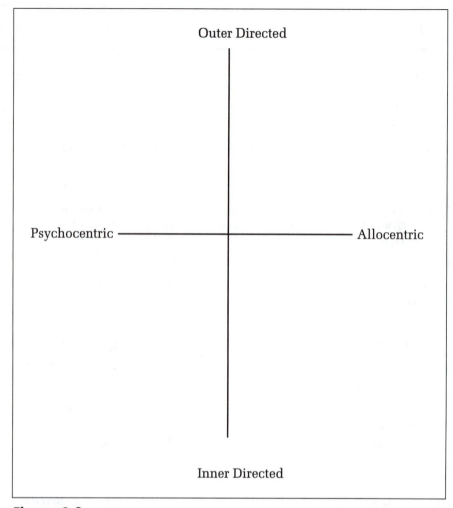

Figure 4-3
Determining a Psychographic Model

> *alcohol would be banned from Munn Field, a popular*
> *tailgating spot where many students—some of whom*
> *never went to the football games—would drink for hours.*
> (Detroit News, *August 29, 1999)*

During the riots, students not only engaged in destructive behavior, but cameras recorded women stripping and engaging in other lewd forms of behavior.

Crowds can turn from peaceful assemblies to riotous mobs. Even when the crowd has nothing to do with political causes, such as a fraternity convention, spring break activities, rock concerts, or festivals, it takes very little for a crowd to feel that it has been persecuted, leading to an eruption. It is essential for event risk managers always to be cognizant that all crowds have the potential to erupt. Indeed, the eruption of a crowd is one of the great nightmares of all risk managers. To understand this better, first remember that crowds sometimes feel persecuted. Usually, when there are crowds, there are security and/or police officers. These security professionals must "rein in" the crowd. That is to say, they must control the crowd's growth and movement. It is fair to say that all crowds have a natural animosity toward the people who try to control them. Thus, just as in the case of a stampede of buffalo, it takes very little in the form of provocation to make the crowd feel that it is being "attacked," and, once attacked, the crowd strengthens its resolve. Crowds, then, have a tendency to feel falsely persecuted. Crowds also usually have very poor sources of information. Thus, at major events such as outdoor concerts, street festivals, or some political rallies, crowds have a tendency to use both tactile and visual hallucinations. Some examples of the hallucination mechanism are alcohol and drugs. In a similar manner, rumors can easily spread that there is an opposing crowd that has become its enemy.

As shown previously, crowds are very similar to fire (one of the main causes of panic and another major concern of risk managers at events). Figure 4.4 demonstrates this concept.

When crowds get out of control, they may either become a mob or begin to panic. Panic can lead to a mob, but panic is not the same as a mob. When mobs take over, there is often some form of an agenda, although the agenda may not be understood by all. The mob's desire is to insight fear. Panic, however, is the result of fear. Mobs are proactive; panic is reactive. Mobs often produce panic by those who are outside of the crowd.

In May 2000, security officials, police officers, and tourism and event experts met to discuss issues of crowd control and risk management. The meeting was held in Long Beach, Washington, and many of the participants came from beachfront communities that struggle with crowd control issues. The following is a list of the

Fire	Crowd
Can easily spread, tends to move from place to place	Can easily spread, tends to move from place to place
Can develop suddenly	Can develop suddenly
Can jump barriers	Can jump barriers
Can be channeled for good purposes, but can get out of control, leading to massive destruction	Can be channeled for good purposes, but can get out of control, leading to massive destruction/riots
Can be both brought under control and tamed	Can be both brought under control and tamed
Recovery can be costly in both time and money	Recovery of property is expensive; furthermore, a great deal of time and money may be needed to recover an event's or place's reputation

Figure 4-4
Fires and Crowds: A Comparative Analysis

components of crowd problems that were shared by the Northwest Pacific coast beach communities. The attendees noted that they were most likely to lose control of a crowd when it contained the following:

- **Mainly young people.** Conference attendees noted that as the proportion of young people grew within the total crowd, so did the potential for violence.
- **Summer/good weather.** Poor weather does not seem to be conducive to out-of-control situations. Nice pleasant weather means people are willing to be outdoors and are often looking for things to do. Again, it should be noted that the atten-

dees were from beachfront communities that are dependent on the weather.

- **Alcohol.** Alcohol and crowds do not mix. Currently, alcohol is the greatest drug threat that event risk managers face. Alcohol is easily available and leads people to drop their inhibitions.
- **Large amounts of bored people.** Beach communities report that large gatherings of people with no clear-cut direction or place to go can be a sign of trouble. Stagnant people, like stagnant water, can be dangerous.
- **Inadequate security.** The larger and better trained the security force, the less likely that a crowd may transform itself into a mob. Studies of the Seattle World Trade Organization (WTO) riots indicate that Seattle simply lacked the human resources at the early stages to prevent the peaceful demonstrations from becoming a riot and to contain those whose intentions were not peaceful.
- **Darkness.** While mob riots can occur at any time, darkness, when combined with alcohol, provides a sense of anonymity, leading to a lowering of inhibitions and contributing to the potential for a riot.

Panic often occurs when human beings are in close physical contact with each other. Being close to others does not mean that panic will occur, but when it does occur, the closer we are to one another the worse will be the panic. When panic occurs, the slow "movement in group" disintegrates and others are dehumanized. In a panic, people have a tendency to take care of themselves and to become blind to the other person's needs. Panic is different from a fleeing crowd. As Canetti notes, in a fleeing crowd cooperation can still exist, but the moment that individual concern takes precedence over the group, then panic breaks out.

Controlling Crowds

Understanding the sociology of a crowd and what turns crowds into mobs and/or causes panic is essential for a risk manager. It is important that each event risk manager develop his or her own specific list of "signs/signals" that indicate that a "large gathering/assembly" is transforming itself into an unruly crowd/ mob. For example, here are some common indications:

- Crowds taking on a drinking-party atmosphere
- Introduction of alcohol or drugs into the crowd
- Loss of personhood; people moving into stampede mode
- Loss of inhibitions, such as public displays of nudity or partial nudity
- Lighting of fires or illegal acts of burning
- Division of the crowd into opposing factions
- Presence of weapons/guns

The last indication is especially important. Guns have the ability to turn a bad situation into a true tragedy. Guns and alcohol do not mix, and when people move into a "group-think mentality" the situation can easily get out of control.

Event risk managers are expected to have invested a great amount of time understanding crowd control. As part of event risk managers' training, they should invest some time developing expertise in such areas as:

- **Crowd types.** Not all crowds are the same. As discussed previously, crowds vary due to demographic makeup, raison d'être, time of year, and time of day. A beach-going crowd may be very different from a city political rally which may be different from a stock car race. Never assume that what is true of one particular crowd is true of another type of crowd.
- **Crowd sociopsychology.** After understanding the particular nature of a specific crowd, the risk manager can then use the principles of social psychology to predict behavior and how resources need to be distributed. Within this category, the risk manager should have a good idea of the behavior and culture of the type of crowd with which he or she is working.
- **Legal issues in crowd control.** How far can the risk manager go? What are the legal rights of the police and security officials? What are the parameters of the law within which he or she must operate?
- **Crowd management tactics.** It is essential that the risk manager think through each situation. Will signage work? Are loudspeakers and barriers necessary? Is this a crowd that

builds fires? How much trash will be left behind and can trash turn into a safety hazard?

- **Crowd control equipment.** There are many firms offering equipment for crowd management. The event risk manager will be working within a limited budget. He or she must know which pieces of equipment are essential, which pieces have multitask uses, which pieces are prone to breakdowns, and which type of equipment will fit into the image that the event is trying to project. For example, a tank might be an effective vehicle for some forms of crowd control, but would be counterproductive at a rally against the use of military hardware. It is a good idea to check with local police departments and other law enforcement agencies as to which brands of crowd control equipment they recommend. It is to the advantage of the event risk manager to use equipment that is compatible with that in use by supporting law enforcement agencies.
- **Use of force.** The risk manager must know when and when not to use force. The WTO riots in Seattle were an example of too little force used at the beginning and too much force used at the end. When combined with poor media management, this misunderstanding made the Seattle situation appear to be worse than it was in actuality.
- **Biochemical risk management.** It takes only small amounts of a biochemical substance to murder hundreds of people, including those in charge. Personnel should know when to enter and when to avoid possibly contaminated areas, types of equipment to use, and what the signs of a biochemical attack may be. Even standard chemicals should be treated with a great amount of care. In case of a riot where basic chemicals such as tear gas are used, the following procedures should be considered during the decontamination process:
  - Clothing should be washed twice by the wearer
  - The washing machine should be run a third time so as to be thoroughly cleaned.
  - Clothing should not be sent to the dry cleaners.
  - The contaminated person should shower with cool water.
  - The shower should be cleaned after use by a contaminated person.

- Security people and risk managers should keep extra clothing at the office to wear home.
- **Vehicular rescue.** Event risk managers often overlook the issue of saving both people inside of vehicles and the vehicles themselves. The event risk manager should have a good idea as to vehicular rescue techniques and should know how to set guidelines as to when a vehicle should or should not be rescued. For example, it is essential that the event risk manager understand how vehicles are positioned and what techniques are available for victim removal and recovery.

The question now becomes: What are the tools that event risk managers have at their disposal to control crowds and stymie crowds from progressively becoming more violent? As might be expected, different authorities have developed differing "tools" for event risk managers. The following ideas for crowd management are the result of years of expertise of risk managers, police departments, and event planners.

- **Higher is better; never sit.** You must be above the crowd's level. Event risk management personnel are best in a position to take charge when they are on horseback or in situations that allow them to be above the crowd. This is especially true if the person can have both height and mobility.
- **Be the conductor and let the crowd be the band.** Orchestrate how the crowd is to move; never let it be still. It is essential that those in crowd control understand not just their role, but everyone else's role, too.
- **Take control of time.** Crowds have no sense of time, but those professionals in crowd control should know how long someone has been in a particular location. The general rule is that the longer a group of people are in one spot, the greater the potential becomes for violence.
- **Use the fear of the "touch or being seized."** People in crowds are fearful of another's touch. The other person may be a criminal, distraction artist, or about to drag one off to jail. The higher the fear of touch, the more likely is the person prepared to follow orders.
- **When possible, control using laughter rather than violence.** The more the crowd is aligned with the event risk manager, the more likely that the event risk manager will be able to

prevent an incident from happening. During the 2001 Super Bowl victory parade, the Baltimore, Maryland, police went out of their way to show the crowd that they were its protector rather than its enemy. In a like manner, the sense of being the protector meant that the police officers in Baltimore never demonstrated fear, but rather gave the impression that they were both friendly and in charge.

The millennium celebrations around the world, especially on the night of December 31, 1999–January 1, 2000, serve as good examples of crowd control. From Las Vegas, Nevada, to Paris, France, from New York, New York, to Sydney, Australia, the predicted catastrophes and riots for New Year's Eve 2000 never materialized. Figure 4.5 provides a listing of some of the reasons that these mega-crowds were handled so successfully **(http://www.csmonitor. com/durable/1999/12/29/fp1s1-csm.shtml)**.

Universities have also invested a great deal of time trying to develop a set of crowd control guidelines. Figure 4.6 lists the techniques Michigan State University and the city of East Lansing are taking to prevent violence at sports events.

GOD SQUADS

Gulfport, Mississippi, faced with a large influx of college students on spring break, has borrowed an idea from Daytona Beach, Florida. The goal is to use police chaplains and mothers to "kill them [those on spring break] with kindness," but do it with "some bass in your voice." Larry Edwards, a police chaplain in Daytona Beach, was called in to share his experiences for dealing with the 500,000 bikers and the 160,000 college students who descend on Daytona Beach each spring. Gulfport's action was prompted by the previous year's spring break, known locally as Black Springbreak 2000, in which traffic was brought to a standstill when a massive street party erupted onto the highway and which resulted in one death. Figure 4.7 shows how the God Squad works.

DEVELOPING CROWD CONTROL TEAMS

Crowd control depends on teamwork. The event risk manager cannot afford to live in isolation. Crowd control begins with good planning and good networking. The professional event

1. Coordinate among various agencies. For example, prior to the millennium celebrations, post offices were on special alert to bombs.

2. Plan and communicate. These celebrations were kept peaceful due to the fact that security professionals were given a good deal of time to plan and to create interagency communication.

3. Demonstrate leadership. Do not let the public panic. President Clinton was at the National Mall and the New York City police chief was at Times Square. Government and security professionals gave the impression that they were on top of the situation, allowing others to not be afraid.

4. Work with the media. The fact that the FBI's successes were publicized acted as a warning against other possible problems.

5. Develop a patrol pyramid. Interagency cooperation and intraagency exercises are essential. Take each possibility seriously and go over every possible scenario.

6. Use a great deal of manpower, especially at the beginning. For example, New York City dispatched some 37,000 out of its 40,000 officers, including 8,000 in the five-block Times Square area. In Phoenix, the entire force of 3,600 sworn and civilian officers worked shifts from 6 A.M. December 31, 1999, through New Year's Day, 2000.

7. Make sure security is clearly visible. Studies show that the public feels safer and behaves better when security is visible. Police officers and security professionals should be aware of what is happening on the streets and be attentive to information about potential crises.

8. Be aware of racial and religious prejudice as an excuse for a riot. During the millennium celebrations, the police were keenly aware that "[m]ilitias, adherents of racist belief systems such as Christian Identity and Odinism, and other radical domestic extremists are clearly focusing on the millennium as a time of action," according to an FBI report.

Figure 4-5
Event Crowd Management and Procedures from the Millennium

risk manager should already have in place cooperative efforts with:

- Local law enforcement
- Event organizers
- The media

- *Extra police, some working undercover.* The greater the number of crowd control professionals, the greater the chances that nothing will happen.

- *Alcohol-free events.* The creation of alcohol-free alternatives is often seen as a way of diverting those who might get caught up in the crowd. It will not stop someone intent on causing trouble.

- *Positive information.* In the case of a university event, large numbers who will attend the event are part of a semistable population. The more information people have about what will not be tolerated, the greater the number of people who will obey the law. Small disturbances are a lot easier to control than large riots.

- *Tailgate hours and sites.* Take control of time. If authorities have control over how long an event can last there is a higher probability for successful crowd control.

- *Dry activities.* These are activities where the school pairs incoming freshmen with upperclassmen for "dry" activities. This method will only work if the first-year student admires the senior.

- *Notification.* Central Michigan and Michigan Tech will notify parents if underage students are caught drinking or if other alcohol policies are violated.

- *Communications.* The University of Connecticut has improved communications between police and students to help prevent riots during Spring Weekend.

- *Economic power.* Emory University in Atlanta took over maintenance and billing of fraternity houses, raised rents by 25 percent, and hired live-in house directors.

Figure 4-6
Sample University Event Crowd Management Control
Techniques

- Anyone who can provide historical or demographic information about the event that is to take place

COLLECTING DATA

Good crowd control depends on good data. A family-oriented picnic or outing will need a very different type of crowd control than a rock concert aimed at teenagers. Historical facts do not mean that one need not continue to collect data. For example, a family-oriented event may be an invitation to those seeking to provoke

1. Create a strong presence of ministers and mothers. This is likely to prevent, for example, groups of young men from ripping blouses off women, a practice young people refer to as "wilding."

2. Practice what you preach. Gulfport viewed films of other communities and knew what to expect.

3. Be good hosts. Part of the God Squad's techniques is to stop problems before they begin. Beaches are not barricaded, and portable toilets are strategically placed on the beach. Special lanes on the local highway are reserved for cruisers.

4. Make sure that the spring-breakers know the laws through easy-to-read flyers and signage.

5. Strictly enforce traffic and public indecency laws.

Figure 4-7
Mississippi's God Squad Techniques

problems. These negative types may choose to come to such an event because they believe that security will be low and that tolerance for negative behavior may be high. It is essential that plans be developed in which event risk management teams will know what to do so as to:

- Monitor the event: prior, during, and after
- Establish and maintain control of local and personal property
- Develop smooth traffic flows and know where to use and not to use barriers
- Protect life and property
- Know whom to call upon to arrest, guard, transport, and process those who may cause illegal disturbances while staying within the confines of due process
- Use physical force and know how much force is appropriate
- Produce an orderly evacuation
- Keep access to and from property/city streets/other parts of a park or field open
- Rescue officers and civilians from building, street, and vehicle environments

- Deal with the media and designate a spokesperson
- Call upon medical personnel as needed

Often, the best intentions do not work out simply because of poor organizational planning. Never assume that the organizational chart is clear to everyone. Make sure that each person on the crowd control team knows who is responsible for:

- Deploying personnel and equipment
- Obtaining intelligence for the smooth running of the event
- Determining the need for and the request for aid
- Assigning tasks and redeploying personnel
- Working with other agencies and/or organizations
- Performing triage (i.e., if only a few things can be saved, who determines what is let go and what is saved)

Never assume that this information is clear and always assign a backup person. All too often, emergencies occur when we least expect them.

Effective crowd control also means that event risk managers must be aware of what the public needs to do to protect itself at events. Following is a partial list of precautions that event risk managers can take:

- **Monitor sexual assaults.** Crowds are a great way for people to touch other people inappropriately. Make sure that there are people not only watching for sexual assaults, but also easily identifiable as capable of taking reports and responding in an appropriate manner.
- **Monitor drugs and alcohol.** Drugs and alcohol make people lose their common sense and do things that can lead to physical security issues.
- **Encourage people to carry identification cards with them.** People should have id cards listing their names, telephone numbers, and addresses. Due to the problems of identity theft, these identification cards must be kept in a safe place. Men should keep wallets in their front pockets; women should keep handbags over their arms, with hand on the bag. A woman should not strap a handbag across her neck, as no loss is worth a broken neck. Extra money should be kept in a sock or shoe or in a money belt that lies within one's clothing.

- **Get injured people to trained medical personnel as quickly as is safe and possible.** Make sure that there is a full written report taken of all injuries, treatments, and reasons for medical decisions (i.e., why a person was moved or not moved).
- **Move people to the edge of the crowd.** If crowd crushes or "moshing" should occur, move people to the edge of the crowd as soon as possible. Be careful of walls and unmovable barricades.
- **Avoid general admission.** It is best to avoid the standing-room-only sections as trouble can often begin in one of these areas. One way to lower the risk of something occurring is to eliminate these sections. While concert promoters will complain that such a policy may lower profits, the elimination of these sections may save lives and reduce litigation costs.
- **Monitor for signs of dehydration.** Younger people, especially people at concerts and at the beach, become so wrapped up in the events that they forget to consume enough liquids. The general rule is that if you are thirsty, you are already beginning to dehydrate. Dehydration leads to confusion, disorientation, fainting, and even death.

Event Risk Management Key Terms

Allocentric person: A person who tends to seek the unusual or the adventurous.

Anonymous crowd: A crowd in which people do not necessarily know each other.

Bating crowd: A crowd that forms for a specific goal, which is clearly marked and easily obtainable, for example, a lynch mob.

Fleeing crowd: A crowd that perceives a threat and flees from it, often in panic. Risk managers should seek to avoid them at all costs.

Heterogeneous crowd: A crowd composed of people who do not necessarily share a common heritage.

Homogeneous crowd: A crowd composed of people who share a common heritage such as religion or a political affiliation.

Moshing environment: Where people, among other things, slam into each other at rock concerts. It can vary in volatility and crowd mood.

Planned crowd: A crowd that has been developed by design, for example, assemblies and juries.

Prohibition crowd: A crowd that refuses to do what is asked, instead obeying a self-proposed prohibition.

Psychocentric person: A person who tends toward the sedate or is highly careful in where he or she goes or what he or she does.

Reversal crowd: A crowd that seeks to overturn the political status quo. These crowds are defenseless but, due to their numbers, gain strength and often gain control.

Wilding: The practice of taking a woman's blouse off against her will. A sign that a crowd may be turning into a riot.

Event Risk Management Drills

1. Assume that you are to host a specific ethnic parade. How would you prepare for it? With whom would you consult? What other community resources might you call upon?

2. You are the risk manager at a major hotel and have just learned that a famous musical group will be coming to your hotel. How would you start to plan? With which other departments in the hotel would you work?

CHAPTER 5

Emergencies

In some Emergency Medical Services (EMS) circles, mass events aren't thought of as definable situations, but as gatherings of potential patients.

—BUTLER, GESNER, AND NREMT, EMERGENCY MANAGEMENT, *NOVEMBER 1999*

IN THIS CHAPTER, WE WILL EXPLORE:

- Issues of emergency medical response (EMR) and risk management
- Types of EMR teams most effective in meetings and events
- Types of people who are at special risk
- Development of a risk management policy for fire safety and prevention
- Poison control issues
- Terrorism's challenge to event risk management

As the journalist Joe Cahill noted, "for the EMS in the city of New York there are really only three nights—the Fourth of July, New Year's Eve and the other 363 nights of the year" (Cahill, 1999, p. 38). While EMR teams are kept busy throughout the year, Cahill recognizes that events, especially large events, provide a tremendous amount of extra stress on those trying to manage medical risks and to care for the public. Events are occasions where participants lower their inhibitions and often do not use common sense. A crowd can easily degenerate into a mob, alcoholic beverages may be abused, nudity and a willingness to perform acts that are contrary to common sense are possible, all of which increase the risk of medical injury. A simple example serves to illustrate this point. Outdoor summer festivals and other events may inspire people not only to wear less clothing than is prudent, but also to forget to use sunscreen or sunblock, resulting in the need for medical attention. In a similar manner, people who tend to drink at these events often become intoxicated from alcohol and therefore increase the need for medical attention. During Las Vegas, Nevada's New Year's Eve millennium celebrations, several deaths occurred when party-goers climbed lampposts in an inebriated condition and then jumped to their deaths.

In the United States, the Fourth of July (Independence Day) and New Year's Eve are major event challenges for EMR teams and for those who seek to manage risk. As such, these holidays serve as a model for event management around the world. To paraphrase the song "New York, New York": If an event risk manager can handle those days, he or she can handle any day.

For example, if we examine the Fourth of July celebrations in many parts of the United States, we will note that across the country even this day's weather is a challenge to risk managers. The day is often hot and dry, prompting people to be out of doors and at water recreation areas. This is the day that pyrotechnics are displayed, both legally and illegally. Not only may crowds be large and tempers short, but risk managers must also worry about everything from fires caused by fireworks in dry fields to too much alcohol consumption, traffic problems, heat stroke, and insect bites. From this perspective, Independence Day celebrations are classical case studies, combining many of the risk management topics in this book.

Few small towns may have the funds to hire a full-time event risk manager for their Fourth of July celebrations. Nevertheless, someone in each community, whether he or she is a professional risk manager or a volunteer, needs to consider the unifying principles of these events. Furthermore, a tabletop exercise permits professional and volunteer risk managers to adapt these concepts to any event that they may need to manage.

Challenges to Event Risk Management

To better understand how some of these concepts fit together, let us begin by examining some of the challenges facing the New York City EMR squads that are assigned the New Year's Eve detail. New York City's New Year's Eve celebration centers around that part of the city known as Times Square, an area that occupies about ten city blocks and is located at the convergence of two major avenues and one major street: Broadway, Seventh Avenue, and 42nd Street. Times Square is not only the heart of New York City, but it serves as a major city transportation hub and as the city's most symbolic crossroads. The New Year's Eve celebration is broadcast around the world, which means that hundreds of thousands of people gather at Times Square both to see and to be seen.

Many of those watching the Times Square crowds are often unaware that the Times Square New Year's Eve celebration is not the only event taking place that night in New York City. Rather, it is one of several events that challenges the city's event risk managers on that night. Because an event such as a major New Year's Eve celebration or an Independence Day celebration encompasses all aspects of risk management, a practical way to gain an understanding of its complexity is to imagine the event as if it were a "momentary city." Figure 5.1 lists some of the comparisons between a major event and a city. After studying this figure, determine what other factors you might include in this comparison.

Central to these events are the EMR teams. These teams are the first response to a medical emergency. While EMR teams are on call every day of the year, for reasons listed at the beginning of this chapter, they experience uniquely challenging conditions whenever there is a major special event.

To address the additional problems posed by a special event to medical personnel, event risk managers must consider the following:

- Remember that life goes on during the special event. EMRs must be prepared to handle the special event, secondary

Major Event	City
Secondary events often produced	Neighborhood areas are separated from major downtown center
Fire equipment needed	Fire equipment needed
Composed of subcrowds	Composed of subpopulations
Coordination needed among medical, fire, and security services	Coordination needed among medical, fire, and security services
Potential for crisis	Potential for crisis
Specific site	Specific city limits
Control of streets essential	Control of streets essential
Chain of command needed to keep crowds under control	City government needed to assure secure environment in which to live

Figure 5-1
Comparing Risks in a City to Risks at a Major Event

events, and just everyday life. This means that the risk manager may not have all of the personnel and equipment that he or she might like to have.

- Obtain extra personnel. Because EMRs cannot handle the special event and the everyday events at the same time without extra personnel, it becomes the job of the risk manager to determine/research how much additional personnel the special event may require and develop a plan to obtain this additional personnel.
- Make certain that your EMR team is present throughout the

special event. When things seem quietest is often when trouble breaks out. Remain in a state of alert until the event is truly over.

- Be prepared to implement triage/treatment and transportation. In case of an emergency at a special event, there is a high probability that more people may need attention than your staff and equipment can handle. Have preset guidelines so that you can determine the order of medical attention.
- Have a coordinated ambulance plan ready and in operation. Determine how you will replace the ambulances that are called into service. Additionally, make certain that you have worked out an ambulance entry and exit strategy.
- Have some way to keep a record of those who choose not to accept medical treatment. You want proof of assessment/ refusal of treatment to minimize postaccident legal issues.
- Make certain that staff and volunteers at the event are fully briefed and that the timing for this briefing is as close to the event as possible. Areas in which you may wish to brief staff and volunteers include:
  - Area layout, with maps
  - Types of expected/potential violence
  - Biochemical hazards
  - Crowd culture
  - Latest weather forecasts
  - Who holds which positions within your chain of command
- Provide safe areas sheltered from the weather for both EMR personnel and victims.
- Design a method to secure unattended official vehicles. The last thing that an event risk manager needs during a special event is to have one of the emergency medical vehicles stolen or damaged.
- Develop a good communications system so that EMR team members can communicate with each other and with fire/ security personnel.

New Year's Eve and the Fourth of July only occur once a year, but concerts, festivals, and sports events take place on a much more frequent basis and attract large numbers of people. A large crowd is defined as having 1,000 or more people. Such large numbers of people mean that the event risk manager should assume that at least some of these people have medical disorders and that any crowd can deteriorate into a mass-casualty incident (Leonard and Moreland, 2001, p. 53).

A football game (university or professional) provides a good example of the momentary city/town analogy. These are events in which over 90,000 people may be present. Small cities have populations of about 90,000 to 100,000 people; therefore, these sports events may pose a certain threat to event risk managers. Although people may only come together for a few hours, these events require a great deal of preparation and budgetary planning. Unlike cities, however, these momentary communities are even more time dependent. In case of an accident or sudden illness, doctors and medical personnel must be on the scene immediately. Crowd density must also be considered. At concerts and sports events, the crowd density is higher than that of any large city's busiest street. Thus, when event risk managers contemplate the challenges that confront them during the life of these temporary communities, they must never fail to take into account such factors as attendance figures, the ratio of attendees to public safety personnel, and the location's capacity.

Anyone who has ever been in a traffic jam knows that often one of the reasons for these bottlenecks is the large number of people who slow down to look at an accident. This same principle must be taken into account when considering medical event risk management procedures. The EMR team must not only treat a sick person who is located in the midst of a crowd, but it also must deal with people stopping to look at the crisis. To make the situation even more difficult, the EMR team will have to navigate around obstacles such as vendors, members of the public giving advice, emotional spectators, and people who may be drunk. Furthermore, there will be a great deal of noise in a very small amount of space. Finally, event risk managers must factor into their equation the fact that it generally takes a longer amount of time to move a person who happens to be in a crowd to an ambulance. Event risk managers must consider the following when meeting with their EMR team:

- Size and layout of event site
- Number of people attending the event
- Number of personnel available, as well as backups
- Resource budget
- Aid from other sources
- Type of response team

When beginning to develop your EMR team, make sure that you meet with the team members. It is essential that you answer the following questions:

- Is the chain of command clearly understood?
- What is the overall budget?
- What equipment and supplies are needed and which supplies are supplemental?
- How will the local law enforcement agency and fire department interact with the EMR team?
- With which events can you compare your event? How are these events similar to other events?
- How can other agencies such as the Red Cross be of help?
- What are the conditions for the event? For example, if this event is a week-long festival, you will need a very different plan than if it is to last only a few hours. In the case of a longer event, several teams will be needed.
- Who are the expected participants at the event? While one never wants to make overgeneralizations, it is also clear that different types of events will attract different types of attendees. It is helpful in determining the types of risk, in particular, health risks, to have a psychographic model of the typical attendee at your event.
- What physical barriers might cause injury? For example, if this is an outdoor festival, are there ditches into which a person may fall, poison plants that can cause injury, or waterways that may prove dangerous? How will these areas be surveyed and isolated? If the event has a nighttime component, then lack of light must also be taken into consideration.
- Where will medical aid stations be situated? What is the farthest that someone would have to go to call for help? Are mobile stations needed? If the event is out of doors, then there may be additional problems in getting help. In the station, the risk manager will also need to decide what equipment the EMR team will need. How many beds should be in a station? By working with a statistician, the risk manager should be able to develop an accurate picture of the amount of materials that he or she will need.

Figure 5.2 provides a sample map showing where to place an EMR team. The general rule of thumb is one EMR team for each 1,000 participants. This equation, however, should be seen as a

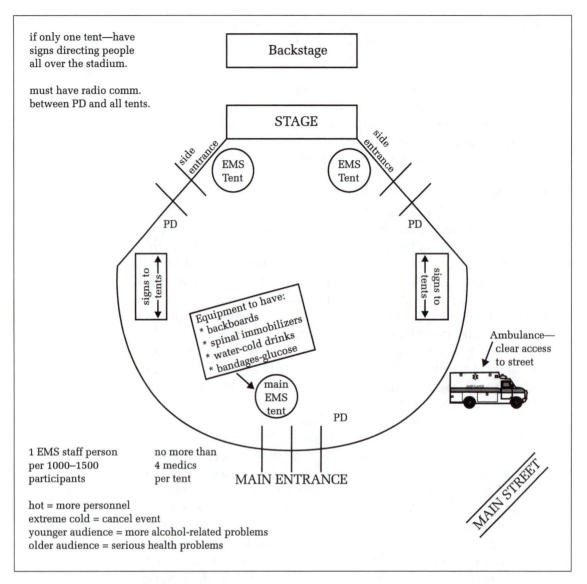

if only one tent—have signs directing people all over the stadium.

must have radio comm. between PD and all tents.

Backstage

STAGE

side entrance

side entrance

EMS Tent

EMS Tent

PD

PD

signs to tents →

← signs to tents →

Equipment to have:
* backboards
* spinal immobilizers
* water-cold drinks
* bandages-glucose

main EMS tent

Ambulance— clear access to street

PD

1 EMS staff person per 1000–1500 participants

no more than 4 medics per tent

MAIN ENTRANCE

MAIN STREET

hot = more personnel
extreme cold = cancel event
younger audience = more alcohol-related problems
older audience = serious health problems

Figure 5-2
Sample Emergency Medical Response Team Map

multivariate equation. Specific demographics must be used to determine the number of EMR teams per thousand participants. Factors to consider are:

- Age of participants in relationship to weather conditions
- Past incidents at this event (i.e., a review of its history)

- Type of event
- Location of event, outdoors or indoors
- Availability of shade if event is held outdoors and in summer
- Political situation (likelihood of attracting opponents)
- Distance of parking from event
- Geographic considerations (e.g., types of walkways, hills, places where one can fall)
- Time of day
- Weather conditions: chilly, sunny, windy, moist

Event managers should add extra EMR teams when the above factors heighten the probability of risk. One formula is to add 0.5 extra team for each additional risk factor and reduce the size of the team by 0.25 for factors that lessen the risk. Nevertheless, the number of EMR teams should not drop below one per thousand participants. For example, if you are the risk manager for an outdoor antique show in August in the southern part of the United States attracting mainly middle-aged people, you might consider:

- One team per thousand
- Time of day: noon, add 0.5
- Potential for violence among participants: subtract 0.25
- Amount of shade: adequate, neither add nor subtract
- Shade availability: low, add 0.5
- Potential for guests to fall: great, add 0.5
- Distance of trip to parking lot: close, subtract 0.25

For this event, we might construct the following equation:

$$1 + 0.5 - 0.25 + 0.5 + 0.5 - 0.25 = 2.00$$

In this hypothetical example, we would require two EMR teams per thousand.

It should be emphasized that the above equation is only a sample equation; the amounts to be added and subtracted for each team must be set by local requirements and should take into account as many variables as possible. The essential thing to remember is that the rule of thumb, one EMR team per thousand, must be modified to meet local demographic, weather, political, and geographic conditions.

Types of Team Responses

UNIT-TEAM RESPONSE

A unit team is based on the idea that a single medical team will take control of the injured person or patient from the moment there is an initial call for help until his or her arrival at the designated medical facility. Sometimes these unit teams are dispersed so that individual teams are positioned in strategic locations. In most cases, however, the team's equipment is at a specific site. Dispersed unit-team strategy is good when bulky tools or equipment is required. Figure 5.3 lists both the advantages and the disadvantages of unit-team responses.

ZONE-TEAM RESPONSE

The zone-team method combines wartime military response methods with civilian EMS methods. A central area is divided into zones, with teams within zones being prepositioned to respond immediately. Each team is prepared to back up the other team as needed.

One way to determine the type of response team that you will need is to consider the number of people who may need medical attention at your event. According to Leonard and Moreland (2001, p. 54), the average number of expected patients ranges from 0.3 to

Advantages	Disadvantages
Less confusion	Team fatigue
Information from patient to team may be more accurate	Possible errors in judgment due to fatigue
	Longer response time
Transportation crew has eyewitness view of the scene and event	

Figure 5-3
Advantages and Disadvantages of EMR Unit Team

1.3 percent of the total number of attendees. Leonard and More-land (2001, p. 57) further note that these numbers must "be adjusted for outdoor events, crowds of less than 30,000 and ambulatory spectators are all factors that have been shown to increase patient numbers over traditional estimates." For example, the Democratic National Convention had approximately 30,000 people in attendance with a treatment percentage of 1.27 percent. A papal mass has about 100,000 people in attendance with a treatment percentage of 1.59 percent. Studies have indicated that there should be at least four paramedics for every 10,000 people attending an event (Leonard and Moreland, 2001, p. 58).

In a similar manner, the event risk manager must not only know the number of people who may be statistically predicted to need treatment under normal event situations, but also the breakdown of individual medical needs for his or her particular event. Should the event risk manager predict "normal" event problems such as headaches and bruises or is there a reason to suspect that other forms of treatment may also be needed? For example, if your event attracts predominately senior citizens, then the needed medical treatments may be different from those needed at a rock concert.

No matter what event risk managers may predict, they must provide the EMR team with enough materials and personnel to coordinate most situations for at least 30 minutes. Finally, event risk managers must consider the type of medical personnel that will be needed. Should the event include only paramedics or registered nurses? Should it also include physicians? How much should 911 be involved in the overall plans? Are there specific times of the day when attendees may need more medical assistance than at other times? These and many other questions must also be considered to prepare properly for the medical needs of the guests (see Figure 5.4).

Fire

Ever since biblical times, people have sought out fire and, at the same time, have been afraid of fire. On the positive side, the harnessing of fire for peaceful uses was one of civilization's great

Inspect	Liaison
Quality of water/food	Local health officials
Loose carpeting or other underfoot hazards	Site engineers, maintenance crews, sanitation crews
Safety of building	Safety inspectors
Loose rocks and obstacles on paths	Grounds department
Quality of lighting	Electrical personnel
Quality of public sanitation services	Health sanitation, waste management services
Debris around the site	Janitorial sanitation services
Condition of warning systems	Fire and police departments
Condition of communications systems	Federal Communication Commission, telephone communications consultants

Figure 5-4
Risk Prevention Checklist

achievements. Fire permitted humans to cook food and to live in less temperate climates. On the negative side, once fire could be transported, it also became an instrument of war. Fire carried (and still carries) multiple risks. Once started, it is almost unstoppable and forms the basis of one of the most deadly weapons known to humanity.

From the perspective of event management, harnessed fire allows people to gather together. Indeed, without some form of fire, most of the world would not have the necessary heat and light for meetings, conventions, and other events. Even in ancient times, the advent of controlled fires allowed people to gather for religious reasons, to form hunting parties, and to hold festivals and markets. It may, then, be argued that the harnessing of fire was one of the basic discoveries that allowed humanity to create collective civilizations. As civilizations developed, meetings took place. At first, these meetings may have occurred around open camp fires, then in designated spots, such as England's Stonehenge, and, finally, in buildings and stadiums.

Indeed, from the Coliseum in ancient Rome to the Superdome in modern-day New Orleans, civilizations have built event venues. These venues have served as centers for sports events, meetings, conventions, expositions, and political rallies. In the past, these stadiums needed to harness fire for light, and along with the gift of fire also came the curse of fire. As long as fire was under control, it offered humanity its gifts of heat and light, but, once out of control, fire became an enemy that could destroy buildings, cities, economies, and life itself.

This double-edged sword, fire's blessing and curse, also has consequences in modern times. For example, the beauty of the mini-bonfires set around the stadium after the home team wins a soccer match never fails to impress visitors to the stadium of Maracanhã in Rio de Janeiro. On the other hand, in 1993, the cities of Atlanta, Georgia, and Irving, Texas, experienced unwanted stadium fires. The Atlanta stadium blaze occurred in the press area and the Irving fire broke out while the Dallas Cowboy cheerleaders were holding field practice. While no one was hurt in either fire, these incidents serve as an example of the high risk of fire, even in modern stadiums and convention centers.

In the two cases cited above, both stadiums were built from noncombustible materials. These fires, however, underline the major point that even though a building may be constructed out of noncombustible materials, there may still be a great many materials found within a modern convention center or stadium that are combustible. For example, in many places where events are held we can find:

- Plastic seats
- Interior materials used in private suites, such as gypsum wallboard or wood paneling
- Upholstered chairs
- Photographic equipment and flammable chemicals
- Office areas that contain combustible materials
- Restaurants/kitchens where grease may be used or combustible material may be present

Often, then, the public believes that event venues are immune from fires. In fact, the reality is quite different. Not only may a building's contents be combustible, but also only part of the buildings may be in use. This means that a fire can break out in one part of the building and not be noticed for quite a while or the fire may burn for a period of time before being discovered. In addition, it may be difficult to bring water to the affected part of the building.

The National Fire Protection Association reports that senior citizens are most at risk in case of a fire **(http://www.usfa.fema. gov/safety/older).** Event risk managers should take into account, then, that the death risk among seniors (some 70 years or older) is more than double that of the average population. A second large category is that of children. As more children and older citizens attend events and stay in hotels, these two demographic groups will present special challenges to event risk managers. Furthermore, event risk managers must never forget that all of the sociopsychological facts discussed in Chapter 1 also apply in the case of fire. For example, a person might not smoke in bed at home, but a person who has had too many drinks at an after-hours convention gathering might easily decide to smoke in bed, thus causing a great amount of risk to him- or herself and to others.

Because people are living longer and remain physically active, event risk managers must never assume that they can ignore the needs of people with special needs. We will examine four such groups: senior citizens, the hearing impaired, the mobility impaired, and the blind or visually impaired. Each of these groups makes major contributions to society and, as such, they now travel more, attend more events, and have found ways that permit them to overcome their disabilities and thus fully participate in all aspects of life. Event risk managers cannot afford to overlook these people's special needs.

SENIOR CITIZENS

Older adults have special needs that present additional challenges to those in the field of fire protection and event risk management. Although the following list can include people of any age, statistics indicate that these items must be of great concern to event risk managers who work with older event attendees. The factors associated with aging include:

- Progressive degeneration in physical, cognitive, and emotional capabilities. Included in this list are such problems as blindness/poor eyesight or deafness/poor hearing. These two handicaps mean that senior citizens can be at much higher risk and have less chance of seeing/hearing signs, warnings, and/or alarms.
- Higher probability that an elderly person will accidentally start a fire.
- Lower probability that a senior citizen may survive a fire, due to physical restraints.
- Consumption of multiple medications by seniors. The taking of multiple medicines may cause side effects, including confusion. These side effects may alter the decision-making process and interfere with one's ability to think clearly during a crisis, increasing the potential for accidents.
- Impairments caused by the combination of alcohol and prescription drugs. Such impairments may lead to an increased likelihood of accidentally starting a fire, not detecting a fire, and not being able to escape a fire.

Because the elderly fire victim often comes in close contact with the heat source that starts the fire, special attention needs to be paid to issues of smoking and portable heating devices. More information is available on line at **http://www.usfa.fema.gov/ safety/older.htm.**

These factors are not only age but also event specific.

Some Facts on Fire in the United States

The United States has one of the highest fire death rates in the industrialized world. In 1998, the U.S. fire death rate was 14.9 deaths per million population. Between 1994 and 1998, an average of 4,400 Americans lost their lives and another 25,100 were injured annually as the result of fire. About 100 firefighters are killed each year in duty-related incidents. Each year, fire kills more Americans than all natural disasters combined. Fire is the third leading cause of accidental death in the home; at least 80 percent of all fire deaths occur in residences. About 2 million fires are reported each year. Many others go unreported, causing additional injuries and property loss. Direct property loss due to fires is estimated at $8.6 billion annually.

There were 1,755,000 fires in the United States in 1998. Of these:

- 41 percent were outside fires
- 29 percent were structure fires
- 22 percent were vehicle fires
- 8 percent were fires of other types

The South has the highest fire death rate per capita with 18.4 civilian deaths per million population. Some 80 percent of all fatalities occur in the home. Of those, approximately 85 percent occur in single-family homes and duplexes.

Following are the most common causes of fires and fire deaths:

- Cooking is the leading cause of home fires in the United States, and careless smoking is the leading cause of fire deaths.
- Heating is the second leading cause of residential fires and the second leading cause of fire deaths.
- Arson is the third leading cause of both residential fires and residential fire deaths. In commercial properties, arson is the major cause of deaths, injuries, and dollar loss.

SOURCE: National Fire Protection Association, *1998 Fire Loss in the U.S. and Fire in the United States 1987–1996,* 11th ed., 2000.

HEARING IMPAIRED

Event risk managers often overlook those guests and participants who are hearing impaired. It is a good idea for event risk managers to consult with groups representing people with hearing impairments to find the best way to serve these people.

We know that hearing-impaired individuals cannot rely on traditional audible smoke alarms. To compensate, some alarms come equipped with flashing lights. Another solution is the vibrating bed and pillows that have been designed to awaken people who are hearing impaired and alert them to the presence of a fire. It is also important for the event risk manager to remember that a portion of the deaf and hard-of-hearing population is also blind or visually impaired. In the case of the smoke alarm, for those who suffer from both visual and hearing impairments, visual strobe lights would be ineffective. Event risk managers should also check with the appropriate authorities to determine which components of the Americans with Disabilities Act (ADA) impact on their jobs.

More information is available on line at **http://www.usfa.fema. gov/safety/hearing.htm.**

MOBILITY IMPAIRED

A third group that presents special challenges to event risk managers is the mobility impaired. People with mobility impairments face challenges, including fire safety. At home, people with mobility problems can take into account the dangers and obstacles that may impair them during a fire, but when traveling these obstacles can become especially dangerous to the mobility impaired. To make matters more complicated, most mainstream fire safety protection devices are designed primarily with the able-bodied person in mind. Thus, it is preferable for event risk managers to have prior knowledge as to who suffers from mobility impairment, and he or she needs to develop a risk management plan that takes their needs into account.

Event risk managers should remember that:

- People with mobility impairments represent a segment of the population with one of the highest risks of dying in a fire.
- The fire safety needs of people with mobility impairments are not addressed through mainstream public fire and life safety education.

- Fire safety engineering has not adequately addressed the capabilities of people with mobility impairments.
- People with disabilities have to deal with extra impediments to their escape in cases of fire.

More information is available on line at **http://www.usfa.fema.gov/safety/mobility.htm.**

BLIND OR VISUALLY IMPAIRED

Event risk managers face many challenges, among which is ensuring the safety of the blind or visually impaired. Those persons who have these impairments realize personal safety is always an issue. Those who cannot see or have trouble seeing must deal with health issues, issues of safety and security, and the realization that, in an emergency, extraction from danger may be difficult at best. For example, in the event of a fire, the event risk manager must be cognizant of the fact that a blind or visually impaired person suffers from an increased risk of injury and death.

The visually impaired person may also inadvertently be the cause of a fire. In cases of impairment, one can clearly note the importance of event risk management. The best way to protect or save a person who has this impairment is to prevent the crisis from occurring. Therefore, you should develop and practice escape plans. Ask yourself, if you were blind, could you find the emergency exits. How much time would you lose seeking exits?

The visually impaired may have a very difficult time if a fire breaks out. By closing your eyes, you can easily determine just how quickly your senses can be overwhelmed and confusion can set in. Take into consideration that high-decibel smoke alarms often make it difficult for the blind individual to process audible clues and instructions effectively.

Furthermore, check to determine if you can equip your event venue with heat resistant Braille or other tactile signs so that the visually impaired guests have multiple sources of directions. These "readable signs" are especially important if other forms of communication should fail. Finally, check with the ADA enforcement section of the U.S. Department of Justice to determine what other safety measures you need to make in order to care for those with one or more impediments.

More information is available on line at **http://www.usfa.fema. gov/safety/sight.htm.**

MANAGING AND CONTROLLING FIRE RISK

Because fire can be so destructive, it is essential that event risk managers invest the time and effort in preventing fires. It cannot be emphasized enough that the best form of fire fighting is fire prevention. Event risk managers should always work closely with local fire officials. The event risk manager should never be afraid to ask questions of fire experts and should never forget that, when it comes to saving lives, it is better to ask questions than to rely on incorrect assumptions.

The following checklist will help you to decrease fire risks and, in case of a fire, to reduce the risk to life and property:

- Inspect smoke alarms and make sure that different types of smoke alarms have been installed. A working smoke alarm dramatically increases a person's chance of surviving a fire.
- Evaluate the fire evacuation plan in terms of the event's demographics. Make sure that the evacuation plan will work for those with impairments, and that warnings can be clearly understood and assimilated by everyone. In a like manner, if children are expected to be present during the event, be aware of the fact that children's skin is thinner and will burn more easily.
- Conduct a tabletop exercise and a practice drill of your fire prevention and evacuation plan. Make certain that you conduct this exercise under various conditions. For example, if a fire broke out at night, how would the evacuation plan be different from that which you might employ during daylight hours?
- Meet with fire officials to discuss their concerns. Develop a worst case scenario and a plan to deal with that scenario.
- Have clear routes for both evacuees and firefighters. Does the fire department have clear and precise maps of where things are, what evacuation routes are to be used, and where firefighting resources are located?
- Make certain that you have checked and reviewed with experts what preventive measures need to be taken to avoid biochemical hazards. In case of a fire, how would you handle the additional problem of biochemicals?

- Ensure that stairs are marked. Is it clearly stated that one should not use elevators during a fire?
- Develop a fire control checklist and review it periodically. Make certain that you regularly inspect the following resources:
  - Sprinkler systems
  - Smoke detectors
  - Fire extinguishers
  - Monitors for the fire extinguishers
  - Ramp/path layouts
  - Available water resources
- Develop recommendations for any special legislative action that may be needed to prevent fire damage in the future.
- Integrate your fire plan with your EMR team plan. Is the EMR team familiar with the fire-fighting plan? Do these two components have the same maps and directions? How well coordinated is the communication between them? Is it clear who is in charge and what the chain of command is in case of an emergency?

In the case of both fire prevention and EMR services, it is a good idea for event risk managers to travel to other facilities of a similar nature. These trips allow event risk managers to see how their colleagues handle problems and provide the event risk managers with professional best practices and benchmarks. The event risk manager may wish to determine the following:

- How well do colleagues handle the large crowds that gather prior to the event and linger at the stadium after the event?
- Are these crowds fire hazards?
- Do these crowds require additional EMR teams and resources?
- What is the relationship between alcohol and fire at colleagues' venue sites?
- How do colleagues mark escape routes?
- How do colleagues coordinate the resources of multiple stakeholders (firefighters, police, security, etc.)?

Developing a policy for event risk management requires careful planning. The following points should always be considered:

- Determine critical needs. The event risk manager needs to determine these needs and prioritize them. No event risk manager will have everything that he or she desires. Know what you must have, desire, and benefit from.

- Establish a good group coordination effort. It is essential that the chain of command and political issues be ironed out before an event. During a critical incident, there is no time for personality conflicts.
- Predeploy resources. Make certain that all resources are in place prior to the event. The last thing you want to do during a crisis is send for resources.
- Have billings established prior to the event. It is essential to know who will charge what and for what services. The sooner these issues are identified and resolved, the quicker the risk manager can move onto the immediate task at hand. Never assume that someone is going to provide a service free of charge.
- Test and test again all warning systems. How loud do warning devices need to be to be heard above the roar of the crowd?
- Develop a backup power plan. If you needed additional power, how would you get it? What alternative power sources do you have in case of blackouts or power cutbacks? Do you have an emergency generator system to make sure that fire alarms, voice communication, fans, exit signs, fire pumps, elevators for firefighters, and emergency lighting will work?
- Determine how smoke will be handled. Is there a smoke control system?
- Know where the phones are located in order to notify the fire department.

Finally, the well-known McDonald's lawsuit involving a patron who was scalded from a cup of coffee should remind and warn event risk managers that burns are not always the result of a fire. There are multiple ways that people can burn themselves. Make certain to review with departments such as catering questions like: How hot is the water going to be? Are there heating units that can accidentally burn a guest or employee? In places where there are open fires and bonfires, make certain that firebreaks are adequate and that weather conditions are closely monitored.

If a person's clothing becomes inflamed, then have the person:

- Stop immediately wherever he or she may be
- Drop to the ground
- Roll over and over again with hands over face and mouth until the fire is extinguished

Poison

In Philadelphia in 1976, former military personnel held a convention in honor of the nation's 200th birthday. Though they never intended their meeting to become a part of history, due to a problem in the cooling system, 221 people became ill and 34 died. It was that convention that gave us the name Legionnaires' disease. The disease, however, has not been confined to Philadelphia. In Stafford, England (1985), over 100 people contracted the disease, resulting in 28 deaths. Legionnaires' disease has also occurred in places such as Australia **(http://www.multiline.com.au/~mg/legion5.html).** In reality, this disease came from contaminated air conditioning ducts and serves as a good example of the fact that we live in a world filled with poisons. While problems with poisons are most likely to occur where there are young children or animals present, Legionnaires' disease is an example that even adults can die from poisoning.

The Carolinas Poison Center provides us the following definition of a poison: "A poison is anything someone eats, breathes, gets in the eyes or on the skin that can cause sickness or death. Poisons can be found in four forms: solid, liquid, spray or gas" **(http://www.carolinas.org/services/poison/info.cfm).** Every event risk manager should have more than a posted poison control center number. The event risk manager should have an established relationship with a toxic center. Notices for all poison control centers should be posted in easy-to-see locations, with large telephone numbers, and, where necessary, be written in more than one language.

Most people are unaware of all the poisons that surround them. For example, almost every adult knows that oven-cleaning agents are poisonous, but few people realize that a common buttercup flower can also be poisonous. Additionally, various things that may be only mildly poisonous to an adult may be deadly to a child, older adult, or pregnant woman.

The main way to avoid poisoning incidents is to focus on prevention. Bottles and containers in which poisonous chemicals are stored should be carefully labeled both in words and with clearly understandable symbols. All packaging should be childproof. The Poison Prevention Packaging Act of 1970 authorizes the U.S. Consumer Product Safety Commission to require the use of child-resistant packaging for toxic substances used in and around the home. This same standard should apply to events whenever children may be present. If the meeting is to be held indoors, carbon monoxide should also be monitored.

As mentioned above, poisons can come in all forms and products. Following is a partial list compiled by the Carolinas Poison Center of some common substances that, if used incorrectly, can be or become poisonous:

- **Personal care products.** Mouthwash, nail polish, permanent-wave solutions, hair-removal products, nail polish remover, cosmetics
- **Household products.** Drain cleaners, toilet bowl cleaners, ammonia, bleach, pesticides, lamp oil, oven cleaners, furniture polish, gasoline, kerosene, antifreeze, windshield solution, fertilizers, lawn chemicals
- **Medicines and vitamins.** Heart and blood pressure drugs, tranquilizers, cough and cold medicines, iron and pain relievers, diabetes medicines
- **Plants.** Wild mushrooms, philodendron, foxglove, castor bean, dieffenbachia, pokeweed, holly berries, Peace lily
- **Environmental poisons.** Carbon monoxide, lead paint

More information is available on line at **http://www.carolinas. org/services/poison/info.cfm.**

Acts of Terrorism

The September 11, 2001, terrorist attacks on New York City and Washington, DC, brought home to much of the world what nations such as Israel, Great Britain, and Ireland have been facing for many years: political terrorism. In the United States, terrorism has been traditionally divided into domestic and international terrorism. In reality, terrorism is terrorism. Terrorism is often defined as the indiscriminate destruction of property and life for the purposes of furthering a political agenda. Because terrorists seek media attention, any event is an open target for terrorists. Terrorists, unlike criminals, are often willing to risk or lose their lives in the pursuit of their goals. Criminals who "work" events seek profit. Terrorists, however, seek to create political chaos. Event risk managers, then, face a new and deadly challenge. Figure 5.5 will help

	Crime	**Terrorism**
Goal	Usually economic or social gain	To gain publicity and sometimes sympathy for a cause
Usual type of victim	Person may be known to the perpetrator or selected because he or she may yield economic gain	Killing is random and appears to be more in line with a stochastic model; numbers may or may not be important
Defenses in use	Often reactive, reports taken	Some proactive devices such as radar detectors
Political ideology	Usually none	Robin Hood model, that is to say, the terrorist sees himself in a positive light
Publicity	Usually local and rarely makes the international news	Almost always is broadcast around the world
Most common forms in events industry are:	Crimes of distraction Robbery Sexual assault	Domestic terrorism International terrorism Bombings Potential for biochemical attack
Statistical accuracy	Often very low; in many cases, the travel and tourism industry does everything possible to hide the information	Almost impossible to hide; numbers are reported with great accuracy and repeated often

Figure 5-5
Major Differences Between Event Crime and Terrorism

	Crime	Terrorism
Length of negative effects on the local events industry	In most cases, it is short term	In most cases, it is long term, unless replaced by new positive image
Recovery strategies	■ New marketing plans, assumes short-term memory of traveling public ■ Probability ideals: "odds are it will not happen to you" ■ Hide information as best as one can	■ Showing of compassion ■ Need to admit the situation and demonstrate control ■ Higher levels of observed security ■ Highly trained (in tourism, terrorism, and customer service) security personnel

Figure 5-5 *(Continued)*

you distinguish some of the major differences between terrorism and crime.

Terrorism has a number of nuances, and it is essential that the event risk manager understand these differences. Figure 5.6 illustrates some of the differences among domestic terrorism, protest terrorism (meetings-cum-demonstrations, or MCDs; see Chapter 7), and international terrorism.

Some Reasons for the Interaction Between Terrorism and Events
- Events are often close to major transportation centers.
- Events are big business.
- Events impact other industries such as restaurants, hotels, and entertainment.
- Events often draw media coverage.
- Events require tranquility or places where business can be conducted in a peaceful manner.
- Events must deal with people who have no history; thus, risk managers often do not have databases on delegates or attendees.

	Domestic	Meetings cum Demonstrations	International
Viewed as	Crime	Politics	War
Goal	Overthrow government or policy	Change policy	Conquest
Preparation time	Very little or none	Great deal of time	Very little or none
Targets	Government Buildings	Meetings	Economic or transportation centers. Tourism most at risk here of a direct attack
Effects on tourism	Major short-term effect; can become a part of dark tourism	Major effect during short- and medium-term memory	Can have long-term effects, especially if repeated

Figure 5-6
Types of Event Terrorism

- Events are based on a constant flow of guests; thus, it is hard to know who is and who is not a terrorist.
- Events are the point where business and relaxation converge, and therefore guests often let down their guard.

DEALING WITH BOMB THREATS OR ACTS OF TERRORISM

Few visitor event venues are prepared for a bomb threat or an act of terrorism. Yet, as the world becomes an increasingly dangerous place, it behooves you to become prepared for such a possibility. In training sessions that you hold with your staff and volunteers:

- Make sure that all employees and volunteers know the policy guidelines. These guidelines should be reviewed on a periodic basis.
- Instruct employees and volunteers not to discuss the matter with anyone, especially the media.
- Practice procedures. The more practice employees and volunteers have, the less chance of panic and the greater the possibility that the person will follow procedures and save lives.

EVENT VENUES

Event venues are perfect sites for both large-scale and small-scale terrorism attacks. Attacks may be of a violent nature, such as the explosion of a bomb, or of a silent nature, such as a biological attack via the building's ventilation system.

When a safety or security incident occurs not only will that particular location suffer, but there will also be a negative impact on the community hosting the event. From a marketing standpoint, safety and security are two sides of the same coin. In other words, if an incident occurs the negative publicity is the same whether it is due to a safety or a security issue.

Develop a set of guidelines for venue safety and security. Review these guidelines first with local law enforcement and then with every employee and volunteer. While an event risk manager cannot invade a person's privacy, the risk manager must be cognizant of the fact that employees or volunteers can be plants (people who have helped plan the attack while working at the event).

The event risk manager then must think through such issues as:

- Policies regarding a crowd in panic
- Notification of the victims' families
- Policies regarding employee and volunteer background checks
- Special security instructions for those working at front desks/ticket booths
- Policies on secondary crises (e.g., after a bomb has exploded, a fire may break out)
- Escape routes

It is essential that policies be developed as to what preventive measures will be taken before an attack, during an attack, and after an attack. The following checklist will be useful in this policy development.

Before an Attack

- Discuss possible solutions with all event stakeholders. The more the stakeholders are involved, the better the chance that there will be cooperation during an attack.
- Have in place a plan for the dissemination of information. Information on sensitive security issues should not be shared with everyone. The event risk manager will need to balance the need to know with the need to maintain security.
- Develop a media recovery plan long before there is a terrorist attack.
- Meet with safety and security personnel. Make sure that you, as a manager, are clear as to what active and passive security plans you have. Do you have a clear evacuation route? Do you have contact information for local law enforcement agencies, fire departments, ambulance services? Make certain that you review your medical equipment and supplies and make sure that you have some form of triage plan in place.
- Check all entrances to event venues. Doors that are off limits to guests should be locked at all times. It is important for the security of the venue that if a terrorist incident should occur there be some way to account for those who may be injured or missing.

During an Attack

- Remain calm. Speak in the lower tones of the voice's register and maintain grace under pressure.
- Listen, without interrupting, in case there is a warning concerning a bomb. Never argue or become defensive.
- Do not be a hero. Instead, call for help when possible. If you are a hostage, give the appearance of cooperation.
- Have a backup person in case the event risk manager is injured or killed.
- Review exit plans on a regular basis. This review is especially important in case of chemical and biological attacks.
- Maintain sense of humor, if at all possible. Humor can help you to keep calm and to think clearly.

- Listen, listen, and listen, then get details. Terrorists will often give out a vital piece of information that can save lives.
- Never display anger.
- Never forget that the attendees are the event's guests. You should attempt to remove guests from the situation as quickly as possible.

After an Attack

- Assess the damage. First, seek to save lives, second, deal with psychological traumas, and finally, assess property damage.
- Implement the recovery plan. Such a plan may include:
    All-clear signals
    Review of all security breaches
    Dissemination of honest and accurate information
- Make sure that all employees, volunteers, and guests understand that you are doing everything possible for their protection. Every person at the event needs to know that you care about him or her. Leadership means listening, keeping all impacted persons in the know, and implementing.
- Make sure that police and security personnel are visible. Good event risk security in this case means that you need to be vigilant but not overbearing. If possible, at least for the next few days after an attack, have security professionals placed at the entrances to all venues and at elevators. It is reassuring to the public when police and security personnel are seen standing rather than sitting.
- Make sure that employees, volunteers, and guests know that you cannot answer every question asked.
- Keep lighting at as high a level as possible. The more light there is, the more people tend to feel secure. Good lighting works on the subconscious as both a protective device and a method of reassurance.
- Take a proactive stance. Keep eyes open for anything that may seem suspicious. In such a case, do not confront the person, but report your suspicions to security personnel.
- Make sure that employee and volunteer identification cards are clearly visible. This is important to reassure the public and provide a sense of professionalism.
- Check the records of all outside contractors doing repair work.

Event Risk Management Key Terms

Chain of command: An organizational structure that identifies decision-makers in order of authority and clearly delineates responsibilities.

Combustible material: Material that can catch on fire.

Incident commander: Called the IC, this is the person who keeps track of the entire risk management team. It is the IC's job to know what is going on at each station and to coordinate the actions of the EMR team.

Medic in charge: The head medic on an EMR team. The medic in charge is often called the MIC and answers to the IC.

Operational supervisor: Another name for the incident commander on an EMR team. Often called the OS for short.

Tabletop exercise: An exercise in which all the key players are given a scenario and asked to act as if it were real.

Unit-team approach: A form of EMR in which one team is responsible for the patient from moment of contact until end of contact.

Zone-team approach: An EMR organizational pattern based on a mixture of military and civilian procedures.

Event Risk Management Drills

1. Assume that you are running an outdoor ethnic food festival for the elderly. What fire precautions might you need to take? What are some of the poison issues that you might consider? How would you organize your EMR team?

2. Assume that you have been hired as the risk manager for a major sports stadium. Design a risk program that deals with issues of fire and health.

3. You are the risk manager and need to determine how many EMR teams you will require. The event is a summer rock con-

cert. Last year, this concert had a number of alcohol-related incidents. The concert takes place in the late afternoon and extends into the night. The concert site is a hill in a geographic area famous for sudden flash thunderstorms. How many EMR teams would you want per thousand participants?

4. A car bomb has just exploded in front of your event center. What are the steps that you would take in protecting the survivors and the rescuers? Develop a time line for your response.

CHAPTER 6

Critical Issues for Event Safety

It is better to be safe than sorry.

—AMERICAN PROVERB

IN THIS CHAPTER, WE WILL EXPLORE:

- Pedestrian safety
- Bites and stings
- Food safety
- Drinking water quality
- Lighting
- Parking lot safety
- Electrical storms and lightning
- Electrical and gas safety

It is difficult to make a theoretical distinction between issues of safety and issues of security. In both cases, there is risk; in both cases, an incident causes similar outcomes. Figure 6.1 shows the similarities in dealing with both safety and security risks.

Incident	Results if Question of Safety	Results if Question of Security
Publicity	Negative	Negative
Litigation	Possible/probable	Possible/probable
Event ruined from perspective of attendee	Yes	Yes
Damage control needed	Yes	Yes
Issues of foreseeability involved	Yes	Yes

Figure 6-1
Comparison of Event Safety and Security Risk Similarities

This chapter explores a number of topics that may not be as "exciting" as other security topics, but they are equally as important. In fact, while there is a minimal probability that most event participants may be confronted with an act of terrorism, almost every event attendee will have to deal with issues such as pedestrian safety and the quality of the water that he or she consumes.

Pedestrian Safety

Pedestrian safety is a major problem and requires careful attention. In Chapter 1, we discussed some of the theoretical reasons that people who are away from home are often less cautious. When it comes to pedestrian safety issues, we have excellent examples to support the theories found in Chapter 1. For example, people at events may:

- Be in a party or jovial mood and thus are distracted while walking
- Walk in groups and tend to talk while walking

- Consume alcohol and thus their faculties may be impaired
- Need special help while crossing the street or dealing with internal pathways
- Stay in multiple hotels, may suffer from issues of anomie, and may not be familiar with local signage, pedestrian laws, and driver responsibilities or lack of responsibilities

In addition, a greater number of children attend conventions and meetings with their parents, and some parents may pay less attention to their children's needs than is desirable.

People at fairs, meetings, conventions, and sports events often exhibit the same sociological patterns as children. All too often, delegates/attendees take unfortunate risks when crossing streets or walking along the side of streets or on paths. For example, just because the pedestrian can see a driver does not signify that the situation is true in reverse. In a similar manner, when a guest is inebriated, he or she may be confused as to the direction from which a sound is coming or may be suffering from other perception skill deficits. If delegates are crossing streets while talking, they may be so involved in the conversation that they misjudge distance, speed of vehicle, and time needed to cross a street. It should, then, come as no surprise that the pedestrian groups most at risk are elementary schoolchildren, adults over age 65, and those impaired by alcohol or other drugs. Pedestrian paths need to be designed in a way that older adults can use them safely. Risk managers should take into account gravel paths and physical impediments that may not be hard on younger people, but may be a safety hazard to the more elderly person.

The American Automobile Association (AAA) Web site notes that: "More than half of all pedestrian deaths and injuries occur when people cross or enter streets while one-third occur between intersections. Both driver and pedestrian errors contribute to these accidents" **(http://www.csaa.com/about/education/pedestrian.asp rights).**

According to the same Web site, a pedestrian is defined as "someone who is walking or using a human-powered device such as a wheelchair, skateboard or rollerskates [sic]. Bicyclists are not considered pedestrians" **(http://www.csaa.com/about/education/ pedestrian.asp rights).** Because of the reasons listed above, pedestrians can cause special event management problems for risk managers. Pedestrians often do not consider walking in crosswalks, observing traffic signals, or paying full attention at an intersection to be a top priority. Furthermore, pedestrians very much live according to the old Spanish proverb, "if the rock hits the pitcher or the pitcher hits the rock, it is still too bad for the pitcher." Thus, while most states insist that drivers must yield for the pedestrian, when there is an accident, it is the pedestrian who most likely is going to suffer. Pedestrians do not only walk in crosswalks. Fairs and meetings with off-site parking often have people walking along the road. In many rural communities, sidewalks are almost nonexistent.

To help save lives, use these simple but effective techniques:

1. When possible, have people walk on the sidewalks. In rural areas where there are no sidewalks, risk managers may want to create walking paths along the side of the road. Make sure that pedestrians walk facing traffic, so they can see oncoming vehicles or an out-of-control vehicle.

2. Encourage bright-colored clothing. Bright colors are easier to spot both during the day and at night. When possible, hand out reflective material for people's shoes or clothing. Do not permit people to walk with headphones as they can mask the sound of an oncoming vehicle.

3. Review where people cross the street. If possible, have crossing guards; if impossible, then consider crossing lights. If neither human nor mechanical aids are possible, then make sure that crosswalks are clearly marked. Cross only at corners or marked crosswalks.

4. Discourage running at street crossings. Running can lead to falling or to pushing another person over. It is essential that people walk at crosswalks rather than run.

5. Have a plan for helping visually and hearing-impaired people to cross streets and walk along paths/roads. Remember that these people need extra care not only outside of the event's grounds, but also in parking lots and on the event grounds if vehicular traffic is permitted.

6. Develop adjacent walking paths so that bicycle and pedestrian traffic do not interact.

7. Use universal signage. Words such as "Walk" or "Stop" are less helpful than international signage. The most common symbol for "Walk" is a stick figure of a person about to walk (usually shown in green), while an outstretched hand (often white on red background) indicates "Stop!"

8. Control speed. The lower the speed in areas of heavy pedestrian traffic, the greater the possibility that a driver may be able to stop before an accident occurs.

The Movie Star's Husband and the Dragon

A number of incidents have happened to pedestrians or people on foot due to lack of common sense. For example, the *San Francisco Chronicle* (June 23, 2001) reported on a bizarre incident involving Phil Bronstein, the executive editor of the *San Francisco Chronicle* and the husband of the actress Sharon Stone. On June 9, 2001, Stone and Bronstein were on a private tour of the Los Angeles Zoo. A zoo employee allowed Bronstein to enter the cage of a Komodo dragon (7-foot-long lizard). The lizard was about to eat a toe on Bronstein's foot when, according to the *Chronicle,* zookeeper, Jay Kilgore, pulled the lizard out of the way.

http://www.sfgate.com/cgi-bin/article.cgi?file=/chronicle/archive/2001/06/23/mn129101.dtl.

Insects and Snakes

INSECTS

Another safety issue that is often overlooked and yet can have great consequences, especially for an outdoor event, is that of insect bites or stings. For example, any child who lives in the southeastern United States knows that sitting on the ground can be dangerous because of fire ants. These small but painful insects can ruin much more than a picnic. Because their bites are so painful and can cause allergic reactions, outdoor events such as concerts and sports events must take into account fire ants as part of any good risk management plan.

A good risk management plan should coordinate dangers from insect bites/stings with the event's management team and planning team. If sitting on the ground poses a danger, then other alternatives need to be found. If a particular type of flower or plant can cause allergic reactions, then alternatives need to be considered. When mitigating insect risks, you should consider:

- The local conditions
- The weather/climate
- The type of people who are attending
- The type of ground covering
- The types of pesticides that can or cannot be used

Fire ants are not the only insect threat to events. Following are some common insects whose bites require immediate attention. It is imperative that event risk managers work closely with EMR units and poison centers in their specific area. The information in this section was adapted from the Web site of the Carolinas Poison Center (**http://www.carolinas.org/services/poison/insect.cfm**).

Black Widow Spider

Identification   The female spider can be identified by its round, glossy black abdomen, which is about one-half inch in diameter, with an orange-red hourglass marking its belly. The male black widow spider is solid in color, and its bite is not venomous.

Results of Bite   The black widow's bite is painful. After being bitten, the victim may experience redness and warmth at the site where he or she was bitten, muscle cramps, twitching, rigid abdomen, difficulty breathing, weakness, headache, nausea, and vomiting.

If Bitten   Wash area with warm, soapy water and call a poison center immediately.

Brown Recluse (Fiddleback) Spider

Identification   The brown recluse spider is small, about one-half inch long, with an oval body and a dark violin-shaped marking on its back.

Results of Bite   Its bite causes pain, redness, tenderness, and a bull's-eye appearance, which progresses to ulceration. Bites may go unnoticed until a lesion develops.

If Bitten   Wash area with warm, soapy water and call a poison center immediately.

Ticks

Tick bites are common and were usually considered harmless. However, with the increase in the reported cases of Rocky Mountain spotted fever and Lyme disease, tick bites must be taken much more seriously in certain parts of the country.

Results of Bite   There is no standard as to when symptoms will appear. The person may begin to experience symptoms at any time, ranging from a few days after the bite to a few weeks. The victim will suffer from flulike symptoms that include headaches, chills, fever, and rash. It behooves risk managers to be on the lookout for Lyme disease and to take appropriate precautions, especially as the victims may not experience any symptoms until long after they have left the event's grounds.

If Bitten   The person "should carefully remove the tick using blunt tweezers. Grasp the tick close to the skin and pull upward with a steady pressure. Check to see that the entire tick has been removed. Clean with warm, soapy water, then apply an antiseptic. Mark the date of the bite and if symptoms develop, contact your doctor immediately." The information in this section was adapted from the Web site of the Carolinas Poison Center **(http://www.carolinas. org/services/poison/insect.cfm)**.

Other Insects

The most common insect stings/bites at outdoor festivals and events are those of bees, hornets, yellow jackets, wasps, and mosquitoes. Although most people find these stings/bites to be nothing more than an irritation, they can cause allergic reactions in some people.

If Bitten   Remove the stinger by scraping a card across the wound (do not squeeze). Wash the area with warm, soapy water. Most people can handle these bites by simply applying a cold compress to control swelling. Some people may want to take an aspirin for pain and an antihistamine, as needed, for minor itching and swelling. If the person is allergic to these types of insects, then he or she will experience a bodywide reaction, severe local swelling, especially around the face or neck, or have difficulty breathing. In any of these cases, alert the EMR squad or call 911 and contact a poison center.

SNAKES

While the chance that a poisonous snake will bite someone at an outdoor event is minimal, snakes, ever since Eve's encounter, hold a special place in the pantheon of panic producers. Many people do not like snakes, are afraid of them, and assume that all snakes are poisonous. While there is no way that a risk manager can prevent a snake from creeping onto the event's grounds, it is essential for risk managers to know what to do and what not to do in the event that a snakebite should occur. Just as in the case of insect bites, risk managers will want to review snakebite treatment procedures with staff on a regular basis. The risk manager need not be an expert in snakebite medicine, but he or she should know to whom to turn and how the emergency medical team should respond. Because there is so much misinformation, combined with legends and superstitions regarding snakes, it is essential that the risk manager review his or her own knowledge base and feelings toward these animals.

The vast majority of poisonous snakes in the United States are pit vipers, belonging to the family Crotalidae. Included in this family are rattlesnakes, copperheads, and cottonmouths (water moccasins). Pit vipers poison their victims through two fangs. About 99 percent of the venomous bites in the United States are from pit vipers.

The other poisonous snakes in the United States are in the family Elapidae, which includes two species of coral snakes. These snakes are principally located in the southern part of the United States. Coral snakes have a less efficient delivery system due to their small mouths and short teeth. People bitten by coral snakes lack the characteristic fang marks of pit vipers. This lack of fang marks often results in an original misdiagnosis. Coral snake bites are rare in the United States, and there is a minimal chance of having to deal with these bites at a major event. Nevertheless, risk managers should know about them because the snake's venom can be dangerous. To further complicate the diagnosis, it is easy to confuse these snakes with their nonpoisonous cousins. For example, the scarlet king snake can easily be confused with the coral snake because of its similar bright red, yellow, and black coloration. Because it is easy to confuse these snakes, risk managers should take no chances and obtain medical treatment for any snakebite.

If a snakebite occurs, it is essential that the risk manager and his or her team remember that these bites can be effectively treated with antivenin. The important thing is to use time wisely and get the person to a hospital or doctor as soon as possible.

The best way to handle the risk of snakebites is to avoid snakes. Some bites take place when someone accidentally steps on or even throws a blanket on a snake and then sits on it. To lower the risk of snakebites, consider:

- Posting signs, reminding people to leave snakes alone. It is a bad idea to try to examine a snake in the wild, and from the snake's perspective, a snake at an event is in the wild.
- Reminding people to stay away from tall grass. It is best to walk along paths and trails.
- Encouraging guests and attendees not to pick up rocks. A snake can strike at half its length.
- Instructing guests on proper snake "etiquette." If a guest encounters a snake, the best thing is to walk around it and give the snake some 6 feet of space.

What Not to Do in Case of a Snakebite

U.S. medical professionals are nearly unanimous in their views of what not to do in case of a snakebite. Among their recommendations:

- No ice or any other type of cooling on the bite. Research has shown this to be potentially harmful.
- No tourniquets. This cuts blood flow completely and may result in loss of the affected limb.
- No electric shock. This method is under study and has yet to be proven effective. It could harm the victim.
- No incisions in the wound. Such measures have not been proven useful and may cause further injury.

SOURCE: Arizona physician, David Hardy, M.D. Available on line at **http://www.fda.gov/fdac/features/995_snakes.html**.

Additionally, make certain that you concentrate on the victim and not on the snake. Do not waste time trying to kill the snake or capture it. Instead, use your time to get the snakebite victim to the hospital as quickly as possible.

Because this textbook is for risk managers and not for physicians, we will not give details regarding what to do for a snakebite. Event risk managers, however, should:

- Know the best route to a local trauma hospital.
- Know how to deal with a traffic snarl.
- Know how to quickly contact a snakebite specialist.
- Conduct a review of the event venue with snakebite experts. The risk manager should go over with these experts what types of snakebites might occur, what he or she should do to aid the physician, and what measures need to be taken to stop additional problems.
- Conduct a tabletop scenario planning exercise with each of the key players.

Once at the hospital the event risk manager may wish to consider:

- Asking staff to contact poison control immediately
- Asking the hospital staff to locate the nearest antivenin resource center

Food Safety

Summer is a great time for outdoor festivals and other out-of-door events. Summer is also a great time for bacteria to spread rapidly and cause food poisoning. Perhaps nothing in the field of safety carries as much risk as does the preparation of consumable products, be they food or beverage. Interestingly enough, although food safety is something that touches almost everyone's life multiple times throughout the day, when eating outside of the home, few people take the time to think about culinary safety issues. Food and water quality can affect the choice of a meeting site. For example, some third-world nations have been unable to attract meetings and conventions simply because the attendees (or so the planning committee believes) are insecure about the quality of the food and/or water.

Food poisoning should be taken very seriously. A young, healthy person may quickly recover from mild food poisoning, while a small child or an elderly person may have more serious health effects. Furthermore, even a case of mild food poisoning or water contamination can signify that a delegate may not be able to attend meetings. When it comes to issues of food and water, perceptions become reality. One well-publicized case of food poisoning or water contamination can ruin the image of a meeting or convention destination or venue for years.

There are few events where some form of food and drink is not available. For example, in Chapter 3 we examined the issue of alcohol consumption at fraternity parties and street festivals. In that chapter, one of the recommendations was to provide foods high in protein as a counterbalance to the liquor. In today's world of meetings and events, the issue is not "should" or "will" food be served, but how it will be served. Figure 6.2 provides information on food-service at meetings.

Following are some questions event risk managers should ask:

What is the health of the people handling the food?
What health precautions do the food handlers have to take?
Who is inspecting the food supply?
How often is the food supply inspected?
What kind of containers is the food served in? Are disposable containers used?
How is refuse/garbage handled? Can this refuse attract rodents or other vermin?

Event risk managers should train cooks and servers for events using the following guidelines:

- Allow people to return food. If a person is not comfortable with the way the food looks or tastes, then he or she should not ingest it.
- Make certain that hot dishes are served hot and cold dishes are served cold. Hot foods should be at least 140 degrees Fahrenheit, and cold foods should be no more than 40 degrees Fahrenheit. In fact, no one should ever eat food that is meant to be eaten hot if it is served cold or food that is meant to be eaten cold if it is served hot. Keep foods out of the danger zone: from +40 to +140 degrees Fahrenheit.

Type of Event	Type of Foodservice	Level of Sanitation Checked
Street fairs	Food carts, homemade foods at tables	From foods made in private kitchens to prewrapped foods
Conventions	Food booths, catering services	Foods under inspection by government agency; assume food providers healthy
Business meetings	Catered foods	Government inspects foods; assume food providers offer healthy inspected food
Sports events	Food stalls	Government inspects foods; assume food providers offer healthy inspected food
Amateur sports events	Food stalls, local foods sold	Wrapped hawked foods; may have licensed or unlicensed food vendors
Festivals	Food stalls, homemade foods	Licensed or unlicensed food vendors
Entertainment events (outdoor)	Food stalls, food booths, catered food	Licensed food vendors, food hawkers
Entertainment events (indoor)	Food booths, catered food	Licensed food vendors

Figure 6-2
Foodservice at Meetings and Events

- Make certain that all food is cooked to the proper temperature. For example, ground meat should be cooked to at least 160 degrees Fahrenheit and poultry to at least 170 to 180 degrees Fahrenheit.
- Make certain that cutting boards and utensils are carefully washed between food preparations. For example, do not permit the same cutting board to be used to cut raw meats/poultry and then vegetables.
- Check the dish and utensil washing process. Risk managers can help cut down the risk of food poisoning simply by checking to make sure that all cooking utensils are washed in hot, soapy water before they are used for another food product.
- Keep raw foods such as poultry, meats, seafood, and eggs away from each other while being stored in the refrigerator. This separation is also valid for these products' "juices." Store the products away from each other and, if possible, on the bottom shelf of the refrigerator. Make sure that "juices" cannot drip from one product to another.
- Find ways, such as barriers, to protect food at salad bars from sneezes and coughs. Make sure that spills are cleaned up and that plates are used only one time.
- Remember that the U.S. Food and Drug Administration (FDA) has cautioned that raw sprouts are connected to outbreaks of *Salmonella* and *Escherichia coli* O157.
- Make certain that all employees and volunteers wash their hands after using the bathroom, that they wear hair covering, and that personal hygiene is enforced. The way that food is presented and the sanitation of rest rooms say a lot about the sanitation of the food. It is essential that the risk manager never forget that the "critical" point in the food preparation process is the health and cleanliness of the person who prepares it.
- Make certain that all ingredients are known and that food servers can answer questions, or know to whom to turn, about the ingredients in all food items. This list should also include basic chemical ingredients such as monosodium glutamate or aspartame, or the presence of specific foods such as milk, eggs, wheat flour, fish, or nuts. Many of these ingredients can be highly allergenic to some people and can cause severe illness or even death. The person who serves food should never be flippant about ingredients or pretend to

know. The best rule is what our parents teach: "If in doubt, throw it out."

- Make certain that all meats are cooked/grilled thoroughly. If grilling meats, it is best to place meats on preheated grills. Make sure to cook all meats, poultry, and fish thoroughly on a hot fire that reaches the proper temperature.

Drinking Water Quality

Closely aligned with issues of food safety is drinking water safety. Many people in the more developed world pay little attention to issues of potable water safety, though the trend toward bottled water may indicate a loss of confidence in the quality of drinking water from the tap. When one considers that water makes up over 70 percent of our bodies' matter, we begin to understand just how important it is. As in the case of oxygen, we cannot live without water. Water regulates almost every part of our bodies. Yet when we are immersed in work or play, we often fail to pay attention to our hydration needs, thereby risking our health.

In the "developing world" or "underdeveloped world," water that is fit for human use is more of a problem. Event risk managers need carefully to examine such issues as:

- The quality of drinking water, including the ice used in drinks
- The quality of water used for preparing food and cleaning utensils and dishes
- The quality of water used for bathing/showering
- The quality of water used for leisure, such as swimming

Perhaps the greatest issue for event risk managers is that many festivals and other events take place outside during the summer's heat, where shade may be scarce. Proper summer hydration then becomes an important issue for event risk managers because:

- Festival-goers may neglect proper hydration.
- There is a tendency to perspire when out of doors and heavy perspiration can deprive the body of up to 16 glasses of water per day.
- Festival and event attendees often do not drink water at regular intervals throughout their outdoor activity.
- Children, especially young children, do not express thirst.

- Pregnant women need additional water and fluid intake.
- Coffee and alcoholic products dehydrate the body.

Event risk managers need to be aware not only of hydration issues, but also how clean and safe water will be delivered to their event grounds/arena. The field of clean water is complicated and there are a number of conflicting studies. Although the risk manager is not expected to be a water quality expert, he or she should have enough knowledge in this field to be able to discuss it in an intelligent manner. Risk managers should know how to ask thoughtful and pertinent questions of the experts to whom they may turn for advice. This section on water quality is designed specifically to raise awareness levels and to provide the reader with the basics of water quality issues. Because a large number of people use bottled water (and it should not be assumed that all bottled water is safe), this section will also provide the risk manager with information about this rapidly growing topic and market. Figure 6.3 lists some illnesses associated with impure drinking water.

Even in the most developed countries, it is not always easy to obtain pure drinking water. Much of the world's fresh water is not fit for human consumption. Because meeting and festival attendees are often from different locales, they are dependent on the event risk manager to assure that the water or liquids that they consume will not make them sick.

To compound this problem, people who travel or are attending outdoor festivals need to consume greater quantities of water, especially in warm or hot weather. Not only must the risk manager worry about the quality of water that is consumed, but he or she must also be concerned that both attendees and staff do not become dehydrated. People involved in festivals or meetings get so caught up in what they are doing that they often forget to drink enough water. Such a mistake can be dangerous, as the general rule for dehydration is that once a person feels dehydrated he or she may already be suffering from the first effects of dehydration. Event risk managers should remember that the following conditions can cause dehydration:

- Athletic activity or any form of physical exertion, including walking
- Air travel
- Warm/hot weather
- Dry weather (where the person does not realize that he or she is sweating)
- Overconsumption of dehydratic liquids such as coffee

Vibrio cholerae	*Cholera*
Escherichia coli	Children's diarrhea Travelers' diarrhea Hemorrhagic uremic syndrome Hemorrhagic colitis
Leptospira interrogans	Leptospirosis
Salmonella paratyphi	Paratyphoid fever
Salmonella typhi	Typhoid fever
Shigella dysenteriae	Bacillary dysentery
Shigella boydii/S. sonnei	Shigellosis
Campylobacter jejuni	Diarrhea
Yersinia enterocolitica	Enterocolitis
Aeromonas	Gastroenteritis
Legionella pneumophila	Legionnaires' disease and Potomac fever

Source: **http://www.globalwater.com/link-10.html.**

Figure 6-3
Some Illnesses That Can Result from Impure Drinking Water

A study of U.S. water drinking habits **(http://www.bottled waterweb.com/statistics.html)** revealed that

- 75 percent of U.S. citizens do not drink enough water.
- 37 percent of Americans often confuse thirst for hunger.
- Lack of water is the primary trigger of daytime fatigue,

a problem for risk managers trying to keep people safe at events.

- A mere 2 percent drop in body water can trigger fuzzy short-term memory. This fact is important when we consider how many people lose cars in parking lots or leave personal items behind.

Event risk managers, then, must take into account issues of both water consumption and water purity. Consuming unsafe water may be worse than lack of consumption. Even in the most developed of areas, risk managers need to know where the water used for drinking, washing, and swimming comes from. Event risk managers should also remember the following key points:

- **Power outages.** If there is a power outage, the water purification plant shuts down, but the water keeps flowing. In situations where there are rolling blackouts, risk managers need to investigate the quality of the drinking water for a number of days after the blackout. Some experts advise that if there is a candle in a hotel room, this may be an indication of a prior power outage.
- **Harmless organisms.** Even in areas where the water is considered safe to drink, the event attendee's stomach may not be accustomed to "harmless" organisms found in another area's water. Fatigue and jet lag may be caused by a change in water.
- **Stream water.** Stream water is never safe. Animals use this water for all sorts of purposes, and one should be suspicious of the drinking water's quality. Remember that some organisms can even resist freezing. Streams also carry chemicals used in agriculture.
- **Well water.** Is well water used? If so, what chemicals or pollutants are in the well water? How safe is it?
- **Reusable containers.** Bottles and canteens from which one may drink multiple times can also be causes of contamination. General rule: If you cannot clean it, do not use it.
- **Bottled water.** Never use locally bottled water in developing countries. Bottled water is like a computer: garbage in/garbage out. That is to say, bottled water is only as good as what was put into it. If there is no way to check on the quality of the water, then use carbonated water as the carbonation process acidifies water and destroys organisms.

- **Pools and showers.** Make certain that water in pools and showers is safe. Swallowing unsafe water in any format is the same, be it consumed in a glass or consumed while showering or swimming.

WATER PURIFICATION

Event risk managers are neither water engineers nor specialists in water purification quality. It behooves risk managers, however, to know something about the water purification process. This basic understanding will give the risk manager the ability to communicate with water specialists.

The event risk manager should know that:

- Purification requires the removal of enteric pathogens (bacteria, viruses, parasites, and other organisms that cause diarrhea).
- Water purification techniques vary, depending on the geographic area and the type of water. The event risk manager may want to determine which technique is best suited for his or her area or type of water.
- Boiling water for at least 10 minutes sterilizes it. The container in which the water is placed must also be sterile.
- Pasteurization (55 degrees Celsius) will kill most, but not all bacteria. If the water comes out of a tap and is too hot to touch, it is pasteurized or close to pasteurized. It should be remembered that neither pasteurized water nor pasteurized milk is sterile.

OTHER PURIFICATION METHODS

When boiling is not practical, chemicals and filters may be used to purify water. First, obtain the best water available. In the wilderness, ideally use water found away from humans and animals. In developing countries, use water from piped taps, wells, and springs. These tend to be less polluted than streams and ponds. Common chemical water purifiers are iodine and chlorine. The U.S. army uses iodine when boiling is not possible. It should be noted that one parasite, *Cryptosporidium,* is resistant to iodine and can cause diarrhea, cramps, and vomiting. This was the parasite that was found in the public drinking water of Milwaukee, Wisconsin, and was responsible for the outbreak of an illness that affected more than 400,000 people in the spring of 1993. It is estimated that large amounts of this parasite are present in the rivers, lakes, and even drinking water of many Western states **(http://www.marinemedical.com/water.htm)**. In most cases, the illness will be mild, but it can be dangerous for people who have recently had operations and have decreased stomach acidity. Iodine-treated water can also be a problem for people with thyroid disease.

Filtration is another popular method and filters do remove most unwanted particles. It should be noted that viruses can pass through filters. Filters require periodic cleaning and the cleaning process can damage the filter **(http://www.marinemedical.com/water.htm)**.

BOTTLED WATER AT EVENTS

A substitute for tap or well water is bottled water. There is hardly a meeting held today in which one does not find bottles of water available for the attendees. In less developed nations, most foreign meeting-goers depend on bottled water. While a risk manager cannot be held responsible for the bottled water industry, he or she should be aware of the following issues:

- There is a great deal of controversy as to the sanitation or purity of bottled water. For example, American Broadcasting Company (ABC) news quoted an Associated Press article indicating that there may be major issues regarding the purity of bottled water **(http://www.abcnews.go.com/sections/living/dailynews/bottledwater990330.html)**.
- The same Associated Press/ABC news story reported that bottled water may lead to dental problems.
- In a separate story, ABC reported that six people in New York had fallen ill to contaminated bottled water **(http://www.more.abcnews.go.com/sections/us/dailynews/bottledwater000915.html)**.
- There is a controversy as to how well bottled drinking water is supervised by the government. In many nations around the world, anyone can sell bottled water without any regulation/supervision.
- If bottled water is sold in one state and comes from another state, then a failure to fulfill the purification process as stated on the label is an infringement of the laws governing interstate commerce.

Needless to say, the bottled water industry strongly disputes these claims. Therefore, risk managers may want to consult members of their legal team to discuss what issues of liability they face should someone get sick from bottled water sold at an event in which they are in charge. It is important for risk managers to be aware of the fact that liability laws in this area, as in other areas, are constantly changing.

Lighting

Many events and festivals extend into the evening hours. In such cases, good lighting is essential in lessening the risk of injury. Yet, we often find paths are poorly lit, and thus place both obstacles and safety hazards in the way of event participants. A rough path may not be hard to navigate during the day, but may become an obstacle course at night. In a like manner, bushes may add beauty to the event's grounds during the daylight hours, but may become both a security and a safety hazard at night. Risk managers should never forget that the public is unfamiliar with the terrain, which means that hazards that are naturally avoided by those who may work at an event may be invisible to those who are attending the event. In addition, risk managers should keep in mind that attendees are operating from an anomic perspective, they may have had too much to drink, or they may be in a state of semidehydration (see above). Proper lighting is also essential for those people working the event. Workers may be exhausted, may be in a rush to get home, and may also be suffering from dehydration.

Event risk managers should also consider:

- Working with an expert in crime prevention through environmental design (CPTED). CPTED specialists can advise the risk manager on where extra lighting is needed, where shadows present a risk, and how to landscape so that the event's participants and employees are safe.
- Mapping the event site. The risk manager should be aware of potholes, danger points, and places where one can easily fall.
- Ensuring that parking lots and paths leading to parking lots are well lit.

- Making certain that bus stops and other transportation pickup points are well lit.
- Designing lighting in a way that protects the event site, but does not create light pollution for areas that are bordering the site.
- Inspecting light bulbs on a regular basis. Light bulbs burn out easily. Make sure that all bulbs are in working order.
- Having a backup plan in case there is a blackout. People may be scattered all over the event's grounds or buildings. Develop an emergency non-electricity-dependent backup system and a way to find stranded event-goers.

Parking Lot Safety

An area that unites security and safety issues is the parking lot. Both indoor and outdoor lots present safety and security hazards and risks. Parking lots are dangerous for the following reasons:

- People tend to drive in parking lots as if there were no rules of the road.
- Pedestrians assume that parking lots are safe and that drivers will see them.
- Event-goers often forget where their cars are parked and some people have a tendency to panic when their car cannot be found. Cars often look alike and alarms are set off when a person tries to enter a car that is not his or her own.
- Sudden storms can create dangers for people who have parked in outdoor lots.
- Poorly lit and inadequately patrolled parking lots can be high security risks for parking lot users, especially at night and at odd hours.
- Children can run off while parents are loading cars and easily be injured.

It is a good idea for event risk managers to develop methods to remind people to lock their cars and remember where their cars are parked. Valuables should not be left in a vehicle, especially if they can be seen through the window. Emergency telephones that are clearly lit and easy to use should be placed around all parking lots. Cameras should also be scanning large lots when it is impossible for personnel to do an adequate job of patrolling the parking lots.

Electrical Storms and Lightning

The weekend of July 7, 2001, should have been a typical day. Nevertheless, the weather had other plans for that day. A series of thunderstorms and strange weather conditions caused multiple delays in various parts of the United States. In New Jersey, a man standing on the beach under clear skies was struck by lightning out of the blue! Meanwhile, on the other side of the Atlantic, in Strasbourg, France, at a Yiddish music festival, eleven people died and more than eighty others were injured when a storm blew a tree onto a makeshift shelter to which people had turned to escape a violent rain and windstorm/tornado.

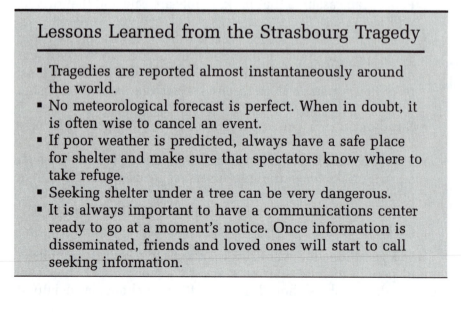

Lessons Learned from the Strasbourg Tragedy

- Tragedies are reported almost instantaneously around the world.
- No meteorological forecast is perfect. When in doubt, it is often wise to cancel an event.
- If poor weather is predicted, always have a safe place for shelter and make sure that spectators know where to take refuge.
- Seeking shelter under a tree can be very dangerous.
- It is always important to have a communications center ready to go at a moment's notice. Once information is disseminated, friends and loved ones will start to call seeking information.

Although lightning is considered an act of God in the United States, there are a number of techniques that risk managers can employ to reduce the risk.

- Consult with local meteorologists concerning when to call off an event, especially if it is slated for outside.
- Have a storm plan ready. No meteorological forecast is perfect. Storms can occur with only minimal warning. What is true of electrical storms is also true of tornadoes. In both cases, once the storm is upon the event there is no time to plan. It is the job of the risk manager to plan ahead, to have adequate shelter available, and to have a means of quickly transporting people, including the impaired, to a shelter.
- Lightning should be taken seriously at its first sign. As the weekend of July 7, 2001, proved again, lightning does not need a rainstorm to strike. People should be moved inside. Electrical use should be kept to a minimum. People should be kept off the telephone and away from water.
- Never hold a festival during a lightning storm. The show business adage that the "show must go on" needs to be modified by risk managers to "the show must go on after the storm has passed and everyone is safe."
- Alternative sources of light should be prepared in case of electrical failure. Needless to say, this is essential during festivals and events that take place at night, but even during the day, alternative sources of lights, such as battery-powered flashlights may be needed. Make sure that the alternative sources of light are also safe. Remember that it was a cow in combination with a kerosene lamp that started the fire that burned down Chicago.

Electrical and Gas Safety

Electrical safety should always be a major concern to risk managers. Electricity is a very powerful form of energy that should always be used with a great deal of caution. Every risk manager should know the people on the electrical staff well. This means those who are installing electricity and those who work with electricity. The

Occupational Safety and Health Administration (OSHA) offers a great deal of information on electrical safety as do local governments. Risk managers should check the OSHA Web site **(http://www. osha.gov)** for the most up-to-date regulations and safety requirements. When in doubt, it is always best to err on the side of caution.

Electrical Safety Checklist

- Make sure that all electrical appliance manuals are read and kept in a place where they can be found if needed.
- Make certain that light bulbs are the correct wattage. Never use bulbs that are of a higher wattage than recommended.
- Make certain that all fuses are the right size for circuits.
- Check electrical outlets on a regular basis.
- Keep all electrical cords away from water and water sources.
- Maintain electrical cords in good working condition and do not overload them.
- Install ground-fault circuit interrupters to reduce the risk of electrocution.
- Make certain that electrical appliances are unplugged when not in use.

SOURCE: Adapted from **http://www.parentsplace.com/health/ safetyrecalls/gen/0,3375,9807,00.html.**

Event risk managers often have very little or nothing to say about the construction of a building, but, at times, they can have input into how electricity is installed. This is especially true of outdoor events. Risk managers should never assume that they are electrical engineers. Knowing what one does not know is, at times, as important as being knowledgeable about a subject. It is important, nevertheless, that risk managers have some basic notions of electrical standards. This basic knowledge allows the risk manager to ask educated questions such as the following:

- Do the electrical installations meet all national and local codes?
- Is there proper ground-fault protection for the specific sites?
- What electrical hazards are there at the site?
- How quickly can equipment/appliances be shut down and what dangers are there?
- Is there the possibility of release of hazardous energy during the festival/event, during maintenance, or during periods of shutdown?

Gas is available in many forms. For example, gas (propane) barbecues can be a problem for the event risk manager at an event such as a "cook-off." Event risk managers cannot be experts on every form of gas heater. They must work with the local gas company to meet or exceed the required safety standards. In areas where there is rented space, risk managers will want to make sure that the owners can prove that the premises have had a gas safety inspection.

Gas Safety Checklist

Prior to purchasing any compressed gas:

- Familiarize all personnel handling any compressed gases with proper procedures.
- Provide proper instruction and training for all personnel handling compressed gases.
- Minimize potential problems associated with hazardous gases by ordering the smallest quantity required.
- Make sure that you have the proper gas detection apparatus.
- Make sure that you are thoroughly familiar with all emergency procedures and devices.
- Check valves and venting and replace valves, outlet plugs, and cylinders as needed.
- Check cylinder storage areas; make sure that they are away from the public.
- Make sure that you have an evacuation plan should an

(Continued)

accident occur. Make sure you have included in this plan:

Emergency telephone numbers

Emergency response organizational charts

Emergency procedures

Listing of key personnel

Training schedules and documentation

Hazardous materials lists (including storage locations, quantities, etc.)

Emergency response equipment lists

Facility maps

In the event of an incident or gas explosion:

- Sound an alarm.
- Evacuate personnel.
- Shut down equipment.
- Determine nature of incident—leak, fire, spill, etc.
- Determine what gases are involved and type of containers.
- Activate your emergency response plan which should include:

Move victim to fresh air and call emergency medical care.

If not breathing, give artificial respiration.

If breathing is difficult, give oxygen.

Remove and isolate contaminated clothing and shoes.

In case of contact with material, immediately flush skin or eyes with running water for at least 15 minutes.

Keep victim quiet and maintain normal body temperature.

SOURCE: Adapted from **http://www.mathesongas.com/mix-safe.htm.**

Event Risk Management Key Terms

Anomic: The state of being in anomie. That is to say, a person is out of his or her element and is not sure how to act.

Foreseeability: Something that a prudent person should have predicted and therefore may be held liable for in a lawsuit.

Event Risk Management Drills

1. Assume you are managing an outdoor summer event and are meeting with your food concessionaire. What issues would you bring to the table? What would be your greatest worries?

2. You have just experienced a rolling blackout and believe that the local water purification plant has also been affected. How would you handle the situation? What methods would you use to assure the public that your event is safe?

3. Develop a lighting program for the parking lot at your event. Note that the parking lot is not far from a neighborhood where there are small children. How would you protect both your patrons and the neighborhood?

CHAPTER **7**

Outdoor Events:
Stage Safety, Pyrotechnics, Parades, and Demonstrations

All the world's a stage,
And all the men and women merely players.
They have their exits and their entrances,
And one man in his time plays many parts,
His acts being seven ages

—WILLIAM SHAKESPEARE, *As You Like It*

IN THIS CHAPTER, WE WILL EXPLORE:

- Stage safety issues
- Pyrotechnic safety
- Parades and parade safety
- Demonstrations and counterdemonstrations

The series of "staged" demonstrations that occurred at the end of 1999 and into 2000 and 2001 are examples of a new type of event risk management. The "G-8" meeting in Genoa, Italy, in which the media reported that one demonstrator died and 300 demonstrators were wounded, is an example of a worldwide phenomenon that must not be ignored by event risk managers. Historians may one day declare the Seattle, Washington, meeting in December 1999 of the World Trade Organization (WTO) to be the start of this new form of meeting-cum-demonstration (MCD). In Seattle, demonstrators turned that city's downtown streets into their stage. These organized rioters serve as an example of dedifferentiation. Just as in *Alice in Wonderland,* during dedifferentiation things become upside down. Anyone watching the news coverage of Seattle soon realized that there was not just one meeting taking place, but, in reality, there were two events occurring at the same time and almost at the same place. The WTO meeting took place inside, but the people who held the world's attention and captured the media were not the international leaders who had come to Seattle, but the gangs and anarchists who took control of the demonstrations and turned that city's streets into a morosely perverse form of carnival. Their goals were not only to halt the WTO's meeting, but also to carefully manipulate the media so as to get their message to the world.

To a great extent, the rioters succeeded. The media were forced to show photographs of bludgeoned protesters, to report that a curfew had been imposed, and to focus on the roving bands of marauders on the streets. In the end, the WTO held its meeting, but Seattle's sterling reputation was tarnished.

Certainly not all outdoor events receive such coverage nor are they this violent. Event risk managers have to deal with multiple types of outdoor events. Some are as "simple" as an Independence Day celebration, a pyrotechnic display, or a crafts fair. Other events will touch on political campaigns, and still others will be "anti-event" events, where protestors turn the streets into a stage, so that they can publicize a particular cause. Figure 7.1 lists some of the multiple types of outdoor events that require event risk managers.

For example, in 1994, George Washington University canceled an outdoor graduation at the last moment due to inclement weather. A thunderstorm turned what should have been a happy occasion into one of anger and frustration because parents, who had flown in from all over the world, soon realized that the university had

Event	Concerns
Parade	Weather Safety of stage and podium Crowd control Traffic control Communications Electrical usage
Festivals and fairs	Weather Alcohol Pyrotechnic devices Safety of stage and podium Crowd control Traffic control Communications Electrical usage Food and beverage
Outdoor graduations and other educational events	Weather Crowd control Safety of stage, including railing and steps Walking paths to stage Electrical usage Communications Alcohol/drugs
Political rallies	Weather Safety of stage and podium Crowd control Traffic control Relationship to law enforcement Communications Electrical usage

Figure 7-1
Typical Outdoor Events

Event	Concerns
Demonstrations	Safety of stage and podium Crowd control Traffic control Communications Electrical Firearms/weapons

Figure 7-1 *(Continued)*

not made alternative plans in case of bad weather. In November of 1999, Texas A&M University suffered one of the worst university disasters in history when twelve students died and at least twenty others were injured when its bonfire collapsed. To make the situation even worse, the collapse of the Aggie bonfire, reported across the world, revealed that no professional event risk manager was in charge of such a large event.

Stage/Building Construction

The collapse of the wedding chapel in Jerusalem, Israel, in May 2001 in which more than twenty people died is a reminder of the importance of building construction and inspection to the field of event risk management. Because events are transitory in nature, much event construction is temporary.

For example, many outdoor events will require the building of a stage that will be demolished after the meeting, festival, or performance. Event risk managers should have a checklist of stage construction issues and must carefully review the Occupational Safety and Health Administration (OSHA) requirements as well as check with local building codes. Monona Rossol, president of Arts, Crafts, and Theater Safety (ACTS) and a noted author, has stated (personal communication, 2001):

> The OSHA regs and the building codes are your guides. Your artistic designs must fit into these. For example, the only variance a stage has from OSHA fall protection regula-

tions is at the front lip. All other potential falls of 4 or more feet must be guarded with rails, nets, or barriers when "non construction workers" such as actors or the general public have access to the area. This is a requirement of the OSHA General Industry Standards (29 CFR 1910).

During stage construction/demolition, the area comes under the OSHA construction standards (29 CFR 1926). [At this time, only construction workers can be present and they must be prevented from falling 6 feet or more by fall protection systems or guards.] The guardrails must meet the OSHA [Construction] Standards. The same with rails for the stairs leading to the stage. And if the pit or any design element does not meet these requirements, the designer should get a variance.

Rossol also reminds event risk managers that stage construction is a form of light construction. Event risk managers should make sure that they consult experts in the field such as riggers and industrial engineers.

Event risk managers should always keep in mind that construction codes and regulations are subject to change. Event risk managers must be aware of the most current building codes for stages used at events, the types of electrical precautions that need to be taken, and what the regulations and codes say about the amount of weight that a stage can support. To fail to take these precautions may cause harm or death and could result in litigation.

It is dangerous for event risk managers to pretend they know more than they do about design and construction. Whenever one is engaging in even temporary building construction, there are multiple risks that must be addressed. For example, are the people using the construction tools safe from electrical shocks, injury, or electrocution? From what type of materials are ladders made? The risk manager will not want people engaged in lighting to use metal ladders. It is important to hold a briefing with people who are doing such work. Never assume that the person involved in lighting/stage construction is a full-time professional. Temporary workers and students on summer vacation are often engaged in this type of work. Thus, never assume anything. For example, remind workers that they should never touch a bare wire or place a cold drink next to an electrical device. Even buildings, which are designed to last, need periodic checkups. Temporary construction such as stages are even more precarious. Make sure that all electrical components are checked daily. Take the time to inspect the construction of the stage. Are there cracks that were not there the day before? Is sagging occurring? Do handrails appear loose? When not in use, have all the electrical plugs been disconnected?

Event risk managers should ask these questions whenever a stage is involved:

- Are flammable materials being used?
- Are there areas that may cause a slip, a fall, or tripping?
- Where are garbage and other wastes stored?
- Where are tools stored?
- Is the stage strong enough to support the weight of both the props and the actors/speakers/guests/band?
- Do the stage and stairs have rails?
- Are the edges of the stairs clearly marked with glow-in-the-dark tape?
- Are the edges of the stage clearly marked with glow-in-the-dark tape?
- Is the space under the stage secure to prevent or reduce access by persons who could be injured?

GUEST HEALTH AND SAFETY SELF-EVALUATION CHECKLIST

I. General Considerations

1. Who is the management representative responsible for health and safety?

2. Is there a labor/management Health and Safety Committee?
___ Yes   ___ No   ___ N/A

3. Is there an evaluation procedure for new materials, productions, and special effects?
___ Yes   ___ No   ___ N/A

4. Are there material safety data sheets on products and chemicals in use?
___ Yes   ___ No   ___ N/A

5. Is there right-to-know training for all employees?
___ Yes   ___ No   ___ N/A

6. Are there special procedures for the health and safety of child actors?
___ Yes   ___ No   ___ N/A

II. Fire Safety

1. Are there written emergency procedures?
___ Yes ___ No ___ N/A

2. Are fire drills routinely scheduled?
___ Yes ___ No ___ N/A

3. Are the emergency exits clearly marked accessible?
___ Yes ___ No ___ N/A

4. Is the sprinkler system functional?
___ Yes ___ No ___ N/A

5. Are there appropriate fire extinguishers?
___ Yes ___ No ___ N/A

6. Are the fire extinguishers in good condition and checked regularly?
___ Yes ___ No ___ N/A

7. Is there adequate training for their use?
___ Yes ___ No ___ N/A

8. Is there a working fire alarm system?
___ Yes ___ No ___ N/A

9. Are there working smoke alarms?
___ Yes ___ No ___ N/A

10. Are there appropriate fireproof curtains, props, sets, and costumes as required?
___ Yes ___ No ___ N/A

11. Are there fireguards or firefighters present at each performance?
___ Yes ___ No ___ N/A

III. Venue Conditions

A. Stage Conditions

1. Is rigging safely secured?
___ Yes ___ No ___ N/A

2. Are props safely secured?
___ Yes ___ No ___ N/A

3. Are lights safely secured?
___ Yes ___ No ___ N/A

4. Are trap doors and pits adequately marked?
___ Yes ___ No ___ N/A

5. Are the grooves in the floor clearly marked?
___ Yes ___ No ___ N/A

6. Are electrical outlets recessed?
___ Yes   ___ No   ___ N/A

7. Is electrical wiring secured to floors and walls?
___ Yes   ___ No   ___ N/A

8. Are electrical cords clearly marked?
___ Yes   ___ No   ___ N/A

9. Are elevations clearly marked and safe?
___ Yes   ___ No   ___ N/A

10. Are raked stages used and safe?
___ Yes   ___ No   ___ N/A

11. Do stage floors have adequate resiliency?
___ Yes   ___ No   ___ N/A

12. Are the stage floors dry and cleared of slippery materials?
___ Yes   ___ No   ___ N/A

13. Are the stage floors free of splinters, nails, or worn-out floor-boards?
___ Yes   ___ No   ___ N/A

B. Lighting

1. Are the stage lights properly focused, angled, and located?
___ Yes   ___ No   ___ N/A

2. Is there adequate lighting backstage?
___ Yes   ___ No   ___ N/A

3. Do lasers meet Food and Drug Administration (FDA) requirements?
___ Yes   ___ No   ___ N/A

4. Is black-light output low in ultraviolet radiation?
___ Yes   ___ No   ___ N/A

5. Are there adequate precautions for strobe lights?
___ Yes   ___ No   ___ N/A

C. Stairways

1. Are the treads and backstage stairs maintained in good condition?
___ Yes   ___ No   ___ N/A

2. Are the stairwells properly lit?
___ Yes   ___ No   ___ N/A

3. Are the alleyways clear of litter and obstacles?
___ Yes   ___ No   ___ N/A

D. Environmental Conditions

1. Is the temperature comfortable?
___ Yes   ___ No   ___ N/A

2. Are costumes modified appropriately for extremes of temperature?
___ Yes   ___ No   ___ N/A

3. Is the humidity level optimal?
___ Yes   ___ No   ___ N/A

4. Is there sufficient airflow with adequate intake of clean outside air?
___ Yes   ___ No   ___ N/A

5. Is the stage area free of drafts?
___ Yes   ___ No   ___ N/A

6. Is the air free of contaminants?
___ Yes   ___ No   ___ N/A

IV. Stage Conditions

A. Stage Traffic

1. Are entrances and exits well choreographed and rehearsed?
___ Yes   ___ No   ___ N/A

2. Are on-stage movements well choreographed and rehearsed?
___ Yes   ___ No   ___ N/A

B. Stunts/Stage Combat

1. Are there written procedures?
___ Yes   ___ No   ___ N/A

2. Are stunts and combat carefully choreographed and planned by qualified personnel?
___ Yes   ___ No   ___ N/A

3. Is there adequate training and rehearsal time?
___ Yes   ___ No   ___ N/A

4. Are there padded landing areas for jumps over 6 feet?
___ Yes   ___ No   ___ N/A

C. Firearms and Weapons

1. Is there a qualified person in charge of all firearms and weapons?
___ Yes   ___ No   ___ N/A

2. Are there appropriate licenses?
___ Yes   ___ No   ___ N/A

3. Is there secure storage for firearms and weapons when not in use?
___ Yes   ___ No   ___ N/A

4. Is there adequate training and procedures for those using firearms?
___ Yes   ___ No   ___ N/A

5. Are the firearms and weapons routinely inspected?
___ Yes   ___ No   ___ N/A

D. Special Effects (Fogs, Fire, Smoke, Etc.)

1. Is there a fire permit when required?
___ Yes   ___ No   ___ N/A

2. Is there hearing protection for noise (e.g., firearms or explosions)?
___ Yes   ___ No   ___ N/A

3. Are materials chosen for optimal safety?
___ Yes   ___ No   ___ N/A

4. Are protective fire gels for skin and hair used in fire scenes?
___ Yes   ___ No   ___ N/A

5. Is sand and artificial snow free of contaminants?
___ Yes   ___ No   ___ N/A

V. Miscellaneous

A. First Aid/Medical Procedures

1. Are there approved first aid kits available?
___ Yes   ___ No   ___ N/A

2. Are there emergency medical procedures?
___ Yes   ___ No   ___ N/A

3. Is there a list of local physicians and medical facilities?
___ Yes   ___ No   ___ N/A

B. Makeup

1. Are there individual makeup kits for each performer?
___ Yes   ___ No   ___ N/A

2. Are ingredients listed on makeup?
___ Yes   ___ No   ___ N/A

3. Is there appropriate ventilation for aerosols (e.g., hairsprays)?
___ Yes   ___ No   ___ N/A

C. Travel and Tours

1. Is there advance inspection of stage, dressing rooms, etc.?
___ Yes   ___ No   ___ N/A

2. Is there adequate rest time between arrival at a location and practice/performance?
___ Yes   ___ No   ___ N/A

3. Are buses and trucks inspected?
___ Yes   ___ No   ___ N/A

4. Are there reasonable standards for accommodations?
___ Yes   ___ No   ___ N/A

5. Is there available sanitary drinking water in the dressing rooms?
___ Yes   ___ No   ___ N/A

SOURCE: This checklist was made possible through a grant from the New York State Department of Labor Occupational Safety and Health Training and Education Program. Copyright © 1988 Center for Safety in the Arts.

Pyrotechnic Safety

Each year in the U.S. around the Fourth of July holiday, the media report that hundreds of people have been injured because they have mishandled pyrotechnic devices. Many events use pyrotechnic materials to provide spectacular effects. Because these devices are designed to burn and explode, they add an element of risk to the safety of the performers, the stage crew, and the audience. The U.S. Consumer Product Safety Commission estimates that in 1999 approximately 7,000 people suffered some form of pyrotechnic injury, ranging from minor burns to blindness. Even when handled properly, there is always an element of risk involved.

These devices are no longer used simply to celebrate national holidays around the world. Events such as the dawn of the new millennium, entertainment spectacles, political rallies, and festivals all use pyrotechnic devices to add a sense of excitement and drama to the "show."

Event risk managers should make certain that the pyrotechnics used have been purchased from reliable companies. The risk manager will want to ensure that the pyrotechnic is clearly labeled and that it has not been stored for longer periods of time than recommended by the manufacturer. These devices should never be used around flammable areas. For example, avoid dry grassy areas. A simple rule to remember is that fireworks (pyrotechnics) burn at about the same heat level as a household match **(http://www.llr. state.sc.us/pol/pyrotechnic/firework.pdf)**.

The British Schools Web site **(http://schoolsite.edex.net.uk/ 500/pyro.htm)** recommends the following pyrotechnic safety precautions:

- Use a commercially built control box with a removable safety key to fire your pyrotechnics.
- Lock the control box in the OFF position and remove the key while loading the pyrotechnics.
- Ensure that there is no chance of an electric current going through the pyrotechnics while you are handling them.
- Ensure that each pyrotechnic position can be clearly seen from the control box.
- Always wear safety goggles or a face shield when loading pyrotechnics.
- Always clean your flashpots before loading them. This reduces the risk of shrapnel.
- If the pyrotechnic is a cartridge designed to be used in a pod, use a real pod; do not just twist wire to the terminals.
- Never fire a pyrotechnic device unless you can clearly see the area is clear of cast and stage crew.
- Never try to refire a dud. Soak it in water and destroy it by tearing it to pieces.
- Never dispose of destroyed pyrotechnic duds in the regular rubbish bin; use the "safe bin" designated by the theater for the disposal of pyrotechnics.
- Never fire pyrotechnics over an audience.
- Never smoke while handling pyrotechnics.
- Store pyrotechnics in their packaging until used.
- Unpack the pyrotechnics in a safe place, well away from flammable objects and sources of ignition.
- Never put pyrotechnics in your pockets.
- Maroons come in a range of sizes. The smallest ones make a very loud bang. The larger ones are very, very loud. Maroons should only be fired in a bomb tank. This is a heavy metal tank with an open top covered with a metal mesh. When fired, they will throw fragments out of the top of the tank. Always put up clear warning notices near the bomb tank; ensure everyone knows you are using maroons,

and ensure that nobody is near the tank when you fire the maroon.

- Gerbs spray white or gold stars in an approximately 30-foot jet for a few tens of seconds. These are spectacular for outdoor performances, but be careful of indoor use as they spray white-hot fragments a long way.

A pyrotechnic presentation can be a spectacular event or a tragedy. Common sense should always prevail. Never use any form of pyrotechnics in close proximity to people. Close means over their heads, around them, under them, or in between. Event risk managers will want to require that there be a full pyrotechnic rehearsal. It is essential that each member of the team know exactly what he or she is to do in case something goes wrong and a member of the staff, a volunteer, one of the performers, or a spectator is injured. Make certain that each person knows his or her responsibilities. For example, is it the pyrotechnician who is responsible for cleaning up after the performance? If not, then the event risk manager may want to review who has this responsibility. The event risk manager should also check with the local authorities to learn what local regulations and other requirements must be fulfilled. In most cases, local fire officials have final authority. Assuming that local officials have just cause, they can stop or cancel any show. Event risk managers should never argue with fire officials. These officials must also be given direct access to all areas of the show and can supervise its safety procedures before, during, and after the performance.

Figure 7.2 provides approximate safe distances when pyrotechnics are used. The figure does not take into consideration special weather conditions and, as stated above, local fire officials have final authority. If a person is on stilts, he or she will need to increase the distance for every foot off the ground. If you have 18-inch stilts and have fire fingers, you should be an additional 2 feet back from the audience. More information is available on line at **http://www.arfarfarf.com/safety/distances.shtml.**

Parades

Most people love parades. Parades seem to bring out the "child" in us. Parades permit us to remember happy times and allow us to feel part of the crowd. Parades are a "show in motion," and, as

Finger-fired, handheld finger props.	At least 4 feet
Chains, staves, torches, or similar props. Chains and fire tools must come no closer than 5 feet to lights or overhead structures.	At least 15 feet
All scenery and decorations are nonflammable or have been treated with a flame retardant.	At least 25 feet
Sparklers, fountains, firecrackers (1.4g Class C "safe and sane"), or as approved by fire marshall.	At least 50 feet
Minimum distance for Class B (1.3g) pyrotechnics. Minimum distance for Class B (1.3g) pyrotechnic set pieces. Add 70 feet for every 1 inch diameter for the shell size, up to a 12-inch shell. Then add 100 feet as a rule and seek specific permission from the local fire safety official.	At least 75 feet
Class B (1.3g) cakes.	At least 100 feet
Class B (1.3g) fire bright work.	At least 125 feet
Class B (1.3g) roman candles. These have a fallout distance of 100 feet.	At least 200 feet

Figure 7-2
Minimal Safe Distances

such, they are one of the earliest forms of theater. The ancient Greeks held parades as part of the opening of a theatrical play. Military organizations throughout the ages have used parades to demonstrate power, to frighten other nations, and, at times, to remind their own population who is in charge. Parades can also have religious significance. For example, both Mardi Gras, held each year in New Orleans, Louisiana, and the Brazilian *Carnaval* originated as symbols of the Christian lenten season. Parades are also part of sports events. The Rose Bowl in Pasadena, California, would be just a mere football game were it not for the pregame parade.

Having this many people come together is both an exhilarating and a challenging experience. Event risk managers must be concerned about crowd control during these events. The sheer number of people present means that there is the possibility of stampedes and riots. Parade management, however, is more than crowd control. To manage a parade, event risk managers must review the safety of both the parade's participants and its spectators. Parade safety requires consideration of the following issues:

- Float safety
- Hazards from objects falling from floats
- Participants' exhaustion
- Lost children
- Traffic safety
- Crimes of distraction
- Noise pollution
- Street cleanup

FLOATS

Event risk managers will want to determine if there are specific float construction specifications and regulations. Many floats have electrical devices: music or special-effects equipment. Just as in the previous chapters, whenever there is electrical usage, make sure that all construction codes are followed and that all safety precautions are in place. The event risk manager should also know if the float uses flammable materials. If so, is there a chance of an interaction between the electrical equipment and the flammable material? What would happen if the float were hit by another vehicle? How safe are the people riding in the float and what is the possibility that the float participants might fall? Following is a partial checklist of issues to review with those who are responsible for constructing floats:

- Make certain that the float's frame is sturdy and that the float's dimensions meet the parade's specifications. Additionally, make certain that tires do not rub against the float.
- Make certain that the float and the truck pulling the float are

properly hooked together and that all mechanical equipment is in good working order.

- Make certain that the gasoline tank is fitted correctly.
- Make certain that all batteries are properly grounded.

FALLING OBJECTS

Closely connected to floats are objects that are thrown from floats into the crowd. In New Orleans, Louisiana, beads and other objects are often thrown from floats to the general public and also from people sitting in balconies who are watching the parade from on high. While in most cases spectators are aware of the beads, they still constitute a hazard to someone who is not expecting to be hit by flying beads. Finally, risk managers need to take into consideration how the parade's participants will be protected from debris falling on them from above the parade route.

PARTICIPANTS' EXHAUSTION

Most parades take place during daylight hours and often in the warmer seasons of the year. This means that those who are participating in a parade often have no time for personal needs. Risk managers have a duty to protect these people. Prior to the parade route being set, risk managers will need to worry about issues of dehydration and personal needs. Sunburn and protection from the sun's harsh rays should be considered when determining the parade route. Will there be adequate shade? Is the use of sunblock required for all participants? What precautions have been taken if someone were to faint due to dehydration or too much exposure to the sun? Finally, does the risk manager have a medical history for each person participating in the parade? Such histories are important not only because they can give the risk manager an idea as to those who should not participate in a strenuous parade. It also helps the risk manager to know if something were to happen, what possible allergic reactions and past medical problems exist.

LOST CHILDREN

Parades traditionally attract families with children. Unfortunately, it takes only a second for a child to disappear. Such a disappearance in a large crowd is frightening to both the child and his or her parents or guardians. Event risk managers will want to develop a system to take care of lost children. This system may include protected areas where parents can seek their children and monitors to care for children while their parents seek them out. Protected childcare areas should be well marked and easy to identify. Needless to say, under no circumstance should a child be turned over to an adult lacking the proper identification. Providing children with id bracelets may also be a helpful tool. As there is always the fear that these bracelets may contain too much information, systems with number identifications can be used. Event risk managers should contact the local police department as to what lost children policies are for that particular community. Volunteers are often helpful in watching for lost children and reuniting them with their parents.

SAFE TRAFFIC CORRIDORS

In large cities, such as New York, traffic corridors must be allowed to cross parade routes. While the local police department will handle traffic control, the event risk manager would be well advised to consider that pedestrians watching the parade may be inebriated and may not be as careful as they should be and that children may quickly escape from a parent's grip. People driving through these corridors are often frustrated or even angry that their trip across town has been slowed down due to the parade. These drivers may rush to cross the parade route before the police close the corridor.

CRIMES OF DISTRACTION

Parades and large crowds are perfect places for crimes-of-distraction artists such as pickpockets. These people are experts in their trade, and interviews with them often indicate that they have no sympathy for their victims or remorse for their crimes. Risk managers should understand that they are up against professionals who do not just happen to come to a parade. Instead, they carefully select their sites and know which areas and times offer the highest statistical probability for success. Event risk managers should discuss the problem of crimes of distraction with local police authorities. Police departments often have undercover agents who work in this field and can be on the look-out for these "artists."

Modern crimes-of-distraction artists often work in groups. They are experts in having one team member distract the victim, while other team members block for the person who will commit the robbery. Artists will seek their easiest prey. They will look for men who have their wallets in their back pockets, people using fanny packs, and women who have purses in their hand instead of over their arm. They will also seek briefcases and cases in which they believe that someone may be carrying a laptop computer.

NOISE POLLUTION

Lots of parades have bands. In most cases, bands should not pose a risk that needs to be managed. Bands that go through neighborhoods where people live, however, may cause frustration or even rage. In such cases, it is a good idea to work with local neighborhood organizations. Develop a plan in which the bands can play without too much disruption to the neighborhood. Even though people who live in such environments should be aware of noise issues, in an "age of rage" these types of issues if not met head on can cause a great deal of hostility or even a tragedy.

STREET CLEANUP

Many parades incorporate animals as part of the event. Large animals can require a considerable number of cleanup tasks. Animal droppings can be a health hazard. Event risk managers need to make certain that those following in the parade's footsteps are not presented with a series of potential hazards and obstacles. Spectators have fun during a parade and not necessarily after it. Once the parade is over, there should be a plan in place to return the streets to the same or even better condition as before the parade. Event risk managers should meet with cleanup crews and local officials prior to the event. They need to know sanitation regulations, and they need to make certain that debris does not create additional risks for both vehicular and pedestrian traffic once the parade has concluded.

POLITICAL PARADES

Although in the United States political parades are rarely connected with violence, in some other parts of the world, parades are used as a political weapon. Northern Ireland is a prime example of a place where this type of parade occurs. Northern Ireland's parades often do more than merely mark a point in history. They are used as a means to express a strong political position and are often accompanied by violence. In the United States, President John F. Kennedy was assassinated while riding in an open car through the city of Dallas, Texas. Political parades require a team of specialists. In the case of the United States, if it is a major political parade, then the local risk manager will need to work with the Secret Service, FBI, and local police departments. In the case of a local election, these national agencies most likely will not be involved. It is recommended that risk managers involve local police authorities in the planning of the parade from its inception and that they consult state and federal authorities if the local police agencies lack parade security expertise.

NIGHT PARADES

Although most parades take place during the day, some parades are held at night, creating new challenges. Following are some of the nocturnal challenges that risk managers should consider:

- **Safety.** Not only at the parade, but along the principal routes taken to and from the parade.
- **Visibility.** Can people see? Is there a chance that they will trip due to darkness?
- **Electricity.** Daytime parades may or may not need electricity, but it is almost certain that nocturnal events will require electrical usage. Event risk managers want to be especially careful that all electrical wires and installations are safe and conform to the proper codes.
- **Crime.** Darkness is the ally of the criminal. As the sun goes down, the risk of crime rises. It is especially important that risk managers work with local police officials to assure the safety of nocturnal events.
- **Pedestrian safety.** We see less well in the dark. A nocturnal parade may mean a great deal of traffic at a time when there is a tendency to see less well, and at the same time, a greater tendency toward strong (alcoholic) drink. Event risk managers must establish a nocturnal pedestrian safety plan that will protect the parade's viewers.

- **Participants' fatigue.** A night parade may finish well into the night and many of those attending the parade may have worked the entire day. Fatigue, then, may be a factor for these participants, and this overtiredness can lead to accidents and injuries. Risk managers want to make sure that the parade's participants arrive at the staging area and leave the finishing area safely. Leaving the "termination area" means that participants have a safe way to return to vehicles, that parking lots are guarded, and that there is adequate safe public transportation available.

ETHNIC PRIDE PARADES AND POLITICAL ISSUES

Parades in Northern Ireland stand out as the prime example of ethnic parades having political overtones. In the United States, the antisegregation movements of the twentieth century used marches (organized political parades) as a way to demonstrate their opposition to racial segregation. Both cases serve as examples of parades with political agendas. Still another form of ethnic parade that may become a challenge for risk managers is the parade that expresses ethnic or sexual orientation pride.

As the world becomes a more dangerous place, the chance of an incident taking place at such parades grows. While it is impossible to seal off a city's downtown, event risk managers should be aware that there is a growing threat by those who may be intolerant of other people's views, orientation, or ethnic or religious heritage. Risk managers should consider who might want to disturb such a parade and what cooperation can be expected from local police departments. Police departments often take a reactive rather than a proactive stance regarding these issues. In such cases, event risk managers will need to incorporate appropriate funding into their budgets to pay for police overtime and to work with the particular group to assure the greatest amount of safety possible.

Demonstrations

A new type of street theater has begun to gain added importance. These are the vast demonstrations that occur concurrently with meetings that are being held. The most famous example of such meetings-cum-demonstrations (MCDs) is the Seattle World Trade Organization (WTO) meeting that took place in December 1999. Not all meetings of this nature have ended in political riots and states of emergency. In 2001, major problems were expected in Washington, DC, during a meeting of the World Bank and the inauguration of President George W. Bush. In May 2001, due to careful preparation by the state of Hawaii, no rioting occurred at the Asian Development Bank meeting. Using these three examples, we can develop a case study of what went wrong in Seattle and why these same problems did not occur in Washington, DC, and Honolulu, Hawaii.

SEATTLE

Before discussing the Seattle, Washington, riots, it must be noted that Seattle was the first city in many years to suffer from a "meeting-cum-demonstration" (MCD). As such, it is unfair to compare the Seattle experience with that of other cities. Seattle had no history of this type of event from which to learn. Other cities holding similar types of events had the advantage over Seattle of learning from Seattle's mistakes. The following critique is not given as a judgment of Seattle, but rather as a way to learn from that city's mistakes.

Seattle began by assuming what is often called a "soft approach" to the WTO meetings. That is to say, Seattle did not want to incite the protestors with large numbers of police on the streets. Looking back at that position from the perspective of history, we are now able to determine why that position was counterproductive. The protestors came as much to be arrested as they did to make noise. The street demonstrations were "political theater" and the lack of police officers (supporting cast members) meant that the protestors needed to increase the violence level if they were to succeed in making a political statement.

Lack of Information

Because the Seattle police lacked adequate internal intelligence gathering, they were often reactive rather than proactive. Thus, when taunted by demonstrators who were well prepared, the police charged into the crowd and attacked not only the perpetrators but also innocent civilians. The fact that pedestrians on their way home were also caught up in the police actions caused a great deal of negative publicity. The same problem occurred when the police overreacted to the city's downtown violence. Indiscriminate use of tear gas ended up radicalizing peaceful protestors and causing public relations damage that then needed to be controlled.

Poor Understanding of the Media

The Seattle Police Department may not have understood the public relations side of the conflict. The media are an important part of street theatrical demonstrations. In fact, the public relations war is as important as the action taking place on the street. Public relations spokespeople should never allow themselves to lose patience with the media. How one acts in front of a camera is as important as how one acts off camera.

Poor Priorities

The Seattle police were so concerned about crowd control that they lost control of the violence that was taking place. The media filmed these acts of violence, and thus a vicious circle began: Violence led to media involvement that led to further violence. The media are to political street theater what oxygen is to a fire: Without oxygen, a fire dies; without media attention, the street theater loses its major raison d'être. Figure 7.3 compares three demonstrations in three major cities.

WASHINGTON, DC

The city of Washington, DC, had the advantage of having experts in controlling demonstrations and of having the Seattle experience to study. Some of its officers were in Seattle and were able to observe first hand what that city's police department did and did not do correctly.

The following interview with Lieutenant Jeffery Herold of the Metropolitan Police Department of Washington, DC, provides valuable insight into this process. Herold is the coordinator for the Metro Police Department's civil disturbance unit and was one of the key players in preparing for the meeting of the World Bank and the 2001 inauguration of President George W. Bush.

> **Q:** *What exactly is your role in MCDs?*
> **A:** As specialists in "disorder control," it is our job to handle everything from crowd management to special events. We

Action	Seattle	Washington, DC	Honolulu
Spontaneous riots	No	No	No
Media attention	Great	Great	Minimal
Police overreactions	Yes	No	No
Large police presence from start	No	Yes	Yes
Sought to take action prior to the event	No	Yes	Yes
Curfew imposed	Yes	No	No
Mass arrests	Yes	Yes	No

Figure 7-3
Analysis of Demonstration Response in Three Cities

are mindful of the fact that any special event has the potential of turning into a situation where disorder or riots can occur.

Q: *What did Washington, DC, do differently from Seattle?*

A: First of all, we were very careful to keep our police department's command staff and the frontline police officers on the same page. As a police trainer, I was able to take the command's plans and present them to the officers during training within a very short time frame. Our officers also receive training in being media aware. They know that what they do may appear on television that night. Second, we had good intelligence gathering. Having a good idea of what and whom we were up against allowed us to plan and to practice those plans. I would say that the keys are good training and good police intelligence. Third, it is essential to equip your officers with the best possible protective gear and to make sure that you take care of their food and water needs. The officers may be on the streets for a protracted period of time, so these details are important and it sends a message to the officers that they have the support of the department and of the community. Last but far from least, our command staff was on the streets with the officers. During the "engagement" periods with the protestors, Chief Ramsey was on the streets with the officers. Seeing the command staff with the frontline officers is a way to keep the officers calm.

Q: *What were some of the other reasons that the Washington metropolitan police were so successful during these two events?*

A: We were proactive rather than reactive. We anticipated what we were going to have to deal with and what the problems would be. In other words, we anticipated the problem and acted prior to it, rather than reacting after the problem had occurred. For example, we were aware that "sleeping dragons" [a device that links people together] would be used. Prior to the events, we seized thousands of feet of "sleeping dragons." To put it simply, I like to say that policing in civil disturbances is a bit like surfing: To catch a wave, you need to be in front of it not behind it.

Q: *What general principles can you share with others?*

A: There are a number of general principles that we learned. These include:

- **Be proactive.** Do not wait until the problem has come crashing down on you; have a plan of action and implement it before the problem occurs.

- **Use a measured response/react in a proper way.** What I mean by this is that your job is to create calm, not a scene. It is very hard before an event to know how much of a response is too little or too much. Some of the ways that may be helpful in deciding how much of a response to use are: (1) Learn from history. See what other similar events have taken place and learn from other's mistakes and successes. (2) Train people to think before they act. (3) Train, train, and train some more. In the area of civil disturbances, you cannot have too much training.

- **Emphasize a balanced approach.** Teamwork can be a major help in not doing something that is counterproductive. Let me give you an example. Let us suppose that there are fifty demonstrators on the street. If you arrest them, you may draw media attention to them. Another alternative is simply to direct traffic around the protestors and let them sit. In other words, there needs to be a balanced approach. You need to consider the safety factor and the publicity factor. If no one is going to be harmed, it may be better to move traffic around the protestors. If you know what the opposition is trying to do, act first to counter it.

- **Do not allow demonstrators to become sympathetic victims.** Realize your opposition seeks to look like victims. Often, it seems that in a media event the group that succeeds in presenting itself as the victim wins. Let me give you an example. In arresting a protestor, dragging the person is more painful than picking the person up and carrying him or her away. Although picking a person up does not harm the person, many of these people will begin to cry out so that on television they falsely appear to be victims of police brutality when in fact they have not been harmed at all.

Q: *With the advantage of hindsight, what might the DC police have done differently?*

A: It would have been to our advantage to have more officers available. Were we to have had a larger number of officers, we would have had greater flexibility. This flexibility would have allowed us to deal with any unforeseen event. Another thing that would have helped is cross-training and better coordination with federal law enforcement agencies. Such cross-training would have meant that we were all on "the same page" and never worked at cross-purposes. At the Honolulu meetings of the Asian Development Bank, federal and local agencies worked well together.

HONOLULU

The big news from the Asian Development Bank meeting in Honolulu was that there was no news. That is to say, good planning and careful risk management were successful in preventing any disturbances. Hawaii has an advantage over Washington, DC, and Seattle in that it is an island. Its geographic location means that both ingress and egress can more easily be controlled and that someone must be willing to spend a lot more money to demonstrate. Hawaii was organized for any possible contingency. Its officials had the added advantage of learning what had happened in places such as Seattle, Quebec, Geneva, and Washington, DC.

Hawaii's philosophy was to stop a problem before it began. This meant that good intelligence gathering was needed. Threats were divided into three levels: green, which meant that the threat was considered to be low; amber, meaning a medium threat; and red, indicating a high risk of trouble. Honolulu officials were well aware that there was a chance of a major problem occurring and the fact that they were not in a state of denial was a major help to the city. Unlike Seattle, Honolulu started off with a large police presence and then backed off. In general, the principle seems to be that a no-nonsense approach in the beginning is the best way to stop trouble from developing at a later stage.

Honolulu not only rehearsed various scenarios, but it also practiced a form of decentralized control. Because field commanders and community officials were all on the same page, decisions could be made in the field almost instantaneously. Honolulu officials also emphasized flexibility. If a particular method was not working, the decentralized command had the right to innovate as needed. Security personnel were not forced to carry out one policy as set by city hall. Honolulu also spent a good amount of time on image management. It was clear to Honolulu officials that there were two concurrent events and they did their best to deprive protestors of media access.

These principles lead us to a number of other generalizable conclusions:

- **Take command of the situation from the start.** It is easier to maintain control than to regain it. Make sure that you have a strong law enforcement presence at the scene from the very beginning.

- **Use surveillance.** People want to be on national television not on local police tapes. Surveillance cameras have a tendency to calm the situation and remind people that they will be held responsible for their actions.
- **Stop trouble before it begins.** For example, if riot rehearsals begin to cross a legal line, stop them as soon as those who are rehearsing break the law.
- **Do not deprive people of their constitutional rights.** People have a right to protest but not necessarily at the spot where they want to conduct the protest. Provide alternative protest locations that are easily controllable and away from the meeting site.
- **Have an adequate budget.** Preventing trouble and protecting meetings can be very expensive, but as we have learned from bitter experience, disarming a potential risk is a lot less expensive than trying to recover a reputation or the cost of media damage control.
- **Train people to watch for those who may be intent on causing trouble.** Troublemakers can often be identified. This is especially true if the troublemaker is intending to harm other people or commit damage to property. Watching people makes those who are intent on causing trouble well aware that they are being watched.

Using the above principles, Honolulu officials adopted the following procedures:

- Health-care organizations were made aware that they might need to provide extra support.
- The potential of a bioterrorism attack was addressed and preparations were made, including which hospitals could handle various types of biochemical problems.
- Pertinent information, such as specific telephone numbers of medical specialists, was well distributed.
- Because the Honolulu convention center contains a large amount of exposed glass, a policy was developed on how to deal with breaking glass and those injured by breaking glass.
- Physicians who could conduct preconfinement exams were enlisted in order to ease the burden on police personnel.
- Information as to where protests would take place was distributed throughout the security community.

- A specific Web site with passwords and user ids was set up for members of the security team prior to the onset of the meeting.
- Staff ids were reviewed so that only authorized personnel had entrance to key areas such as communication centers and health-care facilities.
- A media plan was designed and community members were educated about it.

Honolulu's efforts were so successful that many people never knew that there had been a threat to the safety and security of the meeting. Due to its extraordinary good risk management, Honolulu proved that good risk management is such that the average person never knew the risk existed.

Following is an interview with Jeff Beatty, one of the major experts in the United States in the protection of the civilian population from acts of violence and terrorism. Beatty is a former Delta Force officer, special agent of the FBI's National Hostage Rescue Team, and CIA counterterrorism officer. He has worked on several Olympic projects and has been a commentator on national television. He is president of Total Security Services International, Inc.

Q: *What were the failures that you saw in Seattle?*

A: It should first be stated that Seattle was the first U.S. city, other than New York, Washington, or Chicago, to face meetings-cum-demonstrations of this type. In that sense, the city served as a proving ground for other cities that would face similar events of this type. Having stated this fact, Seattle underestimated the strength and determination of the opposition. Furthermore, the city stuck to its plan. That is to say, it lacked the flexibility to change course as the troubles grew. Finally, there was a reluctance to use the National Guard in a timely manner, before things got out of hand.

Q: *You were intimately involved in the security planning for the May 2001 Asian Development Bank meeting in Honolulu. What are the general principles that people concerned with risk can learn from Hawaii?*

A: From the perspective of risk, were there to have been a major incident of the type we saw in Seattle, the state stood to lose a great deal of business. Hawaii's tourism industry cannot afford a major assault on its image. Furthermore, Hawaii hopes to make itself the major meeting center of the Pacific, the Geneva of the Pacific. This was its first major potentially contested or "threatened" meeting and it could not afford to have tear gas flowing along Waikiki. Were this to have happened, the Hawaii fledgling meeting industry and its existing extensive tourism industry would have been severely hurt. As far as general principles are concerned, I would say:

- Make sure that the responsible opposition has a way to express its opinion. In Hawaii, they went the extra mile and allowed people from the opposition to have adequate time to address the conference.
- Do not be arrogant. History has shown us that today's opposing opinions may be tomorrow's mainline opinions. Be humble enough not to look foolish twenty years down the road.
- Make groups with other issues stakeholders in helping to assure a peaceful meeting. In Hawaii, there is a group that seeks sovereignty; these people were convinced that no matter who rules Hawaii, the entire state would lose if the Asian Development Bank meeting were a failure. Separate the people who have other grievances from those who seek to create problems. In Honolulu's case, the "hearts and minds" of the public were convinced that a successful meeting, not a disrupted meeting, was good for Hawaii.
- Have an adequate budget, especially if this is the first meeting of the sort that might be "threatened." Start-up costs include the price of specialized equipment and training. There is also the question of police overtime pay, publicity, etc. Assume that the cost of maintaining a secure meeting will run into the millions of dollars. It should be stated that the cost of getting it wrong is at least ten times more expensive than the cost of getting it right. Factor in the cost before bidding on the meeting.
- Get public safety officials involved early. It is important to bring the public safety community into the planning stage from the moment that a community has won its

bid. Once it is certain that the meeting is to take place in a community, there is no time to waste on petty disputes or questions of money. It is counterproductive to downplay the costs of the meeting, and no meeting should be allowed to cannibalize other major safety and security projects/programs. The city is still operating while the meeting is going on.

Q: *What role did hotel and convention risk managers play in the Asian Development Bank meeting?*

A: The Hawaii Hotel Security Association (HHSA) and its risk managers were involved in the planning. HHSA people received information as it came in. Because of the cooperation, all the affected hotels upgraded their security plans. Hawaii also learned from the Olympic Park incident [Atlanta Olympics] and was determined to leave no secondary soft targets. By having good cooperation and communication, the HHSA made sure that there were no weak spots within the security system. A sign of Hawaii's incredible success was that during the meeting there were no related arrests.

Q: *What other agencies played a role?*

A: It was not just the locals who made this event a great success; the Federal Bureau of Investigation (FBI) did an outstanding job of supporting the state of Hawaii. The FBI helped by:

- Increasing its presence in Hawaii during the meeting
- Conducting a threat and vulnerability assessment prior to the meeting
- Providing technical capabilities that were beyond the state's resources
- Coordinating other federal resources

What the FBI did for the state of Hawaii should be the model for states that desire to bring in meetings of this type.

Q: *What other information might you want to share?*

A: One of the reasons that Honolulu succeeded was that they never underestimated their opposition. They studied the people who might want to cause trouble and who could become a potential ally. They had good surveillance work. Another fact that should be mentioned is that both Honolulu and Washington, DC, employed integrated plans for potential use of the National Guard prior to the event. The National Guard must be brought into the planning process right from the beginning. A good rule to follow is: Deploy the National Guard to preserve order not to restore order. Good risk management means that the National Guard is pre-positioned to maintain law and order, not to try to restore it after law and order have broken down. Governors don't call out their National Guard after the river has overflowed its banks and then ask them to fill sandbags. They deploy the Guard to prevent the disaster. The same principle applies to planning for civil disturbance. In Seattle's case, the National Guard was brought in after the rioting began; in the case of Hawaii and Washington, DC, the National Guard was on hand and ready to be used to make sure that incidents never got out of control.

Q: *Concerning Washington, DC's handling of the World Bank meeting and the 2001 presidential inauguration, what did they do to make sure that protests did not get out of hand?*

A: Washington, DC, was prepared for any problems. They did not underestimate their opposition and were willing, within the law, to do preemptive operation strikes. For example, when large groups of 600 people or more assembled without permits, the police broke them up. If something went on in the protesters' headquarters that did not have a permit, the police moved into the situation. Washington used its civil disturbance units with skill. By preemptive operations and mass arrests, they were able to head off trouble before it began.

Q: *Do you see meetings-cum-demonstrations as a growing problem or one that has reached its peak?*

A: It will be a problem for the foreseeable future. There will be ups and downs, but every major city that will hold major meetings must be prepared to deal with these challenges. Cities such as Boston, Honolulu, and Washington, DC, have shown that this can be done successfully.

Event Risk Management Key Terms

Aggie bonfire: A huge (60 foot) annual bonfire held at Texas A&M University and built by students without benefit of a professional risk manager. It attracted tens of thousands of spectators. In November 1999, the bonfire collapsed, killing twelve students and injuring more than twenty other students.

Bioterrorist attack: An attack on the civilian population in which some form of deadly bacterium or virus is used.

Floats: Moving displays or scenes that form a parade.

Pyrotechnics: The formal name for fireworks.

Riggers: People who put up lights for a performance.

Street theater: Demonstrations that are aimed at the media, although they purport to be aimed at a specific group of meeting delegates.

Winning minds and hearts: Getting public opinion on your side; getting the public to support a security action plan.

Event Risk Management Drills

1. You have just been informed that a national political party has awarded your convention center with its national convention. You are aware that the thousands of delegates will be holding parades. You are also aware that protest demonstrations are planned. Design a risk management plan for these two aspects of the convention.

2. A popular music group will be performing in your city at an outdoor festival. Part of the group's show is to sing to the accompaniment of pyrotechnics. The show is expected to attract some 10,000 spectators and will be broadcast live to other parts of the nation. How would you handle the stage planning and the electrical planning for this show? What pyrotechnic restrictions would you place on the artists?

CHAPTER 8

Tomorrow's Event Risk Management

. . . the future of risk management lies in the processes rather than the products.

—NEIL CARLSON, WRITER AND CONSULTANT

IN THIS CHAPTER, WE WILL EXPLORE:

- Paradigm shifts in event risk management
- The difference between risk and crisis management
- New demographic trends and their impact on event risk management
- The impact of foreign visitors on meetings and events
- The impact of the Internet and computers
- Issues of biochemical weapons

In 1981, Alvin Toffler published his now-classic work of academic futurism: *The Third Wave.* In *The Third Wave,* Toffler argued that the world was going through a basic socioeconomic paradigm shift.

Toffler used the term *paradigm shift* in the Kuhnian sense of the word. For Thomas Kuhn, the late physicist, a paradigm shift referred to a subtle change leading to a major change in the way a professional group views its particular weltanschauüng. For example, Kuhn wrote of the paradigmatic shift from Newtonian physics to Einsteinian physics. Toffler used the notion of a paradigm shift and adapted Kuhn's ideas to socioeconomic theory. According to Toffler, the first wave was a socioeconomic unit based on an agricultural society in which tools of the trade were made on a piece-by-piece basis. This first-wave preindustrialized society was the world of the craftsman. In preindustrial society, products were few, made to last, expensive, and, for most people, a rarity. According to Toffler, the first wave, or the agrarian preindustrial society, is the time frame in which most of human history has taken place and in which many parts of the world still live.

This first-wave society gave way to what Toffler called the industrial period, or the second wave. The second wave, which began in England, was the period of time when products were produced en masse. Second-wave products were reminiscent of Henry Ford's saying that one can buy a Model T Ford in any color that one wishes, as long as the color is black. The second wave, according to Toffler, replaced the agrarian *weltanschauüng,* or worldview, with a new paradigm, that of the industrialized world. This new second-wave paradigm relied heavily on manufacturing products, maintaining consistency, and satisfying the needs of the masses. The second wave is to what many of the emerging nations aspire.

Around the 1970s, a new paradigm, based on the computer, began to replace the second wave, at least in the more academically advanced nations. Toffler argued that, as we entered the computerized world, another paradigm shift occurred, that of the third wave. In third-wave society, products are mass produced, but instead of coming out as, in the words of the 1960's Pete Seeger song ". . . ticky-tack, and . . . the same," products were individualized to meet the need of the particular consumer. Thus, two people may have the same computer, but because each one has software for his or her own use, the computers may look the same, but, in reality, they are not. They are different machines occupying the same hardware. From Toffler's point of view, this third wave symbolizes society's ability to "mass produce individuality."

By the end of the twentieth century, other changes had occurred so fast that many began to question if Toffler's third-wave concept would soon be washed away by the postmodernist's notions. Theorists such as Umberto Eco and Jean Baudrillard went a step farther than Toffler. Postmodernists argued that not only could products be produced en masse and yet be different, but what was true of products could also be true of intangible ideas and even professions. In this still newest possible post-Tofflerian paradigm, we see "individualized mass production" transforming itself into a new form of individualization: that is to say, from the production of goods to the furnishing of services. Furthermore, this post-Tofflerian form of individualization had an accompanying corollary: the notion of dedifferentiation.

Postmodernists mean by dedifferentiation that while the "same becomes distinct," these individualized distinctions now become blended with other distinctions so as to blur the lines that separate one individualized notion from the other. Dedifferentiation is the "trademark" of a fourth-wave society. To understand this concept in concrete terms, consider the movie *Fantastic Animation,* in which live actors are digitized in such a way that body "errors/blemishes" are perfected/smoothed over. Viewers of the movie no longer know if they are seeing a "real person" or the digitized form of what once was/is a real person. In this new dedifferentiated world, even the past, present, and future blend together. In a dedifferentiated society, the borders between truth and fiction, between reality and "hyperreality," in Umberto Eco's terminology, are now one and the same.

Paradigm Shifts in Event Risk Management

Toffler's theory of the third wave combined with postmodern theory is a good introduction into our examination of twenty-first-century risk management. As long as human beings have roamed the earth, the issue of risk has been with us. When Abel met up with Cain (the world's first meeting?), they both took a risk. Indeed, one might argue that the biblical text is, to a great extent, a story of well-managed and often mismanaged events and meetings. Then, as now, the cost of mismanagement was very high, all too often resulting in death. Just as in Toffler's notion of the first wave, biblical and classical ideas concerning risk were limited. Each risk was individualized; each risk was an action in and unto itself. Figure 8.1 gives a simple outline of first-wave risk management. In it, you will note that there is a direct relationship between the risk and the incident's cure.

With the rise of a second-wave society, event risk management developed a paradigm that paralleled second-wave society. Just as in the second wave, risk management reflected the ideal of a standardized product. Risk managers identified the risk, watched the risk manifest itself, reacted to the risk, and worked with other professionals to set examples so that the same risk would not occur again. Equipment was standardized and reflected the idea of taking care of the greatest number of people for the least amount of money. Figure 8.2 traces the classical model used prior to the advent of modern event risk management.

There is often a transition between second- and third-wave models. In that case, the model might resemble that shown in Figure 8.3.

The third wave represented a new paradigm shift for the industrialized world, which was reflected in the way risk management was carried out. Event risk management now needed to identify risks that came in multiple variations; reactions would be tailored to specific risks by using standardized equipment that

Figure 8-1
First-Wave Event Risk Management
Paradigm

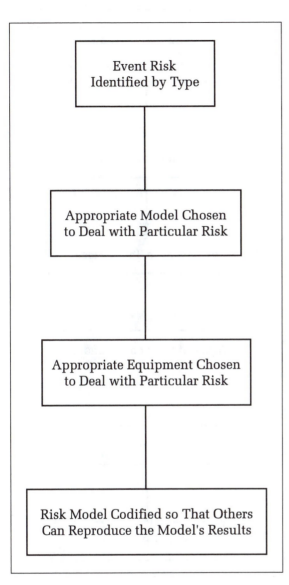

Event Risk
Identified by Type

Appropriate Model Chosen
to Deal with Particular Risk

Appropriate Equipment Chosen
to Deal with Particular Risk

Risk Model Codified so That Others
Can Reproduce the Model's Results

Figure 8-2
Second-Wave Event Risk Management
Model

could be programmed to suit each situation as it arose. Profes-
sionalization of the product created people who would share ideas
with colleagues and offer multiple answers to universal risk management questions. In this third-wave society, risk management
was less the physical action but rather an attempt to understand
risks that occur whenever people gather together. The risk manager's technique would employ a whole palette of analysis tools so

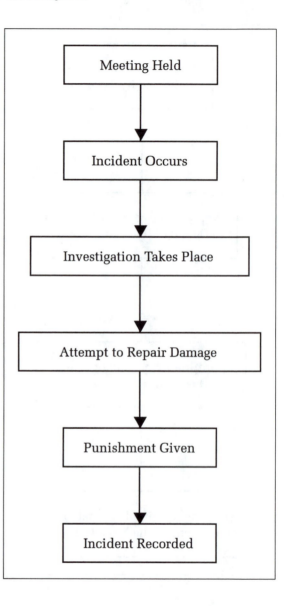

Figure 8-3
Paradigm to Modern Event Risk
Management

that the risk manager might assess the probability of these hazards manifesting themselves. By using a host of methodologies, the risk manager could now attempt to predict what would be the consequences of such a hazard taking place. See Figure 8.4.

The Australia/New Zealand Risk Management Standard (1999, p. 4) provides an excellent third-wave definition of risk manage-

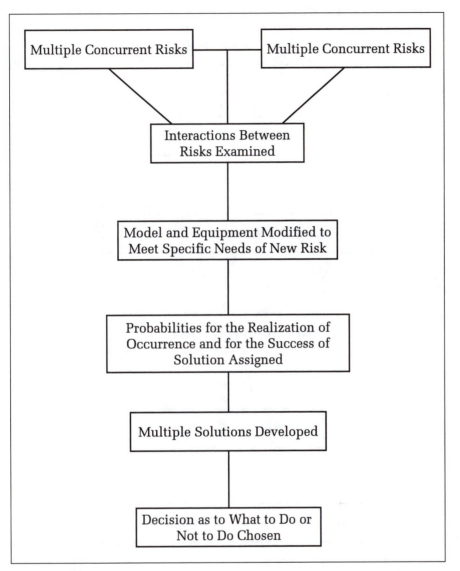

Figure 8-4
Third-Wave Event Risk Management Paradigm

ment. It defines risk management as: "The culture, processes and structures that are directed towards the effective management of potential opportunities and adverse effects" (**http://www.customs.gov.au/media/speeches/cv_sw1.htm**). Figure 8.5 gives some idea of a third-wave approach to risk management. How might you

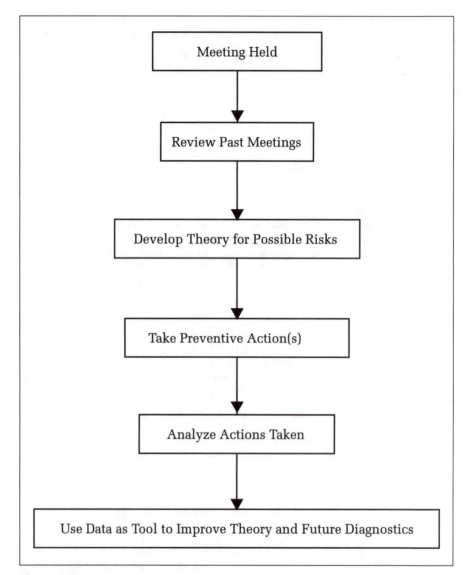

Figure 8-5
Modern Event Risk Management Paradigm

modify it? Notice that the word "meeting" in the first box of the figure refers to an event risk management team meeting, and in the second box the word "meetings" refers to events of a similar nature.

We may now argue that event risk management is entering into a fourth wave or post-third-wave phase. This newest paradigm does not totally reject the paradigm of the third wave. Rather, it adds to it. In the fourth wave of risk management, risk management becomes truly interdisciplinary. The risk manager's role is greatly expanded. Safety and security issues blend together with travel and tourism issues. Festivals and meetings become both part of the workplace and an opportunity for leisure time activities. Even the definition of a delegate becomes harder to determine, as many delegates turn business meetings into family vacations, and an ever-growing number of conventions offer spouse and children's programs as part of the meeting. Furthermore, with meetings often spread across a city and delegates traveling outside of a "host location," it is unclear where the risk manager's job begins and where it ends. Are risk managers in charge of the convention/meeting/festival wherever it may be or are they in charge of the site's headquarters or principal location? To put this question in a more epistemological way: What is a meeting or an event—the place, the participants, or the interaction between the two? Following is a partial listing of how this fourth-wave paradigm is changing the role of event risk managers. Fourth-wave risk managers will need to:

- List and think through the multiple tangible and intangible factors that can go wrong separately and together. The risk manager must think of the interactions between hazards. How does one risk interact with another? What new risk results from this interaction?
- Act as "psychological caregivers." In a society where an ever-increasing number of people have access to information, it becomes harder to hide risks from the public. Such knowledge, while beneficial, can also increase anxiety among the public. It often becomes the job of the risk manager to reassure the public that simply because one is aware of a hazard does not mean that the hazard will occur. Event risk managers now face a new risk: that fear of risk may create a whole new set of risks. In other words, partial knowledge may produce the risk of public anxiety and even panic. Fourth-wave event risk managers must manage both the risk and the perception that the risk will happen.
- Be aware of the fact that they are now part of a marketing team. Event managers have choices in which site to pick. Event risk management now becomes a marketing tool to

assure those doing site selections that their meeting center will offer a hassle-free environment. Event risk managers are a silent partner in the marketing of a location for a meeting or event. The more hazards are controlled, the quieter the situation, the easier it will be (assuming all other things being equal) to sell the locale. People now use safety and security as one of the reasons for choosing a particular site.

- Become part of the overall planning for the event. This means that risk managers must take everything into account from, for example, actors' pyrotechnic needs to the globalization of the meetings and events industry and the realization that lack of knowledge of the local language has become a risk for delegates from abroad.

Figure 8.6 shows some of the basic overall changes in attitudes toward event risk management.

Second-Wave Paradigm	Third- to Fourth-Wave Paradigm
Event risk manager seen as a necessary economic burden	Event risk manager seen as an additional marketing opportunity
Role is to create difficulties for imaginative people	Role is to allow the imagination to flourish in a safe and secure environment
Emphasis on product	Emphasis on process
Emphasis on machines such as television surveillance	Emphasis on strategies
Develop plan and maintain follow-through	Develop several plans and emphasize flexibility and ability to change quickly as the situation changes

Figure 8-6
Comparison of Event Risk Management Paradigms

Future Risks for Event Risk Managers

What are some of the risks that event planners may face in the future? Although no one can predict the future, we can study past and current trends to aid us in making intelligent guesses. For example, in Chapter 5 we refer to risk management's role in facing the threat of terrorism. Prior to September 11, 2001, most event risk managers did not spend a great deal of time on terrorism issues. In the post–World Trade Center world, the threat of terrorism—from bombs, nuclear attacks, and biochemical weapons—is very real. This means that risk managers must not only worry about standardized crowd control issues, but must also now face a new world in which killing is done for the purpose of making a political statement.

A word of caution is in order here. Predictions are only as good as the theory that defines which information becomes data and the quality of the data collected. As noted in Chapter 2, no one can collect all the necessary data or even determine with absolute certainty which information should be considered data. The best we can hope to do is study the past as a guide to developing our theories.

Good risk managers know that each day brings with it change and, as these changes are noted, new analyses must be performed. Flexibility is, then, a key to determining future trends. It is a mistake for risk managers to become so attached to a particular paradigm that they simply refuse to modify it. There is no one way to study risk.

Multiple subjects and academic disciplines are needed. Risk managers can be called "walking academies," as they must combine disciplines such as statistics and sociology, nutrition and economics, engineering and travel, psychology and event management. All these disciplines play a part in helping the risk manager to work hard at appearing to do little. That is to say, a successful risk manager is able to assess a risk and prevent its manifestation in such a way that the public remains almost totally unaware that the risk exists. The bottom line is that in risk management there is no one right answer. Today's correct analysis may be tomorrow's incorrect conclusion. What risk managers can do is be open to change and "own" constantly changing problems.

Risk is a constant fact of life, but how that risk manifests itself is ever changing. We may think of risk management as the opposing side of crisis management. In fact, crisis management may be defined as a managerial technique that comes from failing to institute proper risk management. Risk management, then, is always about the future; crisis management is about the present. Risk management is the attempt to solve or minimize a problem before it occurs; crisis management reflects the need to solve a problem once it has occurred. In Chapter 7, we saw a good example of this difference when we examined the role of the National Guard in Seattle and Honolulu. Seattle called in the guard after the fact. In Seattle, the National Guard was a form of crisis management. Honolulu, on the other hand, carefully deployed the guard so that it would not have to be used. In Seattle's case, mass arrests took place and the city's downtown suffered a large amount of media and physical damage.

In Honolulu's case, most people around the nation never even knew that the Asian Development Bank meeting was occurring.

Good risk management is ever changing. When risk managers assume that yesterday's successes ensure those of tomorrow, they have failed their profession. Instead, risk managers must constantly be aware of new demographic and political trends, the direction of the economy, and the rising and falling of sociological tides. Computers have radically changed the way risk management is practiced around the world. Data today can be collected and stored in ways undreamed of only a few decades ago. Powerful statistical programs can help risk managers analyze trends and determine threats that would have easily been missed by their colleagues of a generation ago. The computer is a major tool in risk management but it, too, carries risks. Not only can the computer be a tool for analyzing risks, but, in the wrong hands, it can also be an instrument for creating risks. Anyone familiar with the numerous computer viruses that spread quickly across the world knows that computers are vulnerable to attack. As the world becomes more computer dependent, the need to protect programs and data becomes a new risk that must be managed. The use of computers presents still another problem for risk managers. This is the problem of data overload. As the world becomes more interconnected, risk managers may have so much data and so much computer technology that they run the risk of becoming technically blind to the obvious.

Not only are computers vulnerable to attack, but they have also led to the often-mistaken belief that "truth" is found solely in quantitative analysis. Quantitative analysis provides risk managers with numerous insights, but no one analytical instrument can provide all the answers. Risk managers need to balance the way they analyze data. Both qualitative and quantitative data will be part of the risk manager's tool bag.

Computers can be instruments that enlighten us, but they can also be excellent tools to obscure reality and hide facts. Used properly, the computer can help risk managers to analyze data coming in to them from an increasingly complex meetings and events industry. If, however, those in charge of the various subcomponents of the meetings and events industry choose to hide problems rather than "own" potential problems, then the risk manager is left with a highly sophisticated form of "garbage in/garbage out." To assure that risks are reported to risk managers, meeting and event planners and organizers are going to have to provide their risk management departments with a great deal of support. This support must include:

- Proper budgets and staff. The cost of managing risk will become more expensive as the risks increase. This is but a small price in comparison to the cost in lives, property, and reputation of ignoring the risk.
- An organizational culture that praises people for recognizing and "owning" problems, rather than chastising them for reporting problems.
- Developing standardized definitions and a vocabulary of terms that has the same meaning across the organizational structure. This standardization of terms will allow risk managers to tailor their programs to the needs of individual meetings and festivals and still communicate in clear and precise terms.
- Praising innovation and flexibility, giving risk managers the freedom to take risks.
- The ability to manage risk with more information while, at the same time, respecting people's privacy and being less intrusive. For example, in a world of meetings-cum-demonstrations (MCDs), risk managers must find ways to check for increasingly smaller and harder to find explosive devices while, at the same time, not invading people's privacy. Reconciliation of these almost paradoxical contradictory needs is often handed to the risk manager at the same time that he or she is requested to hold down costs.

To a great extent, Figure 8.7 represents the classical event risk management model, which was summed up by Colin Vassarotti of the Australian Customs service. Although Vassarotti was writing for Australian Customs, his ideas are adaptable to event risk management. Vassarotti begins by noting that risk managers need

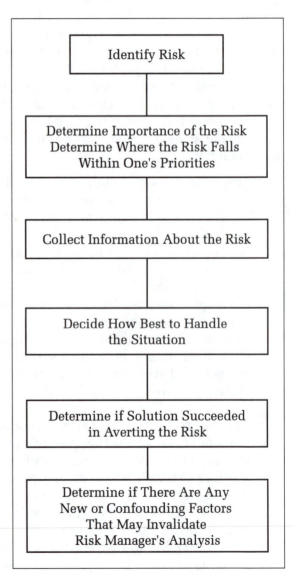

Figure 8-7
Classical Event Risk Management Model

to place their problem within a situational context in a way that specialists can determine what the risks are for a specific circumstance. Once they have contextualized the risk, they can attempt to determine both probability and ensuing results. For example, might the risk be high but the result not terribly dangerous or might there be a low risk that could result in a catastrophic situation? Too much sun might be an example of the first form of risk, while the attack on the World Trade Center would be an example of the second form of risk. Once risk managers have determined how resources are employed according to risk probability, then they must create a scale of risks. On this scale, they need to ask questions such as: Where should the event risk manager place his or her priorities? Where should resources be spent? Vassarotti then notes that risk managers must develop a plan to solve or control the risk. Once that plan is put into action, risk managers will want to measure the success of the plan. That is to say, risk managers need to know if the plan is doing what they want it to do. How do they know that the plan is producing the desired results? Finally, risk managers need to be in constant communication with all those who have a stake in the plan's success. Risk managers should ask themselves questions such as: Are stakeholders satisfied? What else might the risk manager be missing or failing to do?

Vassarotti's final point is especially important as in a fourth-wave society risk managers neither work alone nor are they part of a fixed risk team. Instead, they are part of a fluid risk team, one that will change as the context of the risk changes.

Event Risk Management in a Changing World

To help event risk managers face some of the problems of the future, we now turn to a partial listing of demographic and sociological changes that may well impact the meetings and events industry. The following topics are not given in order of importance.

Part of dedifferentiation is that the risk manager must know the techniques of the future without losing the wisdom of the past. In a fourth-wave form of risk management, issues will fade in and out as to their order of importance.

Demographic Changes   Not only are the demographics of the United States changing, but also demographers have tracked similar trends in most of the postindustrialized (third and fourth wave) world. Among the most important trends for event risk managers are demographic changes. Some of the ways that event risk managers will need to confront these changes have already been noted in previous chapters. Major world demographic changes include:

- **An aging population.** The baby boom generation is now beginning to reach retirement age. This immense demographic bulge, born between 1946 and 1960, means that many of the attendees at both festivals and meetings will soon require extra physical and medical attention. As this is a more allocentric generation (see Chapter 1) than previous generations, these new retirees will be more active than their parents were at a similar age.

- **An increase in foreign delegates.** Due to the availability of air travel, the dropping of visa requirements by many Western nations, the creation of the European Union, and international commerce, the world is seeing an explosion of cross-border travel. Most national departments (ministries) of commerce consider this increase to be highly positive. International meetings not only allow for the free exchange of ideas, but also help nations with their balance of payments. Most nations see foreign visitation as a "renewable export industry" in that the local economy is aided by an inflow of foreign currencies. Nevertheless, cross-border meetings present a whole set of new challenges to the risk manager. Among these challenges are:

  - **Food and hygiene habits.** These vary from nation to nation. It is wise for the risk manager to have an idea of the delegates' country of origin. Do not group nations together. Latin American nations have distinct national habits, as do Asian nations. Never assume that what is correct for one national group is correct for all other national groups.

  - **Higher health risks.** People who cross borders may bring with them diseases unknown in the host country. Often, the person may be well when boarding the airplane and without being aware that he or she is in an incubation period may carry a disease to the meeting site. Local medical personnel may be unaware of the new illness and may fail to diagnose it properly, thus exposing others.

- **Language problems.** Even if the visitor speaks the language of the conference, confusion can take place, especially at moments of crisis. It is wise for the risk manager to learn at least one other language and to develop a list of local people whom he or she can call upon to help with language difficulties. Most people tend to forget words or become flustered in a foreign tongue during moments of stress.
- **Signage issues.** Foreign delegates may not always understand local signage. At international meetings, both the metric and the English measurement systems need to be used. International symbols can also help eliminate confusion.
- **The rise of single parents.** Because there are so many more single parents, business meetings have had to make provisions for children. Single parents often have no alternative but to bring small children to meetings. Careful observers can note the change in such things as nurseries as part of the corporate culture and diaper-changing tables in men's rest rooms. The increase in the number of children at conferences means that risk managers will have an additional worry, that is, providing bonded day-care providers and assuring parents that their children are safe and well cared for while they are at work. To add to the safety issues, risk managers may have to deal with noncustodial parents who decide to use the meeting as a way of "kidnapping the child," children who get lost, and children who wander close to swimming pools or other hazardous areas.

Biochemical Weapons   These weapons have often been called the poor man's atomic bomb. Biochemical terrorism is a real threat at any meeting. As shown by Legionnaires' disease, humans are highly vulnerable to attacks on heating and air conditioning systems and somewhat vulnerable to attacks on water supplies. As the world becomes a more dangerous place, risk managers will have to take the threat of a biochemical attack with much greater seriousness. The bombing of the federal building in Oklahoma City, though not a biochemical attack, is a good reminder that out-of-the-way places are also vulnerable. People working as risk managers at major events such as the Olympic games, national political conventions, or even large state fairs should not only take this type of threat very seriously, but also develop a number of tabletop exercises. Risk managers should be aware of the fact that, in the event of a biochemical attack or suspicion of such an attack, many of the procedures followed are different from other forms of risk management. For example, paramedics and security personnel should not enter the area of a suspected attack without proper gear and equipment.

Changing Travel Patterns   Although the meetings and events industry is distinct from the travel and tourism industry, they are part of the same family. In a postmodern world, the distinctions between these two industries tend to become blurred. For example, small-town convention and visitor bureaus (CVBs) use events such as annual festivals as a major marketing tool. In larger cities, major events, such as a Super Bowl or World Series, are a major part of that community's visitor industry. In the same manner, large meetings, be they political or of a business nature, are more than a mere chance to get together. Delegates buy hotel rooms, eat in restaurants, go to shows, and shop in local stores. It is important, then, that the event risk manager realize that the travel and tourism industry will view him or her as part of its industry.

Computers   Needless to say, the world is becoming more dependent on computers. Computers are used to turn switches on and off, to calculate payrolls, to keep track of ticket sales, to assign hotel rooms, or to inform front desks which sessions at a meeting are already filled and which sessions still have space available. A large part of the world's information and correspondence is delivered through computerized e-mail. E-commerce, in fact, touches almost every aspect of the meetings and events industry. Risk managers are aware that the computer is not only their lifeline, but is also open to multiple risks. For example, a computer virus sent through e-mail can wreak havoc and cause many millions or billions of dollars worth of damage. Risk managers should not only have all data backed up and off site, but work with a computer specialist to take as many precautions as possible.

In the world of meetings, computers present still another challenge. Laptop computers have become a prime target for theft. For example, writing in *Security Management,* Chad Callaghan, vice president of loss prevention for the Marriott hotel chain, notes: "most of the people leaving these laptops [at meetings] would not walk out of a room and leave $2,000 in cash unattended. Yet anecdotal evidence reveals that most guests believe that their laptops are safe even when unattended and they do not want the inconvenience of securing the laptop while they go to lunch or on a break" (Callaghan, 2001).

Computers are and will continue to be a double-edged sword. They will be information holders used in the fight against risk and, at the same time, they will present new risks to risk managers.

Customer Service   Future event risk managers will need even greater patience and customer service skills. Few people understand exactly what event risk managers do. Instead, they are the people to whom delegates and customers turn when things go wrong. Baby boomers and their children will continue to dominate the meetings and events industry. Event risk managers will need even greater person skills. For example, they will need to know how to say "no" with a smile. A large part of the risk management profession, then, will be based on listening skills, customer service skills, and the ability to convince clients to do what is in their best interest.

Cybertheft and Cyberterrorism   As the world becomes more dependent on computers and the Internet, not only is the "hardware" open to the risk of theft, but events themselves may become the victims of scams and cyberattacks. The list of possible cyber–risk management crises is almost without limit and will change on a constant basis. Vigilance and awareness of these scams/attacks are essential for risk managers.

Drugs and Other Forms of Illegal Contraband   Not everything that happens at a meeting or festival is planned or desired. There are often two events taking place at the same time. There is the legitimate meeting or festival/event and then there is the ever-growing number of people who use the protection of the crowd for illegal purposes. Risk managers in the future will have to deal with an increasing number of safety problems caused by people who have used illegal drugs or use the event as a cover to deal in illegal substances. As the use of these illegal substances increases, there is also the added factor of police raids during the event or a gang war taking place in the midst of a festival. Closely tied to the substance abuse problem, but distinct from it, is the issue of lack of respect for authority. This lack of respect often translates into safety factors that go well beyond rudeness. As the population ages, it may feel increasingly vulnerable to gangs and groups of people who feel that they can take advantage of others.

Economic Considerations   Event risk management, especially in a fourth-wave society, will be a very expensive proposition. Not only will people and goods be at risk, but services and ideas/ intellectual property will also need to be guarded. Risk managers will find themselves continually seeking larger budgets, requesting additional sophisticated equipment and greater expenditures for education. Risk managers will need to become experts in multiple disciplines. Should the labor shortage continue, the well-educated risk manager will not only be well trained, but will become a highly prized commodity. This means that corporations and government agencies will compete with the events and meetings industry to hire the best risk managers. Risk managers who stay abreast of the newest material and are capable of ferreting out useful information from less useful information will become highly sought-after commodities on the labor market. Risk managers, however, will need to be able to justify every expense. When proposing budgets, tomorrow's risk managers will have to know how to explain to others why a particular strategy, piece of equipment, or training course is necessary. That explanation will entail not only knowing how to explain the reasons for the new idea/piece of equipment, but also explaining to laypeople how the idea/ equipment will work. Risk managers, then, must justify to management why it should risk its money on risk management.

Internet Access   Closely tied to the computer are the World Wide Web (WWW) and the Internet. In many ways, the Internet has become a staple for meetings and the marketing of major events. Web sites appear almost instantaneously; information, including photographs, crosses national borders without any form of control; tickets and reservations are now purchased on line. The Internet's great success has resulted in a number of new risks. Risk managers now need to know—or have a staff person—who can deal with issues such as encryption and credit card security. To make matters even more complicated, new risks develop so quickly that the event risk manager may not know that the risk exists.

Intellectual Property Rights and Economic Espionage   A great deal of information passes from one person to another at meetings. In most cases, the delegates have a right to be at the meeting and to obtain the information. In a second- or even third-wave economy, the stealing of intellectual property or the sending of people to meetings as spies was rare and did not cause great concern among risk managers. Fourth-wave economies, powered by computers and instant communication, however, are different. If the first-wave economy was based on control of land for agriculture, the second-wave economy sought resources for industrial production, and the third-wave economy was based on the provision of services, the fourth-wave economy is one in which control of intellectual property and ideas becomes key. In these new economies, knowledge is power. In a fourth-wave economy, the criminal often does not care about the laptop computer as much as he or she cares about the information found within the computer. Tomorrow's meetings will be burdened by the fact that delegates may wonder how much they risk in being candid. Delegates will demand of risk managers assurances concerning the security of their ideas. A major task of the risk manager will be to ferret out the legitimate delegate from the industrial spy who is recording every word, not for the sake of knowledge but as a way of stealing ideas.

A word of caution, there is no pure fourth-wave economy. Nations are composed of pockets of first-, second-, third-, and fourth-wave economies. This realization means that risk managers must be flexible enough to determine risks according to the particular type of meeting/event that is taking place. Furthermore, the risks of the newest wave do not cancel out the concerns of the other waves. For example, at a fourth-wave conference delegates may be concerned about the stealing of intellectual property, but they will be equally concerned about the sanitation of the food and/or the quality of the water they drink. Figure 8.8 illustrates this point.

Improved Levels of Performance   One way that event risk managers may be able to justify the large increases in budgets that the future will demand is by arguing that risk management means an overall performance increase throughout the industry. Wise risk

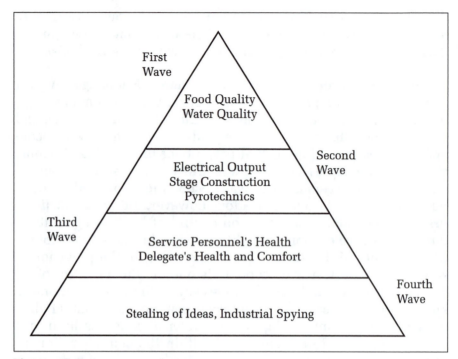

Figure 8-8
Types of Risks Faced by Risk Managers

managers will demonstrate how risk management, if properly used, can hold down costs across the board, from workmen's compensation to litigation. Proper risk management will be one of the ways that the meetings and events industry will be able to do more, use equipment better, and offer improved results with fewer costs to machinery and human beings. Risk management will also answer the need for an ever-growing accountability, especially if the trend toward litigation continues. Stated in its simplest format: Good risk management is an effective way to reduce costs.

Multiple Cultural Societies   As immigration follows free-trade patterns, the nation-state is giving way to "minority conglomerates." Although these new societies may share a common piece of land, they often share only to a minimal degree common values and even languages. This process, called Balkanization, means that signage and warnings may have to be given in more than one language and that risk managers cannot work under the assumption that what is legitimate in one segment of society will be legitimate for other segments.

Terrorism The acts of terrorism in New York and Washington, DC, on September 11, 2001, may indicate that major events will continue to be at risk well into the twenty-first century. As noted in Chapter 5, terrorism is distinct from crime in that it almost always carries a political message and that the terrorists see themselves as heroes. Terrorists seek publicity, which means that the higher the profile of the meeting (especially if it is an international meeting), the greater the publicity that an act of terrorism will produce. Terrorism can come in many forms: from the detonating of a remote car bomb to an explosion set off by a homicide bomber to some form of biochemical attack. Closely related to acts of terrorism but distinct from terrorism is the meeting-cum-demonstration (MCD) syndrome discussed in Chapter 7. Like acts of terrorism, these street theater antics seek publicity. There are, however, some major differences between them, as shown in Figure 8.9.

Event risk managers will have to be constantly on guard. They will need to consider which groups their event might inspire to conduct an act of terrorism and what part of the event system is most likely to be attacked.

Wrap Up

As noted, risk management has come a long way. To conclude this book, it behooves us to review where risk management has been and where it may be going.

PAST IMPRESSIONS

- Event risk management was traditionally viewed as adding nothing to the economic bottom line.
- Event risk management was traditionally viewed as a necessary "evil." As clients tend to shy away from places that are not safe, the overt presence of risk management personnel was seen as a marketing disaster.

Terrorism at Event Site	Meeting-cum-Demonstration(s)
Occurs within site	Occurs outside of site
Seeks to harm those attending to gain publicity	Seeks to prevent delegates from attending
Meeting site under direct responsibility of the risk manager	Demonstrations occur outside of meeting site and therefore have only an indirect link to the meeting's risk manager
Often have a violent political agenda	Rarely have a violent political agenda; rather seek to promote a nonviolent cause
Allies may be other violent groups	Allies may be other groups with other agendas that buy into program or are "pushed" into program due to communication gaps
Seeks publicity for a cause, rarely for the perpetrator; publicity gained through act of violence	Seek publicity for a cause(s) and participants are ready to go to jail as an act of nonviolence
No chance of peaceful rechanneling of energies	Authorities can work with MCD participants and offer them other alternatives

Figure 8-9
Comparison of Acts of Terrorism and MCDs

- Event risk management operations upset the ebb and flow of business, creating stressful situations and, at times, angry customers.
- Many attendees at meetings and events live in a state of "risk safety" denial while at a meeting/event. Risk management professionals, by the nature of their work, must assume that there are risks without destroying the image of a safe meeting/event.

- The event risk manager's colleagues in other departments may be less concerned about matters of risk than is the risk management team. This means that priority conflicts may develop. Without good internal communication, risk managers may be viewed as creating hassles for other members of the meeting/event professional team.

One purpose of this book is to help event risk managers change these negative impressions. The following goals can be met by risk managers:

- Making a good first impression by meeting with the event's personnel at the earliest time possible
- Developing relationships with other departments
- Putting themselves in the other person's shoes, that is to say, in the shoes of the other event's departments
- Remembering that phrases like "I'm only doing my job" may be true, but will win few friends and allies
- Showing appreciation to colleagues
- Asking for colleagues' input
- Developing methods to enhance teamwork among everyone working within and around the event
- Meeting regularly with colleagues to develop creative solutions
- Developing e-mail briefings and face-to-face coordination times
- Projecting an attitude of "service," never one of superiority
- Knowing how to use the basics of face-to-face and telephone-to-telephone communication
- Knowing how to interpret body language
- Knowing how to say "no" and not make an enemy
- Knowing how to deal with different cultures
- Learning about the local community and knowing how to promote it

No one can say for certain what the risk manager's role will be in the future, but risk management is, like life itself, a process. As life changes, so will the risks we encounter; as the nature of the risks changes, so, too, will risk managers. One thing is certain: Not to change is a risk that the meetings and events industry cannot afford to take.

FUTURE TRENDS

Following are some of the issues that risk managers may face in the near future:

- **Greater diversity in the population, leading to cultural misunderstandings.** For example, risk managers will have to deal with a multilingual society. Such a society will not only require international signage, but will also create confusion as to customs, hours of operation, and multiple definitions of acceptable behavior.

- **Greater emphasis on food and water safety.** Due to the large amount of attention paid to these issues in the media, there is a growing concern among the population as to the quality of food and water that is offered to people eating outside of their place of residence. The public will want to know how food is protected, how safe the water is, and who is responsible for its safety.

- **Greater number of single working women attending business meetings and events.** The term "single working women" does not refer to a woman's marital status, but rather to the fact that she is traveling alone. As the working population becomes less unigendered, risk managers will need to take into account everything from possible assaults on single women attendees from issues of better lighting to the assignment of hotel rooms.

- **Greater potential for airborne or contagious diseases.** Risk managers will need to consider that, as meetings and events take on a greater international flavor, diseases will travel from one society to another. The host society may often be poorly prepared or unaware of an illness brought to it by a traveler. Risk managers at international meetings will need to consider attendees' lists to determine if these people may be coming from societies that have diseases not known to the host society.

- **Energy and energy conservation.** Risk managers will need to worry about brownouts and blackouts, power failures, and what these failures' impacts will be on everything from air conditioning and food safety to computers and personal security.

- **New forms of economic fraud.** Risk managers will need to worry about issues such as credit card fraud and international currency exchanges. As the world's economy becomes more interlinked, new forms of monetary fraud are bound to appear.

- **Graying of the population.** As the population ages, risk managers will need to place greater emphasis on emergency medical teams.
- **Merging of risk management with policing.** As phenomena such as meetings-cum-demonstrations (MCDs) become more prominent, risk managers will have to work closely with police departments to assure that demonstrations outside of meetings do not destroy what risk managers are working to protect inside the meeting's site.
- **Protection against computerized attacks and breakdowns of computer systems.** The meetings and events industry continues to become ever more dependent on the use of computers and electronic communication. While these systems are extremely helpful, they are also subject to "virtual" viruses and electronic attacks. Furthermore, increasingly smaller computerized hardware makes thievery continuously easier.
- **Protection against terrorism and biochemical attacks.** As the world becomes more politicized, both meetings and events, even in out-of-the-way locations, will become targets of acts of terrorism or political violence. To make this situation more complicated, sophisticated delivery systems mean that all heating and cooling ventilation systems are subject to infiltration, resulting in massive amounts of damage.
- **Need for better forecasting of weather and terrestrial conditions.** The recent trend toward global warming has produced major climatic changes that impact the safety and security of the meeting or event and of those who must travel to attend the meeting or work at or attend the event.
- **Use of robotics.** Risk managers in the future will have a whole host of nonhuman helpers. These robots may do everything from security checks to analyzing the safety of food. While robots will provide a great deal of nonhuman protection, they will also create a need for "robotic risk protection." In other words, new risks will develop around the robotic world.

According to Donald T. Ahl, CPP, director of safety and security at the Las Vegas Convention and Visitors Authority (LVCVA), risks will continue to grow in the twenty-first century. The LVCVA's convention center is the largest single-level convention center in the United States and hosts some of the largest meetings in the world.

Q: *How is risk management organized at the LVCVA convention center?*

A: At the Las Vegas convention center, we take a team approach to risk management. The team consists of experts from our security, legal, facilities, finance, and human resources departments. This team meets on a regular basis. At team meetings, we discuss general risk management issues, analyze specific risk management issues, and coordinate our risk management efforts. The safety and security department has the primary responsibility at the Las Vegas convention center (LVCC) for the overall coordination of risk management and documentation of incidents. This effort is directly supported by the LVCVA customer account managers and the services group. These entities work together to "police" (review/guard against) potential claims. The primary component of "policing" potential claims is to know what is actually happening in the building.

Q: *What are the advantages/disadvantages of such an organizational system?*

A: Our system's advantage is that all of us (those who are in relevant departments) address multiple aspects of risk management concerns. This method permits the greatest amount of input and the flexibility to see the problem from multiple points of view prior to taking any action. The disadvantage is that the system may not be as fast as other systems.

Q: *What is your role in risk management? How would you describe your job?*

A: As mentioned, I am responsible for all issues dealing with safety, security, and traffic operations. One extremely important part of my role is to guard against fire. Remember that we hold a lot of conventions and many of our meetings have a great amount of material that is brought into the building. A full facility user typically brings in over 500 semitrailer loads of product and display material. This equates to several million pounds of freight that is set up, displayed, and subsequently removed in a 7- to 12-day period. We diligently do everything possible to guard against a fire breaking out or, were it to occur, to mobilize the resources to neutralize it as soon as possible.

Q: *How do you see risk management changing in the meetings and events industry?*

A: The safer the meetings, the stronger the industry. As types of exhibits change, we are going to have to find newer and more innovative ways to deal with these changes. Risk management has made people throughout the meetings industry aware of the fact that safety is everyone's business.

Q: *What educational tools do you expect will be most helpful to risk managers over the next 20 years?*

A: We need to learn from each other. Risk managers must meet on a regular basis and we must develop quick and simple ways to exchange information. This is now a worldwide profession and we will need to think on a global basis.

Q: *Is risk management seen as a marketing tool or as a drain on the bottom line?*

A: Some people view risk management as a drain on the budget. It is quite difficult to use risk management as a marketing tool because it starts out with a negative proposition; that is, it asks the question: Is the attendee truly safe at this meeting/location? Often the feeling has been that if one does not talk about it (risk management) there is a great likelihood that the convention delegates will not even ask about it.

Q: *What is the role of the risk manager vis à vis other safety and security people such as police, firefighters, loss prevention people, etc.?*

A: Perhaps more than anything, risk management is based on the principle of coordination and of being aware of what each person does in his or her role. Good risk management, in a large convention center, is based on people working together, gathering intelligence about what is happening in the building, and training all employees that everyone is responsible for safety.

Q: *Is there anything else that you might like to add?*

A: I think that the layperson often does not realize how complicated are the meetings and events risk management team's task. One way of illustrating this point is to consider that each year we host the COMDEX (computer show) event. This meeting is the equivalent of two Super Bowls held on the same day for 5 days straight. Included in this equation are not only the protection of human life and the facility, but also making sure that the millions of dollars of exhibits are safe. In summary, I would say that we at the LVCVA strive to make our facility clean and hazard free at all times. We have regular inspections done by different entities, and we handle any identified concerns immediately. Another area that we consider vital is the elimination of anything that should not be in the building or that could harm the building's visitors, employees, or its physical structure. Finally, I want to emphasize the importance of good documentation when an incident does occur. We make sure that all incidents in our building are fully documented with a security report that includes either audiovisual and/or still pictures.

Event Risk Management Key Terms

Balkanization: Term used by political demographers to refer to one society breaking into multiple parts and each part promoting its own culture or language.

Dedifferentiation: The merging together of reality and fiction into a new form of "hyperreality." In a dedifferentiated society, distinctions often become blurred.

Meeting-cum-demonstration: A late-twentieth-century phenomenon where demonstrators for a cause seek to disrupt a meeting in order to gain sympathy, portray themselves as victims, and disrupt the scheduled meeting or event.

Paradigm shift: The change of a professional worldview or set of assumptions about the world.

Postmodernism: A term that comes originally from the world of art. In the world of risk, it moves to the abstraction of ideas and the fact that clear boundaries between concepts no longer exist.

Risk assessment: Using both quantitative and qualitative techniques to analyze data and make a determination.

Risk handling: That portion of the process where the program manager attempts to reduce or contain the risks that have been identified, quantified, and analyzed.

Risk identification: Using the opinions of experts to determine risks.

Event Risk Management Drills

1. In the fourth wave, which aspect of risk, the opportunity or the adverse outcome of risk, will risk managers emphasize?
2. You have just learned that you have been asked to run a convention center in a less developed nation. How would you determine which wave best describes that part of the world? How would this knowledge help you to be a better risk manager?
3. The text lists a number of changes in twenty-first-century risk management. Which of these changes do you think will most impact risk management? How can you prepare for them?

APPENDIX 1

Web Resources

The following are useful event risk management Web sites. Web sites continuously change both content and URL addresses. The author accepts no responsibility for material found in any specific Web site. The following Web sites do not necessarily relate directly to event risk management, but rather provide useful information for the event risk manager. Event risk management means learning from different academic and professional fields and applying this information to the specific event.

CHAPTER 1

This Web site provides information about the risk of traveling throughout the world:
http://www.state.gov

This is the Web site of the American Risk and Insurance Association:
http://www.aria.org

This Web site provides information about the Federal Emergency Management Agency (FEMA):
http://www.parma.com

This Web site provides information about the Texas Risk Management Education Program:
http://trmep.tamu.edu/index.htm

This is the official Web site of the Society for Risk Analysis:
http://www.sra.org

This Web site covers articles that deal with risk. It is the risk news Web site:
http://www.riskworld.com

This Web site focuses on risk for nonprofit organizations:
http://www.nonprofitrisk.org

This Web site provides articles on risk that may be of use to event risk managers:
http://www.riskvue.com

This Web site provides insights into what is happening in Australian risk management:
http://www.riskmanagement.com.au

This Web site provides information regarding workplace violence and risk: http://www.opm.gov/workplac

This Web site gives insights into how to handle workplace violence and theft: http://www.ojp.usdoj.gov/bjs/abstract/thefwork.htm

This Web site shows how one can avoid the McDonaldization process in everyday life: http://www.mcspotlight.org/media/books/ritzer_excerpt.html

This Web site provides insights into how to manage the risk of natural disasters on islands: http://www.geic.or.jp/docs/juha.html

CHAPTER 2

This is the official Web site of the International Association of Assembly Managers: http://iaam.org

This is a good Web site for crowd management strategies: http://www.crowdsafe.com

This is a Web site dedicated to consumer's rights and protection: http://www.lectlaw.com/tcos.html

This is a good Web site to help you with issues of interpreting body language: http://members.aol.com/nonverbal2/center.htm

This Web site deals with violence against women and children: http://www.cheshire.gov.uk/domvio/safety.htm

CHAPTER 3

This Web site provides information and data about alcohol abuse issues: http://www.niaaa.nih.gov

This Web site provides material on clinical and experimental research concerning alcohol-related issues: http://www.alcoholism-cer.com

This Web site provides information on alcohol abuse recovery for those addicted and for families of the addicted: http://ola-is.org/index.htm

This Web site provides information on alcohol abuse recovery for those addicted and where to get help: http://www.alcoholics-anonymous.org

This Web site provides alcohol-related information for college and university students: http://www.factsontap.org

This Web site, aimed at college students, provides a great deal of information on how to help someone who has become inebriated: http://healthcenter.ucdavis.edu/alcoholpoisoning.html

The Mothers Against Drunk Driving Web site is a comprehensive Web site for alcohol-related data, policy, and issues:
http://www.madd.org

This Web site provides information on event/party risk management for university fraternities and sororities:
http://www.fipg.org

This Web site provides information on event/party risk management for university fraternities and sororities:
http://www.gwu.edu/~cade

This is the Web site of the national clearinghouse for alcohol and drug information:
http://www.health.org

CHAPTER 4

The following Web sites all deal with issues of young-adult music events. The information is changed on a constant basis. The reader is advised to check these various Web sites for updated discussions and information.
http://teenmusic.about.com/teens/teenmusic/library/weekly/aa071000b.htm?iam=dpile&terms=%2B%22crowd+management%22
http://teenmusic.about.com/teens/teenmusic/gi/dynamic/offsite.htm?site=http://www.crowdsafe.com/thewall.html

CHAPTER 5

These three Web sites are excellent sources of information on all aspects of risk from poisons:
http://www.publicaffairs.ubc.ca/reports/98mar5/dpic2.html
http://www.safekids.org/tier2_rl.cfm?folder_id=166
http://www.carolinas.org/services/poison/info.cfm

CHAPTER 6

This is a useful Web site on how to plan for pedestrian walkways and bicycle safety issues:
http://www.nhtsa.dot.gov/kids/biketour/pedsafety/index.html

This Web site provides information on laws concerning bicycle safety and pedestrian and other forms of nonmotorized transportation:
http://www.azfms.com/DocReviews/Mar96/art13.htm

This Web site examines snakes and snakebites. It contains useful information for event risk managers who are working with outdoor events:
http://www.fda.gov/fdac/features/995_snakes.html

The following Web sites provide information on food safety issues and contain updated information that event risk managers will need to know for events where food and beverages are served:
http://www.fda.gov

http://www.fsai.ie/press_releases/
280498.htm
http://agnews.tamu.edu/stories/
CFAM/Sep0199a.htm
http://www.hi-tm.com/homeprep/
home-XIV.html
http://www.afpc.tamu.edu

The following Web sites provide
updated information on potable
water issues. They provide the
event risk manager with lists of
water-related concerns and how to
avoid aquatic risks at events:
http://www.marinemedical.com/
water.htm
http://www.bottledwaterweb.com/
statistics.html
http://www.abcnews.go.com/
sections/living/DailyNews/
bottledwater990330.html
http://more.abcnews.go.com/
sections/us/dailynews/
bottledwater000915.html

This Web site provides the risk
manager with information and
checklists dealing with electrical
safety:
http://laborsafety.about.com/
industry/government/cs/electricalsh

CHAPTER 7

The following Web sites offer the
event risk manager information on
stage construction and stage
maintenance safety issues:
http://webware.princeton.edu/
theater/electric.htm
http://webware.princeton.edu/
theater/inspectf.htm
http://artsnet.heinz.cmu.edu:70/1/
csa/arthazards/performing

http://artsnet.heinz.cmu.edu:70/0/
csa/arthazards/performing/theatchk

These Web sites address the
issues of pyrotechnics. They offer
guidelines on how to reduce
pyrotechnic risks:
http://schoolsite.edex.net.uk/500/
pyro.htm
http://www.llr.state.sc.us/pol/
pyrotechnic/firework.pdf

This Web site explores some of
the issues of meetings-cum-
demonstrations (MCDs):
http://www.garynorth.com/y2k/
detail_.cfm/6980

CHAPTER 8

This Web site provides
information on how the
Australian government sees future
risks in the area of customs
control:
http://nasdocs.faa.gov/nasiHTML/
risk-mgmt/vol1/9_chapt.html

This Web site offers a major
financial firm's vision of some of
the risks that may be facing the
world in the future:
http://www.pwcglobal.com/
extweb/manissue.nsf/DocID/
0696686C3999413E8525689E0038
F45A

This Web site provides research
into the future of risk
management issues:
http://www.rff.org/crm_news/
index.htm

This Web site, developed by FEMA, permits you to download a course on emergency management principles and applications for tourism, hospitality, and travel management industries: www.fema.gov/emi/edu

This Web site offers a continual update on travel and event security and conferences of interest to event risk managers around the world: www.tourismandmore.com

Alcohol and Beverage Commission Addresses and Telephone/Fax Numbers by State

ALABAMA

Alabama Alcoholic Beverage
Control Board
2715 Gunter Park Drive West
Montgomery, AL 36109
Phone: (334) 271-3840
Fax: (334) 277-2150

ALASKA

Alaska Department of Revenue
Alcoholic Beverage Control Board
550 West 7th Avenue, Suite #350
Anchorage, AK 99501
Phone: (907) 269-0350
Fax: (907) 272-9412

ARIZONA

Arizona Department of Liquor
Licenses and Control
800 West Washington, Fifth Floor
Phoenix, AZ 85007
Phone: (602) 542-5141
Fax: (602) 542-5707

ARKANSAS

Arkansas Department of Finance
and Administration
Alcohol Beverage Control Division
Technology Center, Suite 503
100 Main Street
Little Rock, AR 72201
Phone: (501) 682-1105
Fax: (501) 682-2221

CALIFORNIA

California Department of
Alcoholic Beverage Control
3810 Rosin Court, Suite 150

Sacramento, Ca 95834
Phone: (916) 263-6900
Fax: (916) 263-6912

California Board of Equalization
P.O. Box 942879
Sacramento, CA 94279-0001
Phone: (916) 739-2582

COLORADO

Colorado Department of Revenue
Liquor Enforcement Division
1881 Pierce, #108A
Lakewood, CO
Mailing Address:
1375 Sherman Street
Denver, CO 80261
Phone: (303) 205-2300
Fax: (303) 205-2341

CONNECTICUT

Connecticut Department of
Consumer Protection
Liquor Division
State Office Building
165 Capitol Avenue
Hartford, CT 06106
Phone: (860) 713-6200
Fax: (860) 713-7235

DELAWARE

Delaware Department of Public
Services
Alcoholic Beverage Control
Commission
820 French Street
Wilmington, DE 19801
Phone: (302) 577-5222 or
1 (800) 273-9500
Fax: (302) 577-3204

DISTRICT OF COLUMBIA

District of Columbia Department
of Consumer and Regulatory
Affairs, Alcoholic Beverage
Control Division
North Potomac Building
614 H Street, N.W., Room 807
Washington, DC 20001
Phone: (202) 442-4445
Fax: (202) 727-7388

FLORIDA

Florida Department of
Professional Business
Regulations
Division of Alcoholic Beverages
1940 North Monroe
Tallahassee, FL 32399-1020
Phone: (850) 488-3227
Fax: (850) 922-5175

GEORGIA

Georgia Department of
Revenue
270 Washington, S.W.
Atlanta, GA 30334
Phone: (404) 656-4262
Fax: (404) 657-6880

HAWAII

Liquor Commission City and
County of Honolulu
711 Kapiolani Boulevard,
Suite 600
Honolulu, HI 96813-5249
Phone: (800) 838-9976
(808) 527-6280
Fax: (808) 591-2700

IDAHO

Idaho Department of Law
Enforcement
Alcoholic Beverage Control
Division
700 South Stratford Lane
P.O. Box 700
Meridian, ID 83642
Phone: (208) 884-7060
Fax: (208) 884-7096

Idaho State Liquor Dispensary
1345 East Beechcraft Court
Boise, ID 83716
Mailing Address: P.O. Box 179001
Boise, ID 83717-9001
Phone: (208) 334-5300
Fax: (208) 334-2533

ILLINOIS

Illinois Liquor Control
Commission
100 West Randolph Street,
Suite 5-300
Chicago, IL 60601
Phone: (312) 814-2206
Fax: (312) 814-2241

Department of Revenue
P.O. Box 19079
Springfield, IL 62794-9019
Phone: (217) 785-7100

INDIANA

Indiana Alcoholic Beverage
Commission
302 West Washington Street,
Room E114
Indianapolis, IN 46204
Phone: (317) 232-2463
Fax: (317) 233-6114

Department of Revenue
Special Tax Division
P.O. Box 6114
Indianapolis, IN 46206-6114
Phone: (317) 232-2435
Fax: (317) 232-2724

IOWA

Iowa Alcoholic Beverages
Division
1918 Southeast Hulsizer Avenue
Ankeny, IA 50021
Phone: (515) 281-2407
Fax: (515) 281-7385

KANSAS

Kansas Department of Revenue
Division of Alcoholic Beverage
Control
4 Townsite Plaza, Suite 210
200 Southeast 6th Street
Topeka, KS 66603-3512
Phone: (913) 296-7015
Fax: (913) 296-0922

KENTUCKY

Kentucky Department of
Alcoholic Beverage Control
1003 Twilight Trail, Suite A-2
Frankfort, KY 40601
Phone: (502) 564-4850
Fax: (502) 564-1442

LOUISIANA

Louisiana Department of Revenue
Excise Taxes Division
P.O. Box 66404
Baton Rouge, LA 70896
Phone: (225) 925-4041
Fax: (225) 925-3975

Louisiana Department of
Public Safety
Office of Alcoholic Beverage
Control
2124 Wooddale Boulevard
P.O. Drawer 66404
Baton Rouge, LA 70896
Phone: (504) 925-4041
Fax: (504) 925-3975

MAINE

Maine State Liquor and Lottery
Commission
Bureau of Alcoholic Beverages
and Lottery
Operations
8 State House
Augusta, ME 04333-0008
Phone: (207) 289-3721
Fax: (207) 287-4049

MARYLAND

State of Maryland
Comptroller of the Treasury
Alcohol and Tobacco Tax Unit
Louis L. Goldstein Treasury
Building
P.O. Box 2999
Annapolis, MD 21404-2999
Phone: (410) 260-7311
Fax: (410) 974-3201

MASSACHUSETTS

Massachusetts Alcohol Beverages
Control Commission
Leverett Saltonstall Building,
Government Center
100 Cambridge Street, Room 2204
Boston, MA 02114-2130
Phone: (617) 727-3040
Fax: (617) 727-1258

MICHIGAN

Michigan Liquor Control
Commission
7150 Harris Drive
P.O. Box 30005
Lansing, MI 48909
Phone: (517) 322-1353
Fax: (517) 322-5188

MINNESOTA

Minnesota Department of Public
Safety
Liquor Control Division
444 Cedar Street, Suite 133
St. Paul, MN 55101
Phone: (651) 296-6159
Fax: (651) 297-5259

MISSISSIPPI

Mississippi State Tax Commission
Alcoholic Beverage Control
Division
P.O. Box 22828
Jackson, MS 39225
Phone: (601) 923-7400
Fax: (601) 923-7423

MISSOURI

Missouri Department of Public
Safety
Division of Liquor Control
Harry S. Truman State Office
Building, Room 860
Post Office 837
Jefferson City, MO 65102
Phone: (573) 923-7400
Fax: (601) 923-7423

MONTANA

Montana Liquor License Bureau
125 North Roberts
Helena, MT 59620
Phone: (406) 444-0700
Fax: (406) 444-0750

NEBRASKA

Nebraska Liquor Control
Commission
301 Centennial Mall South
P.O. Box 95046
Lincoln, NE 68509-5046
Phone: (402) 471-2571
Fax: (402) 471-2814

NEVADA

Nevada Department of Taxation
1550 East College
Carson City, NV 89706-7921
Phone: (775) 687-4892
Fax: (775) 687-5981

NEW HAMPSHIRE

New Hampshire State Liquor
Commission
Robert J. Hart Building
Storrs Street
P.O. Box 503
Concord, NH 03302-0503
Phone: (603) 271-3134
Fax: (603) 271-1107

NEW JERSEY

New Jersey Department of Law
and Public Safety
Division of Alcoholic Beverage
Control

140 East Front Street
P.O. Box 087
Trenton, NJ 08625-0087
Phone: (609) 984-2830
Fax: (609) 633-6078

NEW MEXICO

New Mexico Regulation and
Licensing Department
Alcohol and Gaming Division
725 St. Michael's Drive
P.O. Box 25101
Santa Fe, NM 87504-5101
Phone: (505) 827-7066
Fax: (505) 827-7168

NEW YORK

New York Division of Alcoholic
Beverage Control
State Liquor Authority
84 Holland Avenue
Albany, NY 12208
Phone: (518) 474-0810
Fax: (518) 402-4015

New York Division of Alcoholic
Beverage Control
State Liquor Authority
11 Park Place
New York, NY 10007
Phone: (212) 417-4002

NORTH CAROLINA

North Carolina Alcoholic
Beverage Control Commission
3322 Garner Road
P.O. Box 26687
Raleigh, NC 27611- 6687
Phone: (919) 779-0700
Fax: (919) 662-1946

NORTH DAKOTA

North Dakota Office of the State
Treasurer
Alcohol Beverage Control
State Capitol
600 East Boulevard Avenue
Bismarck, ND 58505-0600
Phone: (701) 328-2643
Fax: (701) 328-3002

OHIO

Ohio Department of Commerce
Division of Liquor Control
6606 Tussing Road
Reynoldsburg, OH 43068-9005
Phone: (614) 644-2360
Fax: (614) 644-2513

OKLAHOMA

Oklahoma Alcoholic Beverage
Laws Enforcement Commission
4545 North Lincoln Boulevard,
Suite 270
Oklahoma City, OK 73105
Phone: (405) 521-3484
Fax: (405) 521-6578

OREGON

Oregon Liquor Control
Commission
9079 Southeast McLoughlin
Boulevard
P.O. Box 22297
Portland, OR 97222
Phone: (800) 452-6522 or
(503) 842-5000
Fax: (503) 872-5266
Alcohol Server Education:
(503) 872-5133

PENNSYLVANIA

Pennsylvania Liquor Control
Board
Commonwealth of Pennsylvania
Northwest Office Building
Harrisburg, PA 17124-0001
Phone: (717) 783-9454
Fax: (717) 787-8820

RHODE ISLAND

Rhode Island Department of
Business Regulation
Liquor Control Administration
233 Richmond Street, Suite 200
Providence, RI 02903-4213
Phone: (401) 222-2562
Fax: (401) 222-6654

SOUTH CAROLINA

South Carolina Department of
Revenue and Taxation
Alcohol Beverage Licensing
Section
301 Gervais Street
P.O. Box 125
Columbia, SC 29214-0137
Phone: (803) 737-5000
Fax: (803) 734-1401

SOUTH DAKOTA

South Dakota Department of
Revenue
Division of Special Taxes and
Licensing
700 Governor's Drive
Pierre, SD 57501-2276
Phone: (605) 773-3311
Fax: (605) 773-6729

TENNESSEE

Tennessee Alcoholic Beverage
Commission
226 Capitol Boulevard Building,
Room 600
Nashville, TN 37219-0755
Phone: (615) 741-1602
Fax: (615) 741-0847

TEXAS

Texas Alcoholic Beverage
Commission
5806 Mesa Drive
P.O. Box 13127
Capitol Station
Austin, TX 78711-3127
Phone: (512) 206-3333
Fax: (512) 206-3449

UTAH

Utah Department of Alcoholic
Beverage Control
1625 South 900 West
P.O. Box 30408
Salt Lake City, UT 84130-0408
Phone: (801) 977-6800
Fax: (801) 977-6888

VERMONT

Vermont Department of Liquor
Control
State Office Building
Green Mountain Drive
Drawer 20
Montpelier, VT 05620-4501
Phone: (802) 828-2345
Fax: (802) 828-2803

VIRGINIA

Virginia Department of
Alcoholic Beverage
Control
2901 Hermitage Road
P.O. Box 27491
Richmond, VA 23261-7491
Phone: (804) 213-4413
Fax: (804) 213-4415

WASHINGTON

Washington Business License
Services
Department of Licensing
P.O. Box 9034
Olympia, WA 98504-3075
Phone: (360) 586-2784
Licensing: (360) 586-6700
Fax: (360) 586-1596

Washington Control
Washington State Liquor
Control Board
1025 East Union
Olympia, WA 98504-3075
Phone: (360) 753-6273
Fax: (360) 586-0878

WEST VIRGINIA

West Virginia Alcohol
Beverage Control
Commission
Enforcement and Licensing
Division
322 70th Street, S.E.
Charleston, WV 25304-2900
Phone: (304) 558-2481
Fax: (304) 558-0081

WISCONSIN

Wisconsin Alcohol and Tobacco
Enforcement
Department of Revenue
4610 University Avenue
Madison, WI 53708
Phone: (608) 266-3969
Fax: (608) 264-9920

WYOMING

Wyoming Liquor
Commission
1520 East 5th Street
Cheyenne, WY 82002
Phone: (307) 777-7231
Fax: (307) 777-5872

APPENDIX 3

Organizations for Event Risk Managers

American Conference of Governmental Industrial Hygienists (ACGIH)
1330 Kemper Meadow Drive
Cincinnati, OH 45240-1634
Publications: (513) 661-7881
www.acgih.org

American Society of Heating, Refrigerating and Air-Conditioning Engineers (ASHRAE)
1791 Tullie Circle, N.E.
Atlanta, GA 30329-2305
(404) 636-8400
www.ashrae.org

American Society for Industrial Security (ASIS)
1625 Prince Street
Alexandria, VA 22314
(703) 519-6299
www.asisonline.org

American Society for Testing and Materials (ASTM)
100 Barr Harbor Drive
West Conshohocken, PA 19428-2959
Publications: (610) 832-9585
www.astm.org

American Welding Society (AWS)
550 Northwest LeJeune Road
Miami, FL 33126
(800) 443-9353
www.aws.org

Entertainment Services and Technology Association (ESTA)
875 Sixth Avenue, Suite 2303
New York, NY 10001
(212) 244-1505
www.esta.org

Environmental Protection Agency (EPA)
www.epa.gov

Fraternal Information & Programing Group
www.fipg.org

Inter-Association Task Force
www.iatf.org

International Association of Assembly Managers (IAAM)
635 Fritz Drive
Coppell, TX 75019
(972) 255-8020
www.iaam.org

International Festival and Events Association
World Headquarters
2601 Eastover Terrace
Boise, ID 83706
(208) 433-0950
Fax: (208) 433-9812
www.ifea.com

International Special Events Society
401 North Michigan Avenue
Chicago, IL 60611
(312) 321-6853
Fax: (312) 673-6953
www.ises.com

National Crime Prevention Council
The Woodward Building
733 15th Street, N.W.
Washington, DC 20005

National Fire Protection Association (NFPA)
1 Batterymarch Park
P.O. Box 9101
Quincy, MA 02269-9101
(617) 770-3000
www.nfpa.org

National Institute for Occupational Safety and Health (NIOSH)
4676 Columbia Parkway

Cincinnati, OH 45226-1998
(800) 35-NIOSH
E-mail: pubstaft@cdc.gov
www.cdc.gov/niosh

Occupational Safety and Health Administration (OSHA)
General Industry Compliance Assistance
Director of Compliance Programs
200 Constitution Avenue, N.W., Room N-3107
Washington, DC 20210
(202) 693-1850
www.osha.gov

Tourism and More
1218 Merry Oaks
College Station, TX 77840
(979) 764-8492
tourism@bihs.net

U.S. Consumer Product Safety Commission (CPSC)
Washington, DC 20207
(800) 638-2772
www.cpsc.gov

U.S. Department of Agriculture, Food Safety and Inspection Service (FSIS)
www.fsis.usda.gov

World Future Society
www.wfs.org

APPENDIX 4

References

GENERAL

Fagence, M., "The Battle for the Tourist: Lessons from the Pacific Region," *Anatolia,* Vol. 9., No. 2, 1998.

Goldblatt, J., *Special Events: Best Practices in Modern Event Management,* John Wiley & Sons, New York, 1997.

Lasch, C., *The True and Only Heaven: Progress and Its Critics,* Norton, New York, 1991.

Ritzer, G., *The McDonaldization Thesis,* Sage, London, 1998.

Rojek, C., *Ways of Escape,* Macmillan, Houndsmills, UK, 1993.

Santana, G., "Tourism: Toward a Model for Crisis Management," *Turizam,* Vol. 47, No. 1, 1999.

Smith, G., "Toward a United States Policy on Traveler Safety and Security: 1980–2000," *Turizam,* Vol. 47, No. 1, 1999.

Sonmez, S., Apostolopoulos, Y., Tarlow, P., "Tourism in Crisis: Managing the Effects of Terrorism," *Journal of Travel Research,* Vol. 38, No. 1, 1999.

Steene, A., "Risk Management Within Tourism and Travel," *Turizam,* Vol. 47, No. 1, 1999.

Sternberg, E., *The Economy of Icons: How Business Manufactures Meaning,* Praeger, Westport, CT, 1999.

Urry, J., *The Tourist Gaze,* Sage, London, 1990.

CHAPTERS 1 AND 2

Ansell, J., Wharton, F., Eds., *Risk: Analysis, Assessment, and Management,* John Wiley & Sons, Chichester, UK, 1992.

Appenzeller, H., *Managing Sports and Risk Management Strategies,* Carolina Academic Press, Durham, NC.

Baudrillard, J., *America,* Verso, London, 1986.

Bramson, R., *Coping with Difficult People,* Dell, New York, 1981.

Chafetz, J., *A Primer on the Construction and Testing of Theories in Sociology,* Peacock, Itasca, IL, 1978.

Eco, U., *Travels in Hyperreality,* Harcourt Brace & Co., San Diego, 1983.

Fast, J., *Body Language,* Pocket Books, New York, 1971.

Frenkel, M., Ulrich, M., *Risk Management: Challenge and Opportunity,* Springer-Verlag, Berlin, 2000.

Greenway, A. R., *Risk Management Planning Handbook: Comprehensive Guide to Hazard Assessment, Accidental Release Prevention, and Consequence Analysis,* Government Institutes, Rockville, MD, 1998.

Griffiths, R., *Dealing with Risk: The Planning, Management and Acceptability of Technological Risk,* Manchester University Press, Manchester, UK, 1981.

Hales, A., Matthias, B., Eds., *After the Event: From Accident to Organizational Learning,* Pergamon, Oxford, UK, 1997.

Imai, M., *Gemba Kaizen,* McGraw-Hill, New York, 1997.

Kipp, J., *Emergency Incident Risk Management: A Safety and Health Perspective,* Van Nostrand Reinhold, New York, 1996.

Kliem, R., *Reducing Project Risk,* Gower, Aldershot, UK, 1997.

Koehler, R., *Law, Sport Activity, and Risk Management,* Stipes, Champaign, IL, 1987.

Mestrovic, S., *The Coming Fin de Siècle,* Routledge, New York, 1991.

Parsloe, P., Ed., *Risk Assessment in Social Care and Social Work,* Jessica Kingsley, London, 1999.

Product Safety: Risk Management and Cost-Benefit Analysis, OECD Publications and Information Center, Washington, DC, 1983.

Reason, J., *Managing the Risk of Organizational Accidents,* Ashgate, Aldershot, UK, 1997.

Rescher, N., *Risk: A Philosophical Introduction to the Theory of Risk Evaluation and Management,* University Press of America, Washington, DC, 1983.

Richards, E., *Medical Risk Management: Preventive Legal Strategies for Health Care Providers,* Aspen Systems Corporation, Rockville, MD, 1983.

Rojek, C., *Ways of Escape,* Macmillan, Houndmills, UK, 1993.

Sjoberg, L., Ed., *Risk and Society: Studies of Risk Generation and Reactions to Risk,* Allen & Unwin, London, 1987.

Tannen, D., *That's Not What I Meant!* William Morrow, New York, 1986.

Tarlow, P., Muehsam, M., "Theoretical Aspects of Crime as They Impact the Tourism Industry," in *Tourism, Crime and International Security Issues,* A. Pizam, Y. M. Mansfeld, Eds. John Wiley & Sons, New York, 1996.

Urry, J., *The Tourist Gaze,* Sage, London, 1992.

CHAPTER 3

Berlonghi, A., *The Special Event Risk Management Manual,* Berlonghi, Dena Point, CA, 1990, revised, 1994.

Bingham, S., Ed., *Conceptualizing Sexual Harassment as Discursive Practice,* Praeger, Westport, CT, 1994.

Conn Coomber, R., Ed., *The Control of Drugs and Drug Users: Reason or Reaction?* Harwood Academic, Amsterdam, 1998.

Crawford, R., *But I'm Only a Social Drinker: A Guide to Coping with Alcohol,* Whitcoulls, Christchurch, New Zealand, 1986.

Frances, R., Sheldon, Miller, S., Eds., *Clinical Textbook of Addictive Disorders,* Guilford, New York, 1998.

"From Turmoil Back to Tourism," Lake Chelan Police Department document, page 1.

Gallant, D., *Alcoholism: A Guide to Diagnosis, Intervention, and Treatment,* Norton, New York, 1987.

Goodwin, D., *Alcoholism,* Oxford University Press, Oxford, UK, 1994.

Hanson, G., *Drugs and Society,* Jones and Bartlett, Boston, 1998.

Hemphill, H., *Discrimination, Harassment, and the Failure of Diversity Training: What to Do Now,* Quorum Books, Westport, CT, 1997.

Hite, S., *Sex and Business,* Prentice Hall, London, 2000.

Kreps, G., Ed., *Sexual Harassment: Communication Implications,* Hampton Press, Cresskill, NJ, 1993.

Marshall, R., *Alcoholism: Genetic Culpability or Social Irresponsibility?* University Press of America, Lanham, MD, 2001.

McDowell, D., *Substance Abuse: From Principles to Practice,* Brunner/Mazel, Philadelphia, 1999.

Miller, N., Ed., *Comprehensive Handbook of Drug and Alcohol Addiction,* Dekker, New York, 1991.

Schuckit, M., Ed., *Alcohol Patterns and Problems,* Rutgers University Press, New Brunswick, NJ, 1985.

Schuckit, M., *Educating Yourself About Alcohol and Drugs: A People's Primer,* Plenum, New York, 1995.

Stevens, S., Wexler, H., Eds., *Women and Substance Abuse: Gender Transparency,* Haworth, New York, 1998.

Stimmel, B., *The Facts About Drug Use: Coping with Drugs and Alcohol in Your Family, at Work, in Your Community,* Consumer Reports Books, Yonkers, NY, 1991.

U.S. Commission on Civil Rights, *Sexual Harassment on the Job: A Guide for Employers,* U.S. Commission on Civil Rights, Washington, DC, 1984.

Webb, S., *Step Forward: Sexual Harassment in the Workplace: What You Need to Know,* MasterMedia, New York, 1991.

CHAPTER 4

Canetti, E., *Crowds and Power,* Farrar Straus Giroux, New York, 1973.

King, E. G., *Crowd Theory as the Psychology of the Leader and the Led,* Melon, Lampeter, UK, 1960.

Le Bon, G., *The Crowd,* translation of *La Psychologie des Foules,* 1895.

McCleeland, J. S. A., *The Crowd and the Mob,* Union Hyman, London, 1989.

McPhail, C., *The Myth of the Madding Crowd,* de Gruyter, New York, 1991.

Mellen Studies in Sociology, Vol. 7, Mellen Press, Lewiston, Maine, 1990.

Nye, R., *The Origins of Crowd Psychology: Gustave Le Bon and the Crisis of Mass Democracy in the Third Republic,* Sage, London, 1975.

Plog, S., "Why Destinations Rise and Fall," *Cornell Hotel and Restaurant Quarterly,* November 1973.

Rudé, G., *The Face of the Crowd: Studies in Revolution, Ideology, and Popular Protest: Selected Essays of George Rudé,* Humanities Press, Atlantic Highlands, NJ, 1988.

Wright, S., *Crowds and Riots: A Study in Social Organization,* Sage, Beverly Hills, CA, 1978.

CHAPTER 5

Brannigan, F., *Building Construction for the Fire Service,* National Fire Protection Association, Quincy, MA, 1992.

Briese, J., Gary, J., Eds., *Fire Protection Management for Hazardous Materials: An Industrial Guide,* Government Institutes, Rockville, MD, 1991.

Cahill, J., "New Year's Eve in Times Square," *Emergency Management,* November 1999.

Cote, A., *Principles of Fire Protection,* National Fire Protection Association, Quincy, MA, 1988.

Dreisbach, R., *Handbook of Poisoning: Prevention, Diagnosis and Treatment,* Prentice Hall, London, 1987.

Gomberg, A., *Evaluating Alternative Strategies for Reducing Residential Fire Loss: The Fire Loss Model,* U.S. Department of Commerce, National Bureau of Standards, Washington, DC, 1982.

Goudsblom, J., *Fire and Civilization,* Allen Lane, London, 1992.

Institute of Engineers, Australia National Committee on Structural Engineering, *Fire Engineering for Building Structures and Safety,* Institute of Engineers, Australia.

Jeynes, J., *Practical Health and Safety Management for Small Businesses,* Butterworth-Heinemann, Oxford, UK, 2000.

Kaye, S., *Handbook of Emergency Toxicology: A Guide for the Identification, Diagnosis, and Treatment of Poisoning,* Thomas, Springfield, IL, 1970.

Leonard, R., Moreland, K., "EMS for the Masses," *EMS,* January 2001.

Proctor, N., *Chemical Hazards of the Workplace,* Lippincott, Philadelphia, 1998.

Sax, N., *Dangerous Properties of Industrial Materials,* Van Nostrand Reinhold, New York, 1979.

Sittig, M., *Handbook of Toxic and Hazardous Chemicals and Carcinogens,* Noyes, Park Ridge, NJ, 1991.

TriData Corporation, *An NFIRS Analysis: Investigating City Characteristics and Residential Fire Rates,* Federal Emergency Management Agency, U.S. Fire Administration, National Fire Data Center, Washington, DC, 1998.

Tuhtar, D., *Fire and Explosion Protection: A System Approach,* Halsted, Chichester, UK, 1988.

Vale, J. A., *A Concise Guide to the Management of Poisoning,* Churchill Livingstone, Edinburgh, 1985.

Wilder, S., *Risk Management in the Fire Service,* Fire Engineering Books and Videos, Saddle Brook, NJ, 1997.

CHAPTER 6

Bazelian, E. M., *Lightning Physics and Lightning Protection,* Institute of Physics, Bristol, UK, 2000.

Cleaves, D., *Assessing Uncertainty in Expert Judgments about Natural Resources,* U.S. Department of Agriculture, Forest Service, Southern Forest Experiment Station, New Orleans, 1994.

Committee to Ensure Safe Food from Production to Consumption, Institute of Medicine, National Research Council, *Ensuring Safe Food: From Production to Consumption,* National Academy Press, Washington, DC, 1998.

Farahan, E., *Residential Electric and Gas Water Heaters,* U.S. Energy Research and Development Administration, Springfield, VA, 1977. Available from National Technical Information Service, Washington, DC.

Frydenlund, M., *Lightning Protection for People and Property,* Van Nostrand Reinhold, New York, 1993.

Glendon, A., *Human Safety and Risk Management,* Chapman & Hall, London, 1995.

Hach Chemical Company, *Drinking Water Analysis Handbook: A Buyer's Guide for Chemical Reagents and Laboratory Apparatus for EPA-Approved and Hach Methods, Side by Side,* Hach Chemical Company, Ames, IA, 1977.

Harris, J., *Performance of Instantaneous Gas-Fired Water Heaters,* U.S. Department of Commerce, National Bureau of Standards, Springfield, VA, 1987. Available from National Technical Information Service, Gaithersburg, MD.

Kämper, E., *Decision Making Under Risk in Organisations: The Case of German Waste Management,* Ashgate, Aldershot, UK, 2000.

Keller, A. Z., *Hazards to Drinking Water Supplies,* Springer-Verlag, London, 1992.

Larson, R., Ed., *Biohazards of Drinking Water Treatment,* Lewis, Chelsea, MI, 1989.

Levitt, A., *Disaster Planning and Recovery: A Guide for Facility Professionals,* John Wiley & Sons, New York, 1997.

McFeters, G., Ed., *Drinking Water Microbiology: Progress and Recent Developments,* Springer-Verlag, New York, 1990.

Organisation for Economic Co-operation and Development, *Food Safety and Quality: Trade Considerations,* Organisation for Economic Co-operation and Development, Paris, 1999.

Sheridan, J., O'Keeffe, M., Rogers, M., *Food Safety: The Implications of Change from Producerism to Consumerism,* Food & Nutrition Press, Trumbull, CT, 1998.

Smith, M., *Crime Prevention Through Environmental Design in Parking Facilities,* U.S. Department of Justice, Office of Justice Programs, National Institute of Justice, Washington, DC, 1996.

Unnevehr, L., *Food Safety Issues in the Developing World,* World Bank, Washington, DC, 2000.

CHAPTER 7

Baldassare, M., Ed., *The Los Angeles Riots: Lessons for the Urban Future,* Westview, Boulder, CO, 1994.

Bement, L., *A Manual for Pyrotechnic Design, Development and Qualification,* National Aeronautics and Space Administration, Langley Research Center, Hampton, VA, 1995.

Getz, D., *Festivals, Special Events, and Tourism,* Van Nostrand Reinhold, New York, 1991.

Goldblatt, J., *Special Events: The Art and Science of Celebration,* Van Nostrand Reinhold, New York, 1990.

Goldblatt, J., *Dollars and Events: How to Succeed in the Special Events Business,* John Wiley & Sons, New York, 1999.

Horowitz, D., *The Deadly Ethnic Riot,* University of California Press, Berkeley, CA, 2001.

Lagaukas, V., *Parades: How to Plan, Promote and Stage Them,* Sterling, New York, 1982.

Lagaukas, V., Ed., *IFEA's Official Guide to Parades,* International Festival Association, Port Angeles, WA, 1992.

Randall, A., Charlesworth, A., *Moral Economy and Popular Protest: Crowds, Conflict and Authority,* St. Martin's, New York, 2000.

Rossol, M., *The Health and Safety Guide for Film, TV and Theater,* Allworth, New York, 2000.

Rossol, M., *The Artist's Complete Health and Safety Guide,* Allworth, New York, 2000.

Salert, B., *The Dynamics of Riots,* Inter-University Consortium for Political and Social Research, Ann Arbor, MI, 1980.

Steele, P., *Riots,* New Discovery Books, New York, 1993.

Tarlow, P., "A Site to See," *Security Management,* August 2001.

U.S. Consumer Product Safety Commission, *Fireworks,* U.S. Consumer Product Safety Commission, Washington, DC, 2000.

CHAPTER 8

Adam, B., Beck, U., Van Loon, J., *The Risk Society and Beyond,* Sage, London, 2000.

Callaghan, C., "Lodging No Complaints," *Security Management,* June 2001.

Ferguson, M., *The Aquarian Conspiracy,* Tarcher, Los Angeles, 1976.

Harris, A., *Special Events: Planning for Success,* Council for the Advancement and Support of Education, Washington, DC, 1988.

Kuhn, T., *The Structure of Scientific Change,* 2nd ed., University of Chicago Press, Chicago, 1970.

Naisbitt, J., *Megatrends,* Warner Books, New York, 1984.

Pizam, A., Mansfeld, Y. M., Eds., "Theoretical Aspects of Crime as They Impact the Tourism Industry," in *Tourism, Crime and International Security Issues,* John Wiley & Sons, London, 1995.

Tarlow, P., "Creating Safe and Secure Communities in Economically Challenging Times," *Tourism Economics,* Vol. 6, No. 2, 2000.

Tarlow, P., Muehsam, M., "Wide Horizons: Travel and Tourism in the Coming Decades," *The Futurist,* Vol. 26, No. 5, 1992.

Toffler, A., *The Third Wave,* Bantam Books, Toronto, 1981.

Toffler, A., *Previews and Promises,* Bantam Books, Toronto, 1983.

Glossary of Pyrotechnic Terms

This information is for informational purposes only. As with any issue involving fire, please check with your local fire marshal before using this information for an event.

Aerial shell: This is usually a cylindrical or spherical cartridge containing pyrotechnic material. Although they can be other shapes as well. A shell will have a long fuse or electric match wires and a black powder lift charge. The shells smaller than 2 inches are considered consumer fireworks (1.4 g). Shells larger than 3 inches are considered Class B (1.3 g).

Airburst: A pyrotechnic device that is suspended in the air to simulate outdoor aerial fireworks shells. These lack a launch tube or a lifting charge.

Approved: Acceptable to the authority having jurisdiction. As an example, if you have been granted a fire permit, you have been approved by the fire marshal.

Assistant: Anyone that works under the supervisor of the pyrotechnic operator.

Audience: The people watching the show. An audience is considered spectators whose primary purpose is to view a performance.

Authority having jurisdiction: The organization, office, or individual responsible for approving equipment, an installation, or a procedure. As an example, the fire marshal could be the authority having jurisdiction for approving a fire show. Also referred to as the AHJ.

Binary system: A two-component pyrotechnic system where the pyrotechnic material is broken down into two separate containers. One is the oxidizer and one is the fuel. The ingredients cannot burn or explode until they are mixed together. This makes binaries safer to store and handle. Also known as a *binary explosive* or *binary materials.*

Black powder: A low explosive consisting of an intimate mixture of potassium or sodium nitrate, charcoal, and sulfur. Commonly associated with muzzle-loading weapons such as a musket or cannon.

Comet: A pellet of pyrotechnic material that is ignited and propelled from a mortar tube by a charge of black powder. Comets frequently leave a trail of sparks as they rise in the air, and they sometimes burst into smaller fragments at their zenith.

Concussion effect: A pyrotechnic effect that produces a loud noise and a violent jarring shock for dramatic effect. A very powerful example would be a concussion grenade.

Concussion mortar: A device specifically designed and constructed to produce a loud noise and a violent jarring shock for dramatic effect without producing any damage.

Consumer fireworks: Any small fireworks device designed primarily to produce visible effects by combustion that complies with the construction, chemical composition, and labeling regulations of the U.S. Consumer Product Safety Commission, as set forth in Title 16, Code of Federal Regulations, Parts 1500 and 1507. Some small devices designed to produce audible effects are included, such as whistling devices, ground devices containing 50 mg (0.8 grains) or less of explosive composition (salute powder), and aerial devices containing 130 mg (2 grains) or less of explosive composition (salute powder) per explosive unit. Consumer fireworks are classed as Explosives 1.4G and described as Fireworks UN0336 by the U.S. Department of Transportation. Formerly known as *common fireworks.*

Electric match: A device containing a small amount of pyrotechnic material that ignites when a specified electric current flows through the leads. An electric match is used to initiate pyrotechnics. Electric matches are often incorrectly called squibs.

Fallout area: The area in which any hazardous debris falls after a pyrotechnic device is fired. The fallout area is defined as a circle that, in turn, is defined by the fallout radius.

Fallout radius: A line that defines the fallout area of a pyrotechnic device. The line is defined by two points. The first point is at the center of a pyrotechnic device. The second point is the point most distant from the center of the pyrotechnic device at which any hazardous debris from the device can fall.

Fire (v.): To ignite pyrotechnics by using an electric match, electrical current, or some other means.

Fire fingers: A device that attaches to individual fingers either made of wire or integrated onto a glove. Each finger will have a wick at the end which is soaked with a combustible fuel such as alcohol, kerosene, paraffin, or stove fuel.

Firing system: The source of ignition for pyrotechnics. In an electrical system, it is the source of electric current used to initiate electric matches or other devices. Generally, the electrical firing system has components, such as a primary key switch, test circuits, warning indicators, cables, isolation transformers, and switches to control the routing of the current to various pyrotechnics.

Fixed production: Any production performed repeatedly in only one geographic location.

Flare: A pyrotechnic device designed to produce a single source of intense light for a defined period of time.

Flash pot: A device used with flashpowder that produces a flash of light and is capable of directing the flash in an upward direction.

Flashpowder: A specific pyrotechnic material in powder form composed of fuel(s) and oxidizer(s). Ignition produces a flash of light, sparkles, an audible report, or a combination of these effects.

Fuel: In pyrotechnics, anything combustible or acting as a chemical reducing agent such as, but not limited to, sulfur, aluminum powder, iron powder, charcoal, magnesium, gums, and organic plastic binders. Fuels are an ingredient of pyrotechnic materials.

Gerb: A cylindrical preload intended to produce a controlled spray of sparks with a reproducible and predictable duration, height, and diameter.

Hazardous debris: Any debris, produced or expelled by the functioning of a pyrotechnic device, that is capable of causing personal injury or unpredicted property damage. This includes, but is not limited to, hot sparks, heavy casing fragments, and unignited components. Materials such as confetti, lightweight foam pieces, feathers, or novelties are not to be construed as hazardous debris.

Holder: Any device used to hold a pyrotechnic device other than a mortar. The purpose of a holder is to maintain the position of a pyrotechnic device. Holders hold preloads, which are self-contained. A holder is not to be construed to be a mortar.

Igniter: An electrical, chemical, or mechanical device normally used to fire pyrotechnics.

Ingredient: A chemical used to create a pyrotechnic material. Such a chemical is not itself a pyrotechnic material.

Integral mortar: A preloaded mortar containing pyrotechnic materials and intended for a single firing only.

Isolated power supply: An ungrounded power supply that provides electricity, in which both output wires are isolated from ground. An isolated power supply can be an ungrounded generator, an ungrounded dc-to-ac converter, or commercial power supplied through an isolation transformer.

Labeled: Equipment or materials to which has been attached a label, symbol, or other identifying mark of an organization that is acceptable to the authority having jurisdiction and concerned with product evaluation that maintains periodic inspection of production of labeled equipment or materials and by whose labeling the manufacturer indicates compliance with appropriate standards or performance in a specified manner.

Lift charge: The composition in a pyrotechnic device that propels (lifts) the effect into the air when ignited. It usually consists of a black powder charge.

Listed: Equipment, materials, or services included in a list published by an organization acceptable to the authority having jurisdiction and concerned with evaluation of products or services that maintains periodic inspection of production of listed equipment or materials or periodic evaluation of services and whose listing states either that the equipment, material, or service meets identified standards or has been tested and found suitable for a specified purpose.

Magazine: Any building, structure, or indoor container used exclusively for the storage of explosive materials as defined in NFPA 495, Explosive Materials Code.

Manufacturer: An individual who performs the following: prepares any pyrotechnic material or loads or assembles any pyrotechnic device.

  Exception 1: In the case of binary systems, the supplier of preweighed or premeasured ingredients, not the person mixing the ingredients, is considered the manufacturer of any pyrotechnic materials created from binary components.

  Exception 2: The person loading binary materials into devices supplied by the manufacturer of binary systems is not considered a manufacturer where such loading is performed in accordance with the instructions of the manufacturer. Note: A federal explosives manufacturer's license is required where a binary system is used and the components are mixed in the course of a trade or business to create an explosive material.

Mine: A pyrotechnic device, usually a preload, that projects multiple pellets of pyrotechnic material that produce sparks or a flame. It is usually supplied with an integral mortar.

Mortar: A tube or a potlike device used to direct and control the effect of the pyrotechnic material.

Oxidizer: Usually an oxygen-rich, ionically bonded chemical that decomposes at moderate to high temperatures. Where such a chemical decomposes, it releases oxygen. In addition to ionic solids, an oxidizer can be a material having covalent molecules containing halogen atoms. An oxidizer is an ingredient of pyrotechnic materials.

Performance: The enactment of a musical, dramatic, operatic, or other entertainment production. The enactment begins and progresses to its end according to a script, plan, or other preconceived list of events. A performance can include encores.

Performer: Any person active in a performance during which pyrotechnics are used and who is not part of the audience or support personnel. Among others, performers can include, but are not limited to, actors, singers, musicians, and acrobats.

Permittee: The person or persons who are responsible for obtaining the necessary permits for a production. The permittee can vary from jurisdiction to jurisdiction. The pyrotechnic operator is not necessarily the permittee.

Preload: A pyrotechnic device supplied by the manufacturer in a ready-to-use condition.

Producer: An individual who has overall responsibility for the operation and management of the performance where the pyrotechnics are to be used. Generally, the producer is an employee of the promotion company, entertainment company, festival, theme park, or other entertainment group.

Production: All the performances of a musical, dramatic, operatic, or other series of shows. There are two types of productions: fixed and touring.

Proximate audience: An audience closer to pyrotechnic devices than permitted by NFPA 1123, Code for Fireworks Display.

Pyrotechnic device: Any device containing pyrotechnic materials and capable of producing a special effect as defined in this standard.

Pyrotechnic material: A chemical mixture used in the entertainment industry to produce visible or audible effects by combustion, deflagration, or detonation. Such a chemical mixture consists predominantly of solids capable of producing a controlled, self-sustaining, and self-contained exothermic chemical reaction that results in heat, gas, sound, light, or a combination of these effects. The chemical reaction functions without external oxygen. Also called *pyrotechnic special effects material.*

Pyrotechnic operator: An individual who has responsibility for pyrotechnic safety and who controls, initiates, or otherwise creates special effects. The operator is also responsible for storing, setting up, and removing pyrotechnic materials and devices after a performance. Also called *special effects operator.*

Pyrotechnic special effect: A special effect created through the use of pyrotechnic materials and devices. *See also* **Special effect.**

Pyrotechnics: Controlled exothermic chemical reactions that are timed to create the effects of heat, gas, sound, dispersion of aerosols, emission of visible electromagnetic radiation, or a combination of these effects to provide the maximum effect from the least volume.

Rehearsal: A practice performance during which no audience is present.

Rocket: A pyrotechnic device that moves by the ejection of matter produced by the internal combustion of propellants.

Saxon: A pyrotechnic device consisting of a tube that rotates around a pivot point to produce a circular shower of sparks.

Shall: Indicates a mandatory requirement.

Should: Indicates a recommendation or that which is advised but not required.

Special effect: A visual or audible effect used for entertainment purposes, often produced to create an illusion. For example, smoke might be produced to create the impression of fog being present, or a puff of smoke, a flash of light, and a loud sound might be produced to create the impression that a cannon has been fired.

Support personnel: Any individual who is not a performer or member of the audience. Among others, support personnel include the road crew of any production, stage hands, property masters, security guards, fire watch officers, janitors, or any other employee.

Touring production: Any production performed in more than one geographic location.

Venue manager: An individual who has overall responsibility for the operation and management of the facility where pyrotechnics are to be used in a performance.

Waterfall, falls, park curtain: An effect of a cascade of sparks that usually are produced by multiple devices fired simultaneously.

Wheel: a pyrotechnic device that rotates on a central axis consisting of multiple gerbs or rockets attached to a framework.

Copyright © 1998–2001 by Wally Glenn unless otherwise noted. All rights reserved. Available on line at **http://www.arfarfarf.com/safety/definitions.shtml.**

Index